Business Cycles and Economic Crises

Throughout the history of economic thought, interest in business cycles and economic crises has sometimes been observed to rise during times of crises, recessions and depressions. However, the treatment of this topic in the literature has generally been merely anecdotal.

This book presents a bibliometric and econometric analysis of the development of business cycle and crises theory and its connection to economic developments, particularly since the early 20th century. The book explores the connection between economic development and the literature, utilising systematic bibliometric and rigorous econometric methods and drawing its data from a wide range of sources. This volume provides quantitative answers to questions which have not previously been subject to a precise and comprehensive empirical analysis.

This book will be of great interest to historians of economic thought for its novel treatment of a much-discussed topic, and its well-founded and transparent results.

Niels Geiger is a postdoc in economics and research assistant at the Department of Economics at the University of Hohenheim in Stuttgart, Germany.

Vadim Kufenko is a postdoc in economics and a research assistant at the Department of Economics at the University of Hohenheim, Germany.

Routledge Studies in the History of Economics

205 The Economic Thought of William Petty
Exploring the Colonialist Roots of Economics
Hugh Goodacre

206 Greed in the History of Political Economy
The Role of Self-Interest in Shaping Modern Economics
Rudi Verburg

207 Aristotle's Critique of Political Economy
A Contemporary Application
Robert L. Gallagher

208 Otto Neurath and the History of Economics
Michael Turk

209 A Brief Prehistory of the Theory of the Firm
Paul Walker

210 Unproductive Labour in Political Economy
The History of an Idea
Cosimo Perrotta

211 The History of Money and Monetary Arrangements
Insights from the Baltic and North Seas Region
Thomas Marmefelt

212 Business Cycles and Economic Crises
A Bibliometric and Economic History
Niels Geiger and Vadim Kufenko

For more information about this series, please visit
www.routledge.com/series/SE0341

Business Cycles and Economic Crises

A Bibliometric and Economic History

Niels Geiger and Vadim Kufenko

Routledge
Taylor & Francis Group
LONDON AND NEW YORK

First published 2019 by Routledge

2 Park Square, Milton Park, Abingdon, Oxfordshire OX14 4RN
52 Vanderbilt Avenue, New York, NY 10017

Routledge is an imprint of the Taylor & Francis Group, an informa business

First issued in paperback 2020

British Library Cataloguing-in-Publication Data
A catalogue record for this book is available from the British Library

Library of Congress Cataloging-in-Publication Data
A catalog record has been requested for this book

ISBN: 978-1-138-65942-1 (hbk)
ISBN: 978-0-367-66576-0 (pbk)

Typeset in Bembo
by Sunrise Setting Ltd., Brixham, UK

Contents

Figures

Tables

Preface

This book is about the economics literature on business cycles and economic crises, and it is an empirical effort to that end. However, we are neither presenting a new theory of these subjects, nor providing statistical tests of already available work. Instead, our contribution is to the history of economic thought. This may seem a bit surprising at first – indeed, the most widely used method for research in the history of economic thought is probably the deep reading of particular texts and the identification of links between them, different authors, their research interests, etc. This may often be supplemented by delving into archives or building upon biographical information to get a more comprehensive picture of an author's background, and, specifically, what they may have meant with one statement or another. What we present in this book instead is a bibliometric study not of individual contributions, but of a large sample of economics as a whole to trace the spread and diffusion of discussions of business cycles and economic crises over time. In doing so, this book ultimately has two aims. First and foremost, we present precisely those results just mentioned – how the economics literature on business cycles and economic crises in general, not just as captured by particularly relevant examples (or what were later deemed to be just that), evolved over time, in relation to actual economic developments, specifically observable fluctuations in the shape of business cycles or economic crises. Secondly, and in doing so, we also wish to strengthen the case for the relevance of bibliometric research in work on the history of economic thought in general. Our results will show, and we will also argue in the discussion of them, that this is of course no substitute for the traditionally established methods, specifically the close and understanding reading of a particular contribution. But, indeed, bibliometric methods seem to be a highly promising complement to this approach, in particular if the history of economic thought strives to capture and explain both the background and also the broad impact of individual papers, and the literature at large.

In assembling, processing and statistically analysing metadata like citations and other bibliometric variables, we have collected and organized a vast array of information on the quantitative history of business cycles and economic crises in the economics literature. Despite the generous scope given to us by our publishers, Routledge, for this book, it is not possible to present every detail in print, and we had to select the most relevant data and findings to be documented here. However, insights into the additional data and further results from our econometric analysis may be arranged upon personal request to the authors. Since we believe that the data and methods we employed here may be used further, and in different contexts, we will be happy to discuss these matters with other researchers interested in a quantitative approach to the history of economic thought in general.

Affiliation and acknowledgements

Niels Geiger is a postdoc in economics and research associate at the Institute of Economics (520H) at the University of Hohenheim in Stuttgart, Germany. He received his doctorate in economics in February 2015 with a thesis on combining behavioural economics with business cycle theory. His current research interests mainly cover business cycle theory and behavioural economics, and especially the history of thought in both subjects. Part of the work on this book was conducted while he enjoyed the warm and welcoming atmosphere at the Academy of Finland Centre of Excellence in the Philosophy of the Social Sciences (TINT), University of Helsinki, Finland, during spring of 2016. Vadim Kufenko received his doctorate in economics in 2017 at the University of Hohenheim and is currently a postdoctoral research associate and a research area coordinator at the Institute of Economics (520H) at the University of Hohenheim. His main research interests include the econometric analysis of time-series and panel data, scientometrics and the analysis of sentiments, inequality, political economy and economic history, with a focus on institutions and demographics.

The authors began their joint work in late 2013 with a paper on the "stylized facts" of business cycles, which was recently published in the *Journal of Business Cycle Research* (Kufenko and Geiger 2017). In late 2014, the authors started to work on the connection between business cycles in the economy and economic research on business cycles, and thus prepared a paper on "Business Cycles in the Economy and in Economics: An Econometric Analysis" for the 2015 Conference of the European Society for the History of Economic Thought in Rome. The paper was published in *Scientometrics* in early 2016 (Kufenko and Geiger 2016). It soon became obvious that this highly interesting and intriguing research area provides many more questions and many more potential answers than could be fitted into just one single paper, so the authors decided to make it their main research project and expand on the original results documented in the paper in various ways. Emily Kindleysides of Routledge was kind enough to offer the ideal frame for such a publication, by offering the authors a book contract for a monograph in Routledge's series on the history of economic thought. During the process of writing and producing this book, we were in regular exchange with Laura Johnson, Lisa Lavelle and Anna Cuthbert of

Routledge, who were always helpful – and, in particular, very considerate and understanding of our requests regarding the completion of this book.

The bibliometric data in this book primarily come from two sources. The first is JSTOR's "Data for Research" portal. (Copyright JSTOR 2016–2017. All rights reserved.) While Niels Geiger visited the University of Helsinki, citation data were accessed from the second source, Clarivate Analytics Web of Science™. (Copyright Clarivate Analytics 2016. All rights reserved.) More detailed records of which data were used are documented in the respective chapters and sections, and are available from the authors upon request. The inclusion of long-memory effects into the time-series analysis is a merit of at least several generations of econometricians. In particular, however, we would like to thank Morten Ørregaard Nielsen and Michal Ksawery Popiel for the FCVAR software package implemented in Matlab. To our knowledge, our work was one of the first applications of this type of analysis to bibliometric series.

Naturally, a book such as this one owes its completion to more than the input of the two authors. We are particularly grateful to Johannes Schwarzer for his various comments and feedback throughout the process of working on this book, as well as for his careful proofreading of drafts. We would also like to thank Mattis Geiger for the discussions we had on statistical power tests, specifically their relevance and especially their interpretation in the context of our econometric set-up. Our original discussion of the research question has benefited from comments by Pedro Garcia Duarte and Harald Hagemann. All remaining errors are, of course, our own.

1 Introduction

Following the 2007–08 financial and economic crisis, even casual observers of economics could have gained the impression that many more authors than before suddenly referred to John Maynard Keynes's writings, particularly the *General Theory* (Keynes 1936). Maybe most evidently, for example, Robert Skidelsky (2009) proclaimed *Keynes: The Return of the Master*. Against the background of the severe economic crisis and subsequent contraction, Skidelsky argued, it was in the writings of Keynes that economists would find answers to the present problems. Indeed, it seemed not just to Skidelsky, but to many economists, that the economic downswing called for a discussion of that approach to understanding the severe contraction. A similar context is apparent when going back in time to the *General Theory*'s original publication. It is evident that this original work itself was written against the very background of severe economic crisis and depression. Even though the direct influence of the Great Depression on Keynes (1936) is debatable (see Caspari 2008: 170), the economic turmoil arguably contributed to why Keynes's work seemed so relevant and quickly gained such attraction (see Johnson 1971: 3f.). What is more, Keynes's *General Theory* is by no means the only example of a major work on fluctuations and crises that is frequently set and seen in its historical context of a large economic contraction. Indeed, while the Great Depression was still near its trough, Irving Fisher had written and published a book influenced by his own first-hand experience (see Blaug 1986: 80f.; Dimand 1994) with the devastating effects of the stock market crash and deflation in *Booms and Depressions* (Fisher 1932).

These prominent examples highlight how economic downturns can inspire works on those events, i.e. contributions to business cycle and economic crises theory (BCCT) or related empirical work. Similar anecdotal evidence can easily be gathered for trends in the opposite direction. During the economically prosperous times of the post-war decades, a prime example is Bronfenbrenner's (1969) edited volume, which raises the eponymous question *Is the Business Cycle Obsolete?* as the book's title. Despite the volume's emphasis on *high* (not necessarily *steady*) growth rates (e.g. see Allsopp 1971), interest in BCCT seemed to have decreased in the 1960s, with growth theory in particular taking centre stage instead. Similarly, having experienced long expansionary phases and relatively mild recessions during the 1980s and 1990s, authors such as Walsh (1999) referenced Bronfenbrenner (1969) in posing the same question (also see Romer 1999). Maybe the most iconic recent example of positive economic developments decreasing interest in BCCT can be found in Lucas (2003: 1), who likewise argued, based on the experience of the previous years of the "Great Moderation" and shortly before the onset of the "Great Recession", that "the central problem of depression prevention has been solved".

While this is a relatively varied list of anecdotal evidence, the above examples still suggest a coherent interpretation. Could it be that it is not just the economy which goes through cycles over the course of its development, but that the discussion of said business cycles – particularly of its most dramatic points and phases, namely crises and contractions – follows a similar cyclical pattern of fluctuations in interest and prevalence? What is more, could this pattern even be linked to the economic developments, following and trailing the latter, in the sense that economic downturns precipitate increased interest in the discussion of business cycles and economic crises, while recoveries and upswings have an adverse effect? This would imply a much more specific and peculiar cyclicality in economic thought than was discussed elsewhere, for example by Neumark (1975: 257f.) or Kurz (2006), who pointed at the idea of old economic ideas resurfacing many decades later, not necessarily connected to actual economic developments.[1]

As it turns out, the notion of a potential link between economic fluctuations and the corresponding literature is almost as old as BCCT itself. In a theoretical work on economic fluctuations, John Mills (1868: 11) noted that "every commercial crisis occurring in this country is promptly followed by a literature of pamphlets". Similar observations pointing out the large amount of publications following each economic crisis were made, for example, by Aftalion (1913: 289f.) and Richter (1923: 153). Realizing the same phenomenon, other authors such as Durbin (1933: 17) warned readers against texts originating in these circumstances, as they might attract relevance not by virtue of their respectability, but because of the (historical) context in which they are published. Looking back at the Great Depression and subsequent years, Bronfenbrenner (1966: 542ff.) described the increased discussion of economic fluctuations as a fad (despite using the term "cycle"; this argument is therefore closer to those of Neumark (1975) and Kurz (2006) referenced above). Overall, observations of economic developments affecting the literature are not limited to BCCT in a more strict sense (i.e. focused on cyclical fluctuations) either. In his *History of Economic Analysis*, Schumpeter (1954: 1172) finds that "[i]n any prolonged period of economic malaise economists, falling in like other people with the humors of their time, proffer theories that pretend to show that depression has come to stay." Nor is the suggested effect limited to the academic literature, as Fabian (1989: 127f.) shows by tracing the influence that the 1837 and 1857 downswings in the United States had on attempted explanations and discussions outside of academia and economics experts. There, economic crises became a matter of reflection not just by all kinds of pundits, but also as widely as in poetry or jokes of the time. Fabian (1989: 127) further argues that these non-economic writers frequently and explicitly acknowledged that it was the "panics" which had made them write their texts. What is more, even within the academic literature, contractions may cause not just increased research in BCCT and related empirical work, but also more casual discussions of business cycles and economic crises. Overall, therefore, an intriguing argument can be made for the hypothesis and story that "panics produce texts" (Fabian 1989: 128), and, more generally for the academic economics literature on business cycles and economic crises, that downswings in economic activity cause an increase in publications and in the reception of literature on business cycles and economic crises, while upswings conversely tend to have the opposite effect.

On the one hand, this argument of the economics literature reacting to business cycles and economic crises is intuitively very appealing. On the other hand, however, there is something strange about the "panics produce texts" story indeed. If economists realized the recurrence of business cycles and economic crises, and if those constitute a phenomenon worth explaining – or even one that is considered essential for a complete analysis of capitalist economies, as for example Schumpeter (1939: v) argued (similarly, also see Böhm-Bawerk 1898: 132; Mitchell 1951: vii) – should that phenomenon not be discussed regardless of the phase of the cycle the economy is currently in? Indeed, following this logic, the academic literature – unlike media such as, especially, news outlets – should be expected to be fairly independent of recent salient events. In other words, searching for answers on what causes, and how to devise policies to deal with, crises is not just relevant – albeit arguably more pressing – in a contraction period. Therefore, if economists strive for a better understanding of aggregate economic fluctuations, they should not stop deliberating on business cycles and economic crises just because the previous year was prosperous. This may be very much in line with what newspapers are supposed to do – i.e. report on the events – but less so with what is expected from academics trying to fundamentally comprehend underlying phenomena. However, even if much BCCT research in the strict sense was not subject to such fluctuations, economics as a whole might still display a corresponding reaction if economic downturns fuel more general writings on and superficial references to these (also note Durbin 1933: 17).

Therefore, despite the intuitive appeal of the "panics produce texts" hypothesis, and even when taking all the above-mentioned anecdotal examples into account, it can be said that, *ex ante*, it is not completely evident whether the economics literature as a whole, and specifically BCCT, reacts to business cycles and economic crises. To gain a better understanding of whether or not there really is a corresponding relation between economic data and the economics literature, reference to anecdotal examples needs to be extended by an empirical analysis that considers more than individual historical contractions such as the Great Depression and seminal works such as Keynes's (1936) *General Theory*. A first contribution in this direction was made by Besomi (2011), who traced frequencies of particular terms relevant in the context of BCCT in the titles of economics publications between 1815 and 2009. Based on a descriptive analysis directly comparing absolute frequencies inside and outside of (respectively, close to and far from) contraction years, Besomi (2011: 56) corroborates the "panics produce texts" hypothesis. A more in-depth, econometric analysis which picked up Besomi's work was subsequently provided by Kufenko and Geiger (2016). Measuring relative frequencies of Besomi's terms in the full texts of economics articles archived on JSTOR, the authors argue that their results may be read to confirm the original hypothesis, but also point to caution in interpreting the findings and highlight the necessity of further research such as a more comprehensive statistical approach (see Kufenko and Geiger 2016: 57f.). This is precisely what the present book will do, namely, extend earlier empirical work (in particular that of Besomi (2011) and Kufenko and Geiger (2016)), and especially provide a more comprehensive and in-depth discussion of the results and their potential implications. The guiding research question is whether or not economic fluctuations have a clearly identifiable, robust effect on the economics literature on business cycles and economic crises, and the book is devoted to investigating, analysing and discussing this question.

To achieve this end, the argument and analysis in this book is structured as follows. Chapter 2 provides a comprehensive overview of the data used and methods applied, and especially of how the "panics produce texts" hypothesis can be operationalized and linked to the data. This includes a general illustration of the relevant sources and tools of bibliometrics and scientometrics, which are presented in some additional detail for the reader who may not yet be familiar with these approaches. All aspects of the methods and data, whether they are related to how the data were accessed, compiled and analysed with econometric methods, are laid out in Chapter 2. This is in order to allow Chapter 3 to fully focus on the presentation and discussion of the empirical findings. Results on the "panics produce texts" hypothesis, i.e. the potential effect of economic fluctuations on the academic literature on business cycles and economic crises, are presented in a descriptive manner with figures and corresponding conjectures in Section 3.1, as well as in the rigorous econometric analysis supplemented by various illustrative tables in Section 3.2.

In the descriptive part of the results, there are several interesting findings in line with earlier observations in the literature that had not built on a similar empirical record. In the 1930s, around 40% and in some years nearly 50% of all economics articles, and well over 30% of all articles in economics journals, contained the term 'depression', which appeared much more frequently then than during any other historical episode. In the following decades, 'depression' came to be used less and less, and even more rarely than 'recession' since the 1970s. Between the 1920s and the 2010s, in line with the question raised by Bronfenbrenner (1969), 1970 marks the year with the lowest frequency of papers featuring the terms "business cycle" or "trade cycle",[2] in both economics journals and economics articles, as well as in the broader categories of business and economics, which include neighbouring disciplines such as finance. Overall, however, the descriptive results provide no generally conclusive evidence.

As regards statistical associations between economic and bibliometric variables, there are a select few robust findings. Concerning articles on economics and neighbouring subjects, changes in the US consumption price index were consistently found to affect changes in the frequency of papers containing the terms 'crisis', 'recession', 'glut' and 'stagnation'. In the same categories, variations in the frequency of papers in which either of the terms "business cycle" or "trade cycle" appeared were found to be affected by changes in investment activity in the United States. Several impulse response functions further indicate effects of non-negligible magnitude and in the expected direction of increased discussions following a downturn. This implies that, at least for these combinations, there may be a "panics produce texts" effect in the literature. However, there is a remarkable lack of more general robust positive evidence from the statistical analysis, especially in bibliometric time series for economics journals.

Aiming at a validation of these and the many other findings, Section 3.3 provides a detailed discussion of various issues relating to the data itself, the operationalization of the research question, and the potential interpretations possible from the results. Chapter 4 then concludes with a summary which argues that, despite compelling anecdotal evidence and positive findings from earlier related research, as well as some individual examples like those mentioned in the previous paragraph, in light of the various caveats raised in the discussion and the overall weak evidence for a systematic, robust effect of economics on bibliometric variables, the "panics produce texts" hypothesis cannot be confirmed as a general rule for the academic economics literature at large, and especially not for the academic literature published in economics journals.

Notes

1 The resurgence in popularity of Keynes's works in the context of the Great Recession may be seen as an instance of both: a revival in popularity of old ideas decades after their original publication, and greater interest in BCCT fuelled by recent economic developments.

2 Throughout this book, the terms of interest are usually put in single quotes when they are referenced in the text. This is in order to highlight that a bibliometric variable with potentially various corresponding strings is concerned. However, when the text refers to specific search strings, which were used for compiling the bibliometric series, those are put in double quotes. See Subsection 2.4.2 for a full overview of the notation.

2 Method and data

This chapter presents our research strategy in detail. To provide some context first, Section 2.1 operationalizes the research question against the background of a short summary of the history of scientometrics and bibliometrics, specifically concerning its applications to economics, respectively the history of economic thought (HET). Empirically assessing the "panics produce texts" (PPT) hypothesis requires both economic data (presented in Section 2.2) and bibliometric records (documented in Section 2.3). Section 2.4 then concludes the chapter by listing how and in what way we process and arrange the data, including the econometric methods. Results are presented in the following Chapter 3.

2.1 The overarching research question

In order to quantitatively answer the question of how economic fluctuations affect the academic literature in economics, we use bibliometric, respectively scientometric, data and methods. Since neither are, as of yet, standard tools in research on the HET, it is worthwhile to include a short overview of what these two fields cover, and how and where their methods and corresponding data have already been employed in research on the HET. Subsections 2.1.1 and 2.1.2 do just that, before Subsection 2.1.3 returns to focus on the issue at hand, i.e. the operationalization of the PPT story as a research question.

2.1.1 On "scientometrics" and "bibliometrics"

Scientometrics is the scientific observation and analysis of science itself by means of quantitative methods. This pertains to both the history and present state of science. One of the major tools employed in this endeavour is bibliometrics, i.e. the statistical analysis of written publications, including both their actual text content and their metadata, most importantly citations and references between items.[1] Non-bibliometric measures which feature in scientometric research may include data on the number of scientists, the volumes of research grants, etc. In comparison with the sociology of science (e.g. Merton 1968, 1988), scientometrics generally focuses on publications, whereas the former is more interested in the behaviour of scientists – see Leydesdorff and Milojević (2015); but also note Merton's (1979) foreword in Garfield (1979). The analysis in this book tackles a scientometric research question by means of bibliometric and econometric tools.

The origin of scientometrics and bibliometrics as dedicated scientific efforts dates back to Eugene Garfield's (1955) paper on "Citation Indexes for Science". Garfield's early work led to the creation of the Science Citation Index (SCI), officially launched in 1964 and originally arranged and published by the Institute for Scientific Information, and now accessible via the Web of Science.[2] It is still one of the primary, most reliable and most commonly used sources for citation data today – see Hamermesh (2015: 3); also Section 2.3. Next to Eugene Garfield, another prominent founding father was Derek J. de Solla Price (e.g. Price 1963). In 1978, fuelled by the rise of computers and the thereby increasingly possible effective analysis of the vast arrays of data which scientometrics deals with, the dedicated journal wearing the discipline's name, *Scientometrics*, was established (see Price 1978). Today, additional periodicals such as the *Journal of Informetrics* focus on scientometrics as well. The tools of bibliometrics are of course not exclusively used in scientometrics, but particularly feature as a staple in library and information science. Furthermore, they have recently been applied to an even broader field: Michel et al. (2011) trace trends in English book literature (including non-academic works) by means of bibliometric methods to quantitatively analyse developments outside of science under the label of "culturomics".

At present, scientometrics constitutes an empirical approach used to quantitatively assemble trends, changes and developments in science in order to gain a more detailed picture of the history and state of science (see e.g. Leydesdorff and Milojević 2015). This also includes such general topics of interest as the identification of thematic structures and research fields like "economics" through bibliometric methods – see e.g. Gläser et al. (2017) for a recent review of that literature. Furthermore, scientometric indicators are broadly used to compare research fields, universities, faculties, journals and individual researchers – whether in ranking comparisons (e.g. the Shanghai "Academic Ranking of World Universities"), hiring decisions or other related issues. The two most prominent measures employed in this context are the "impact factor" (IF) and the "*h*-index". Both are simple index numbers which do convey some information, but should also be interpreted with care, as much of the discussion within the scientometric literature itself shows – for example, see Zuckerman (1987) on the advantages and shortcomings of citation data; also see Alberts (2013) and Gagolewski (2013) for more recent discussions of the limitations of simple indicators.

The IF, mostly encountered as a journal IF and regularly provided not only in bibliometric databases, but on publishers' own websites, is a measure which relates citations that a body of literature received to the number of citable items in that body (see Garfield 1972). In the standard form that is often documented, for example for journals, the IF for a given year t is the number of citations received in year *t* by articles published in that journal during the two preceding years $t-1$ and $t-2$, divided by the total number of articles published in that journal in years $t-1$ and $t-2$. That is, a journal's 2015 IF is the number of 2015 citations to 2014 and 2013 articles in that journal, divided by the number of 2014 and 2013 articles published in the journal's respective issues (or, more generally, citable items instead of articles). Of course, other, similar numbers can be constructed just as easily, e.g. by using a five-year IF, etc. This measure is simple and straightforward, and provides a very general impression of the reach and impact of a body of literature (e.g. a journal's issues within some time period). However, there are a number of apparent problems once more than a superficial impression is to be gained from the index. These apply even if all relevant citations could be observed without any error, bias or other shortcomings, i.e. even if it was certain that empirically measured citation counts reflect actual citation counts (and, what is more, that these accurately reflect intellectual influence).

The major caveat which can be raised about IFs is that they are averages which do not capture either any other aspects of the distribution they are describing or differences in underlying determinants. For example, different disciplines – and even subdisciplines within the same general research fields such as economics – often have vastly different citation practices (see e.g. Kaur et al. 2013). If, in one discipline, there was a higher frequency of co-authorship and a generally higher average citation or reference count per paper (as is usually the case when comparing natural sciences with social sciences), IFs in that discipline – whether for journals or authors – will tend to be higher than in the other, which does not really say much about a journal's or author's impact within their relevant area or peer group.[3] This matters, of course, when university hiring decisions are based on IFs, and candidates from different disciplines – or even just subdisciplines, e.g. from macroeconomics and industrial economics – apply for the same position. Furthermore, differences between disciplines also feature in publication lags, which additionally affects IFs, depending on how they are calculated. For example, due to the short-term view captured by the standard two-year form of IFs, economics journals tend to have lower IFs than those in the natural sciences (see Hamermesh 2015: 27), in part because lags between acceptance and publication are often much shorter in the latter – as opposed to the 18 months between submission and publication which are common in economics (see Björk and Solomon 2013). Therefore, unless a paper is written and submitted very soon after a publication it cites, it will not affect the latter author's or publication's IF.

Citation patterns, however, differ not only between subdisciplines, but also indeed within them. This is best illustrated by differences in IFs of a (sub)discipline's journals, where the majority of papers in lower-ranked journals are cited just as (in)frequently as those in higher-ranked journals, but the higher-ranked journals (by IF) often feature a few extraordinarily frequently referenced items. As Hamermesh (2015: 26) notes, "[t]he main reason that a few economics journals are ranked more highly than all others is that a very few papers in these journals generate immensely more citations than other papers published in those journals or elsewhere. A very few outliers determine our perceptions of journal quality, a perception that ignores the tremendous heterogeneity of articles within and across journals." This heterogeneity is not captured by simple IFs, which is why an individual article's quality cannot be reliably (i.e. without considerable probability of misattribution) derived from the journal's IF. Wang et al. (2016) even show that "novel" papers (defined as those which contain new and often unprecedented combinations of citations), which are more likely – at a greater overall variance in citation counts – to be major contributions to science in the long run, are often published in journals with a relatively low IF. Quite generally, Palacios-Huerta and Volij (2004) therefore point out that rankings based on IFs do not build on a sound theoretical basis and are just one among many other conceivable ways of ranking journals' (or authors') intellectual influence.

Given the discussion about the adequacy of IFs, alternative, more refined measures have been suggested recently. For example, Guerrero-Bote and Moya-Anegón (2012) propose the SJR2 indicator, which works similar to Google's PageRank algorithm. Instead of only considering simple citation numbers, these are weighted by the prestige of the citing journal (i.e. that journal's own SJR2) as well as the proximity (i.e. similarity in citation profiles) of the cited and citing journal (see Guerrero-Bote and Moya-Anegón 2012). The SJR2 is highly correlated with simple IFs, but documents different rankings between journals. For the empirical analysis in the present book, the SJR2 index is used as one reference to identify premier journals in economics (see Subsection 2.4.1).

The second prominent simple index number, the *h*-index, was originally proposed by Hirsch (2005). It is usually calculated for individual authors and used as a proxy to compare their scientific productivity. When ordering all of an author's works by number of citations, the present *h*-index is equal to the number x of items of that author which have been cited at least x times. This results in a single number which may be considered as a better measure of a scholar's scientific productivity than the mere number of papers (which does not capture quality) or the total number of citations (which may be highly skewed by one single very successful contribution). It is thus, to some extent, a measure of both quality and quantity combined. While the *h*-index is most prominent, there are similar examples of the same family of indexes which are sometimes used as well: Egghe (2006) proposed the *g*-index, where g is the unique largest number so that an author's g most cited publications are cited at least g^2 times in total. By giving higher weight to very frequently cited articles, g is usually larger than h.

Like the IF, the *h*-index and similar numbers are subject to a series of issues, too, for which they are frequently criticized. While between two authors, the one with the higher *h*-index will have a higher number of relatively frequently cited publications, the other may actually have more very highly cited publications. Problems like these are especially relevant when comparing authors across (sub)disciplines. This holds in addition to the fact that the *h*-index does not account for these differences in citation behaviour in the first place. Normalizing citation counts by each (sub)discipline's average citation count can then lead to rank reversals among authors. Perry and Reny (2016: 2723) thus criticize popular scientometric indicators like the *h*-index for being "ad hoc measures based almost entirely on intuition and rules of thumb" and instead propose a new "Euclidean" index to measure research performance by taking the square root over the sum of the squares of citations of each of an author's papers. This index, Perry and Reny (2016) argue, can overcome several shortcomings (e.g. ranking reversals) of the *h*-index and related concepts.

2.1.2 The place of bibliometrics in history of economic thought research

Given the aim of scientometrics and bibliometrics to quantitatively describe science itself with scientific methods, it appears to be a relevant approach to and tool for the history of science – including, of course, the HET. However, the use of bibliometric methods in research on the HET has been rather limited so far, as a cursory reading of the field's most prominent journals – even more so if supplemented by a search for scientometrics- or bibliometrics-related key terms within these journals – quickly indicates.[4] A look at conference programmes of relevant meetings further confirms the impression of a marginal role of bibliometric research. Instead, work on the HET usually analyses a small sample of contributions in-depth, and this approach is sometimes supplemented by archival sources or biographical and general historical records. As an anecdotal but illustrative example of this, consider Marcuzzo's (2008) paper, which identifies four broad categories of methods used in research on the HET: "textual exegesis", "rational reconstruction", "contextual analysis" and "historical narrative". Interestingly, although Marcuzzo (2008) uses some descriptive bibliometrics to describe the subject of the HET herself, she does not list quantitative or bibliometric research among the categories of approaches she identifies.

However, there are nonetheless a number of interesting and often highly illuminating contributions which provide new and additional insights on various questions discussed in the literature dealing with economics and the HET – particularly, related to the availability of respective data, more recent HET. The following list is not comprehensive, but it should still provide a good impression of the different contexts and questions where bibliometric and scientometric methods are employed in the HET, which should also highlight the value of such approaches.

Already five decades ago, George Stigler (1965a), maybe "the most famous advocate of scientometrics in economics" (Diamond 2000: 323), had pointed out the potential of quantitative methods in his *Essays in the History of Economics* and provided a categorized list of the contents of five relevant journals (see especially Stigler 1965b). Stigler and Freidland (1975, 1979) subsequently published further work which empirically approached HET topics using citation measures acquired through manually counting references in published articles (see Hamermesh 2015: 3). The first dedicated HET journal to publish on the topic was probably *History of Political Economy* (*HOPE*) with Stigler and Freidland's (1979) "The Pattern of Citation Practices in Economics". Bordo and Landau (1979) provided their "Exploration Towards a Quantitative History of Thought" using 1945–1968 citation data in the next *HOPE* issue. Subsequently and ever since, bibliometrics featured more frequently in *HOPE* than in other primary HET journals – see e.g. Oehler (1990), Biddle (1996), Sandelin and Veiderpass (1996), Backhouse (1998) and very recently Claveau and Gingras (2016).

A year after Stigler (1965a), Bronfenbrenner (1966) documented "Trends, Cycles, and Fads in Economic Writing", which were illustrated with two tables and two figures. Bronfenbrenner (1966) used the American Economic Association's (AEA) "Index of Economic Journals" to categorize papers (similar to today's JEL codes) from 1866–1963 as well as dissertation records from 1960–1965 documented in the *American Economic Review* in order to identify trends and cycles of interest in different subdisciplines of economics, specifically in what was considered orthodoxy or the mainstream. Of particular interest for the research question and analysis in the present book is that Bronfenbrenner (1966: 546) points out that the discussion of economic fluctuations greatly increased throughout the Great Depression – but he classifies this observation as a fad, and does not argue for a recurring theme of generally increased discussion of the matter during economic downturns. Despite the use of the term "cycle", therefore, Bronfenbrenner's (1966) analysis was not limited to BCCT, and the length of the cycles in the literature which he observes is far greater than the five to maybe ten years business cycles are usually associated with, too (see e.g. Bronfenbrenner 1966: 542).

A somewhat comparable analysis which specifically refers to both Stigler (1965b) and Bronfenbrenner (1966) was provided by Diamond and Haurin (1995), who document changes of the popularity of different economics subdisciplines by coding and tracing research interests of AEA members as registered in the AEA directories at different points in time between 1905 and 1989. Most notably, Diamond and Haurin (1995: 118) find an increase in theory between 1956 and 1969, followed by a subsequent decline. They also find that interest in HET had decreased since 1955 and throughout 1969–1974, but slightly increased at very low levels again afterwards.

Just like in scientometrics in general, the digital availability of data sources allows for more applications and more comprehensive analyses in HET research. Extensively using Social Science Citation Index (SSCI, see Subsection 2.3.3) data, Kim et al. (2006) identify the most cited papers in economics since 1970 and document their characteristics, background, etc. Similar data are used by Laibson and Zeckhauser (1998) to point out the relevance of some influential behavioural economics research. A more detailed analysis of behavioural economics since Herbert Simon in the 1950s, based on SSCI and JSTOR (see Subsection 2.3.2) data, is provided by Geiger (2017). Wight (2002) uses SSCI data to trace citations to Adam Smith's work between 1970 and 1997. In other contributions, Hoover (2004) uses JSTOR data to trace the frequency of papers using terms such as "cause" or "causality" in economics journals since 1930, an approach very similar to what is employed in this book (see Section 2.4). Silva and Teixeira (2008) provide a bibliometric overview of the economics literature on structural change since the 1970s. Diamond (2009) compares the influence of Keynes and Schumpeter over time, using SSCI data. Similarly, Becker and Knudsen (2004) had already examined occurrences of the name "Schumpeter" in top economics journals between 1898 and 1998. Based on SSCI citation counts, Jovanovic (2012) tracks the reception of Louis Bachelier's work on financial economics. Using JSTOR data, King et al. (2012) document the increase of mathematization (and concepts closely linked to it, such as statistics or the use of the term "model") in economics throughout the 20th century and until 2012, specifically for the years following World War I until the 1980s. Hoover (2014) traces citations to Trygve Haavelmo's work since the 1940s using JSTOR data. Emphasizing and analysing somewhat different variables, Sandelin and Ranki (1997) document changes in Swedish economics between the 1940s and early 1990s by observing shifts in the languages of cited articles (and also the countries where cited authors work), as well as of Ph.D. theses, etc. (see also similarly Sandelin 2001). Biddle and Hamermesh (2016) analyse the history of microeconomics after World War II, with a focus on the role of theory, by outlining and quantitatively testing earlier arguments brought forward in the HET literature. Concerning the very recent history of economics, Cardoso et al. (2010) use EconLit and SSCI data to investigate which regions of the world had contributed how much to influential economics research since 1991. Duarte and Giraud (2016) provide bibliometric time series from 1991 to 2011 to assess the place of HET itself within mainstream economics.

Furthermore, even when it is not the main part of the HET analysis which is presented, scientometric and bibliometric data and methods are sometimes still present in respective contributions in order to provide an additional illustration of the main arguments. For example, Colander (2004) supplements his paper on "The Strange Persistence of the IS-LM Model" with term frequency data from JSTOR and EconLit. More comprehensively, Qin's (2011) work on the history of econometric approaches to the Phillips curve discussion is supplemented with citation data. Therefore, it is clear that scientometric and bibliometric data and tools have a wide applicability in research on the HET.

Outside of what may strictly be considered the HET (even if only for how recent a time period the study deals with), scientometrics and bibliometrics sometimes feature in other research on economics, too. Indeed, it may even be argued that economics and scientometrics are complementary, because, for example, scientometrics can provide information relevant to allocating scarce resources, e.g. concerning research funds, and economics can provide theoretical explanations for scientometric findings, e.g. concerning researcher behaviour (see Diamond 2000). A few examples will suffice to illustrate this.

In an early application using citation data in economics, Gerrity and McKenzie (1978) ranked economics departments in the South of the United

States. In a very economic bibliometric analysis of economics, Hamermesh et al. (1982) investigate the relation between economic rewards received by economists and bibliometric variables such as their citations. Similarly, Diamond (1986) estimates a "dollar value" of citations by comparing different researchers' salaries and earnings. Peritz (1990) compares citation records of funded with those of unfunded economics research, and finds that the former is cited more frequently. Beckmann and Persson (1998) identify the 13 most cited journals in economics. Using economics as an example, Cahlik (2000) discusses which methods are suitable to identify a discipline's fundamental articles (also see Subsection 2.4.1). Oswald (2009) deals with the question of assessing a country's research output by analysing bibliometric data on economics. Diamond and Toth (2007) employ a logit estimation to identify determinants such as citation counts and where a Ph.D. was obtained to explain which AEA members were elected presidents in the 1950s. Hamermesh (2013) documents changes in co-authorship, authors' age structure and methodology in top economics journals between 1950 and 2010. Sun and Xia (2016) analyse how citations of cited papers, authors' IFs and similar measures relate to a paper's citation count in economics. Gnewuch and Wohlrabe (2017) analyse the connection between characteristics of titles of economics papers and citation counts. Brogaard et al. (2018) analyse citation counts of economists before and after they were granted tenure. Very generally, Hamermesh (2015) provides an overview both of (early) uses of citation data in economics, as well as some general guidelines for their use.

Among all previously published bibliometric works on economics, the most relevant one for the analysis in this book is that by Daniele Besomi (2011). Building on an identification of key terms relevant to BCCT which is presented in the early part of that paper, Besomi (2011: 113–117) proceeds to document absolute annual frequencies of these terms within the titles of a wide array of contributions (journal articles, books and even pamphlets, etc.) listed primarily on JSTOR and EconLit and dating back to 1815. In discussing the results, Besomi (2011: 55ff.) finds that the frequency of key terms related to business cycles and crises indeed increases in connection with economic contractions. An extension of Besomi's (2011) work has subsequently been suggested by Kufenko and Geiger (2016). The analysis which follows in this book further expands on Kufenko and Geiger (2016), as the following sections will demonstrate.

2.1.3 Operationalising the bibliometrics of business cycles and economic crises

Ideally, to fully answer the research question derived from the PPT hypothesis – or any question which concerns general developments in the HET – one might want to read all economics papers carefully and, through a profound understanding of business cycle theory and related literature, classify and categorize these items correspondingly. Owing to the vast amount of both historical and contemporary literature, this is, of course, impossible. Indeed, there exists a major trade-off: the broader the trend which one wants to analyse, the less feasible it is to conduct a full in-depth analysis of all its constituent parts. This is precisely where bibliometric analysis enters the picture as a very helpful tool: it allows an analysis of a broad spectrum of hundreds of thousands of articles by standardized methods and metrics – at the expense of the detail and the researcher's individual insight with which the single elements can be analysed. It is straightforward to see, therefore, that the application of bibliometric methods in the HET is not a substitute for, but a complementary approach to, those traditionally employed in the field such as the careful in-depth reading of selected texts. Indeed, as Merton (1979: vii) put it in his foreword to Garfield (1979), "[s]pecialized historical and sociological studies can supplement explicit citations with tacit ones, the kind that can be reconstructed from textual evidence such as eponymous allusions, terminology bearing the stamp of the source of an idea, and the like."

The utility of this, as it were, co-operation between bibliometrics and more "traditional" HET approaches becomes apparent in the discussion of how to actually operationalize the PPT hypothesis and our research question of whether and how the economics literature on business cycles and economic crises is connected to economic fluctuations. Here, it is evident that appropriate bibliometric variables can hardly be identified without a prior theoretical understanding of the literature to be analysed. Thus, if the history of BCCT and related work is to be traced with bibliometric data, as is the aim of this book, it should be clearly defined when and how a paper is classified as belonging to that very category, which presupposes a theoretical background and knowledge of the relevant literature. Building on this, then, both the number of such papers as well as references and citations to these can be counted, analysed and discussed.

There are multiple ways to classify a particular paper as belonging to a certain category such as BCCT. The arguably most precise one is based on an in-depth reading of the said article – i.e. the standard approach in most HET work. However, as pointed out above, this is in no way feasible for a bibliometric analysis of the scope employed in this book. Therefore, more superficial approaches are necessary, which will be presented in Section 2.4. The primary tool employed is to identify and classify contributions by the terms they use. In doing so, we refer to and build on Besomi's (2011) list of key terms related to BCCT. The respective bibliometric data used here are presented in Section 2.3. On the other hand, answering the research question also requires an empirical assessment of economic fluctuations, of course: the data used for this other half of our approach are presented in Section 2.2. Next to describing how the relevant bibliometric series are constructed, Section 2.4 also lays out the different statistical methods employed in comparing the economic and bibliometric data. The descriptive and econometric analyses return a long list of quantitative empirical results documented in Sections 3.1 and 3.2. In the final step of the analysis, the results are validated and discussed in Section 3.3. Here, BCCT, as

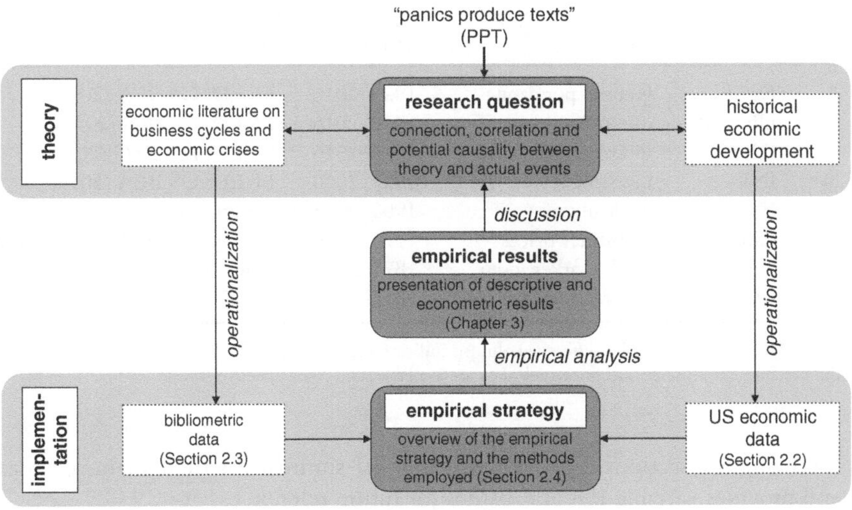

Figure 2.1 Schematic overview of the research question and its implementation.

well as previous HET research on the issue, will feature prominently once more, for it is this theoretical background which allows one to meaningfully relate the empirical results to the research question and therefore to ultimately conclude the book in Chapter 4. Figure 2.1 summarizes this approach, starting from the PPT hypothesis, and including the various steps which are documented in detail in all of the following.

2.2 Economic data: measuring business cycles

In order to assess the effect of business cycles and economic crises on the economics literature, it is of course inevitable to first operationalize and quantify said business cycles and economic crises in the economic data. In both theoretical and empirical literature on such fluctuations, there are multiple variables which feature frequently and in prominent position, irrespective of whether business cycles and economic crises are to be traced in the data, explained by reference to the data or a theoretical construct which can then be approximated with these data, or even if attempts at prediction are made. Corresponding with the literature, we thus consider seven economic variables to trace business cycles and economic crises in the data, and additionally employ an index based on an assessment of various indicators to trace contraction periods: income per capita, unemployment rates, industrial production, investment activity, bankruptcy rates, the consumer price index, the Standard & Poor's stock market index, and a dummy variable for contraction years (i.e. downswings). Each of these variables, their relevance for the analysis at hand, sources, availability and additional remarks (where necessary) are laid out in detail in the

Table 2.1 Reference list of economic variables

ID	*Name*	*Variable*	*Period*	*Source*
A	INCPC	income per capita	1929–2016	FRED; US BEA (2017a)
B	UNEMP	unemployment rate	1948–2016	FRED; US BLS (2017)
C	INDP	industrial production	1919–2016	FRED; Fed BoG (2017)
D	INV	investment	1929–2016	FRED; US BEA (2017b)
E	BANKR	bankruptcies	1900–2005	Garrett (2007)
F	CPI	consumer prices	1774–2016	Officer and Williamson (2017)
G	SPC	stock market index	1871–2016	Shiller (2015)
H	CON	contraction years	1855–2015	NBER

Note: For each variable, the different columns indicate their assigned IDs, their short name identifier, the variable, the time period for which data are available, and the respective source.

following Subsections 2.2.1–2.2.8. Table 2.1 summarizes their main metadata and provides variable IDs and names for future reference.

The question of operationalizing business cycles and economic crises has two more layers in addition to selecting appropriate variables, though. The first one concerns the time period and is rather easy to settle: the longer the available series, i.e. the larger the sample size, the better. Therefore, as long as a time series is available without any relevant structural breaks in the data, we use the maximum available length. As the respective subsections show, however, this leads to considerable differences in the years covered by the various series. In general, it would also be desirable to have all data at as high a frequency as possible. However, here the bibliometric variables (see the following Section 2.3) become a limiting factor, for they are mostly available consistently only on an annual basis. Therefore, we will also use annual frequencies for the economic data in our analysis.

The second additional point to consider and discuss is somewhat harder to tackle. It concerns the question of the appropriate geographical entity to trace. For the analysis in this book, we use US data as our proxy for economic activity – as previously done in Kufenko and Geiger (2016). This does, of course, introduce some inaccuracy with regards to our research question, because economists surely do not only know about fluctuations in the United States, but also about those in other countries. Ideally, we would like to include global or at least aggregate OECD data, while also striving to differentiate country-specific business cycles.

Nonetheless, using US data seems like a good compromise between data availability and a large and especially relevant (particularly in terms of the literature) economy for multiple reasons. The first is the high availability of the data, and the length of the available time series, sometimes reaching back into the 19th century without any problematic structural breaks in the data (especially when compared with, for example, OECD or even global aggregates).

Secondly, the United States is the major and leading economy of the world, and has been for over a century. By considering US data, we can therefore trace economic activity in the world's largest economy for much of the time period for which a large sample of bibliometric data is available – especially when the papers constituting our bibliometric data are mostly in English (see Section 2.3). Furthermore, and in connection with this, US developments have also been a central concern in much research on business cycles and economic crises, not least because of the National Bureau of Economic Research (NBER) and the research conducted and originating there. More broadly, close to half of all journal articles on the EconLit database (see Subsection 2.3.1) which contain either of the strings "business cycle" or "trade cycle" (a term which was mostly used in British literature until the first half of the 20th century, as for example in Keynes (1936) or Hicks (1950)) also contain "United States", and the ratio is similarly high for the term "recession". In the economics journals on JSTOR (see Subsection 2.3.2), among the articles which contain "business cycle" or "trade cycle", respectively, "recession", the relative frequency of those featuring "United States" is even higher than 50%. This indicates that the United States is a frequent point of reference for discussions of business cycles. And, finally, many of the most influential journals (as can be taken from, for example, the SJR2 journal ranking – see Subsection 2.4.1) are from or are published in the United States.

The main purpose of the economic variables illustrated in the following is to provide an overall measure of economic activity subject to business cycles and economic crises. If anything, it is these variables which should be among the primary suspects expected to have an effect according to PPT on the economics literature. Furthermore, it will also be interesting to identify potential differences in how a particular variable is connected to developments in the literature, e.g. if changes in one economic variable lead to more substantial changes in one or another bibliometric variable. All series were last updated from their online sources on March 4th and 5th, 2017.

2.2.1 Income per capita

The first economic variable included in our analysis is a general measure of aggregate macroeconomic activity: real disposable income per capita. Data are taken from the Federal Reserve Bank of St. Louis Economic Database (FRED), specifically the Real Disposable Personal Income: Per Capita series which covers the years 1929–2016.[5] A major advantage of this particular variable is its comparatively long historical record. The alternative series of gross domestic product (per capita), which is often used as a similar indicator, only dates back to 1947. The data supplied by FRED are originally from the US Bureau of Economic Analysis (2017a). We use the standard annual series (due to the bibliometric data being available at an annual frequency) which is given in 2009 dollars and not seasonally adjusted.

2.2.2 Unemployment rate

The second variable is another measure of aggregate economic activity which also features very frequently in both theoretical and empirical work on business cycles and economic crises, as well as in reports on these events outside of the academic literature: the unemployment rate. Upswings during a business cycle are usually thought of as periods where, in line with the economy's expansion, employment increases and unemployment decreases. In a downswing, then, the opposite occurs and unemployment tends to increase while the economy contracts. The series we use covering annual values for the period 1948–2016 is taken from FRED,[6] and originally provided by the US Bureau of Labor Statistics (2017). Specifically, the series represents the average percentage of unemployed persons aged 16 or older among the civilian labour force during any given year. It is somewhat unfortunate that such an important series does not even partly cover the period of the Great Depression. Data for earlier years can be constructed from publications by the US Bureau of the Census (e.g. US Bureau of the Census 1975), but then contain a structural break in 1947–48. The time series we built from these earlier records caused problems with the stability of vector autoregressions when we combined them with the 1948–2016 data (i.e. they did not pass econometric tests of quality or consistency). Therefore, we only include the consistent series available via FRED here.

2.2.3 Industrial production

Another variable which is a staple in discussions of business cycles and economic crises is the index of industrial production (INDP). Relative to the service sector, production in manufacturing and other industries is usually considered to be more volatile in response to (or even as the major driver of) aggregate fluctuations over the course of a business cycle. Annual data covering 1919–2016 are taken from FRED,[7] which uses records from the Board of Governors of the Federal Reserve System (2017). Industrial production is provided as an index, which captures real output for manufacturing, mining, and electric and gas utilities. Among other uses, INDP serves as the enumerator for estimating capacity utilization (based on an assessment of the industry's capacities), which is another variable often cited in discussions of business cycles and economic crises, especially contraction periods, both inside and outside of academia. The INDP data we use are normalized to 100 with 2012 as the reference year.

2.2.4 Investment

An economy's investment activity is a crucial focal point in much work on business cycles and economic crises. In many, especially older, theories, investment activity is considered to be relatively volatile compared with consumption expenditures, and is therefore a major factor in aggregate fluctuations of gross domestic product or gross domestic income. This also connects to INDP, because many investment goods are produced in the industrial machinery sector. Put simply, the argument would hold that, as firms perceive or expect higher demand, they will strive to expand their capacities, thus increasing investment demand, which may further amplify the original effect, etc. (naturally, the precise chain of causation and argument differs between theories; but this is not the point of the present book, and specifically not of this data overview). In contrast, during a downswing, firms will tend to cut back greatly on their investment demand and prioritize satisfying any consumption goods demand within available capacities. Given the prominent role thus taken by investment activity, it is a natural candidate to include in our analysis. The data series we use is real gross private domestic investment taken from FRED,[8] but originally provided by the US Bureau of Economic Analysis (2017b). The series is available as a chain-type quantity index with the reference year 2009 normalized to 100 and covers 1929–2016.

2.2.5 Bankruptcies

The number or relative frequency of bankruptcies is rarely featured in analyses of business cycles and economic crises, but seems naturally suited to a discussion of downswings and contractions in particular. During an upswing, both firms and consumers are usually more likely to take up a loan, and, especially if a crisis hits suddenly, they may go bankrupt in the subsequent downswing. Garrett (2007) provides a long time series for personal bankruptcies per 1000 persons of the total US population which covers 1900–2005. Similar to the income per capita and unemployment series, this is a variable which reflects a macroeconomic aggregate average, but nonetheless also serves as a measure of how fluctuations in economic activity affect individual agents.

2.2.6 Consumer prices

Next to these important real variables, we also include two primarily nominal time series. The first of these is an aggregate price index. There are multiple options available here which could be included in the analysis, starting from the GDP deflator and ranging to indexes for different relevant goods or sectors. We choose the consumer price index (CPI) here, mainly for two reasons. The first is data coverage: the US CPI series by Officer and Williamson (2017)[9] covers 1774–2016. Secondly, consumer prices feature in both BCCT as well as empirical work when monetary variables are concerned, and they have become a primary target variable for monetary policy in recent decades. Just as our selection of variables in general is of course only a sample of economic activity overall, especially over the course of a business cycle, the CPI is only one example of a price index. But given the long time series in particular, it seems like a very reasonable candidate to single out and include. The series from

Officer and Williamson (2017) that we use here is provided as an index, with the 1982–1984 average normalized to 100.

2.2.7 Stock market index

Especially two of the most severe and most frequently discussed economic crises and subsequent contractions, the Great Depression of 1929 and the 1930s, and the Great Recession of 2007–08 and the following years, are usually associated with major financial crises. Therefore, a representation of economic activity to assess business cycle fluctuations and economic crises can hardly be complete without also including a series for developments on financial markets. For the United States, the Standard & Poor's stock market index (S&P) seems to be a good compromise between offering a long time series and covering stocks from a larger sample of companies. Specifically, we use data on the S&P Composite Stock Price Index, which lists 1500 companies and covers about 90% of US market capitalization (the Dow Jones, in contrast, contains only a fairly small number of companies, namely 30 at present). Annual data are taken from the work of Shiller (2015), as available on Robert Shiller's website,[10] and cover the period 1871–2016.

2.2.8 Contraction years

The NBER, specifically its Business Cycle Dating Committee,[11] is the primary authority on dating the turning points (peaks, i.e. the time of crises, and troughs), and thus up- and downswings, for the US economy. Its time record for business cycles[12] dates back to December 1854. From then on until June 2009 (the latest recorded point of interest, a trough), it has documented 33 cycles (defined as the period between two peaks or two troughs) of varying lengths. Since World War II, for example, cycles have generally been longer (close to seven years), and expansions (upswings) over five times as long as contractions (downswings). Before World War I, in turn, cycles were much shorter on average (just about four years), and expansions lasted just five months longer than contractions. However, this does not say anything about the respective strength of an upswing or severity of a downswing, i.e. by how much GDP, unemployment, investment activity, etc., were affected.

The dating of troughs and peaks is based on the NBER's definition of contractions, i.e. the period in between. This downswing is characterized by a large decline in activity across the whole economy. Economic activity, in that context, is assessed based on the development of various variables, including GDP, employment, etc. There is no fixed rule which is applied to decide when a contraction begins, or when a change in the opposite direction is to be considered only a short-term interruption of an up- or downswing. But, clearly, the NBER's Business Cycle Dating Committee uses a wide range of indicators to provide an overall assessment of the state of the economy. Including the contraction period timings as a final variable for our analysis thus means that we include a generally recognized index measure of US economic activity over the course of a business cycle.

Since the NBER dates and timings are provided for months, and the bibliometric data used here are generally only available on an annual basis, contraction *years* need to be identified first. For our analysis in this book, we define a contraction year as one in which a contraction occurred for at least four consecutive months. The empirical findings of Section 3.1 are not sensitive to changes in this definition (see Subsection 3.3.2.1). Table 2.2 documents the NBER demarcations in the first column, and the years consequently defined as "contraction years" based on the criterion of four consecutive months. Since the first point identified in the NBER series is a trough in December 1854, the contraction years series used in the further analysis begins in 1855. Furthermore, as the NBER data were last accessed on January 2nd, 2018, when the last identified point had still been the June 2009 trough (and, correspondingly, the most recent announcement had been the one from September 20th, 2010, which identified that trough), the series includes 2015 (the last available year for some bibliometric series, see Section 2.3) as the final year.

Since the contraction dates provide an index variable for economic activity, this series offers a fairly long period for which at least one general measure of economic fluctuations over the course of a business cycle is available. We therefore use the period 1855–2015 as the maximum frame for our analysis. As the previous subsections have shown, most series are available only for shorter time frames, and their comparison with bibliometric variables can thus only cover shorter periods. It should be noted that the contraction years index does not render the seven other economic variables obsolete. The individual variables allow for a differentiation of whether or not the literature reacts to particular aspects of business cycles more readily. Furthermore, due to the binary nature of the contraction variable, effect strengths cannot be differentiated as precisely, and it cannot be used in the econometric analysis in the same way (see Section 2.4).

2.3 Bibliometric data sources

Large parts of the economics literature are now archived, documented and indexed in digital databases. The most prominent and encompassing among these are EconLit (the AEA's database), JSTOR, the Web of Science (WoS, hosted by Thomson Reuters until 2016 and by Clarivate Analytics since), Elsevier's Scopus, and Google Scholar. All of these sources provide broad metadata coverage. The latter three further specialize in citation records, whereas the first two (EconLit and JSTOR) are directly linked with full texts which can be searched and accessed in addition to the metadata. These five sources therefore appear as natural starting points for a bibliometric analysis – and indeed feature frequently in previous bibliometric research (see Subsections 2.1.1 and 2.1.2).[13]

The following five Subsections 2.3.1–2.3.5 sketch the databases' comparative advantages and disadvantages, which can be organized by reference to three

Table 2.2 Years defined as "contraction years"

NBER contraction period	*Contraction years*
June 1857 – December 1858	1857, 1858
October 1860 – June 1861	1861
April 1865 – December 1867	1865, 1866, 1867
June 1869 – December 1870	1869, 1870
October 1873 – March 1879	1874, 1875, 1876, 1877, 1878
March 1882 – May 1885	1882, 1883, 1884, 1885
March 1887 – April 1888	1887, 1888
July 1890 – May 1891	1890, 1891
January 1893 – June 1894	1893, 1894
December 1895 – June 1897	1896, 1897
June 1899 – December 1900	1899, 1900
September 1902 – August 1904	1902, 1903, 1904
May 1907 – June 1908	1907, 1908
January 1910 – January 1912	1910, 1911
January 1913 – December 1914	1913, 1914
August 1918 – March 1919	1918
January 1920 – July 1921	1920, 1921
May 1923 – July 1924	1923, 1924
October 1926 – November 1927	1927
August 1929 – March 1933	1929, 1930, 1931, 1932
May 1937 – June 1938	1937, 1938
February 1945 – October 1945	1945
November 1948 – October 1949	1949
July 1953 – May 1954	1953, 1954
August 1957 – April 1958	1957, 1958
April 1960 – February 1961	1960
December 1969 – November 1970	1970
November 1973 – March 1975	1974
January 1980 – July 1980	1980
July 1981 – November 1982	1981, 1982
July 1990 – March 1991	1990
March 2001 – November 2001	2001
December 2007 – June 2009	2008, 2009

Note: The left column shows contraction periods on a monthly basis as provided by the NBER dating; the right column lists "contraction years", which are here defined as a year in which there were at least four consecutive contraction months.

main evaluation criteria. First of all, the coverage itself is important, i.e. how many journals, books, etc., and over which time frame, the respective sources index. Secondly, the quality of the metadata the databases provide, i.e. whether they reliably trace authors, titles, publication years, citations, etc., is discussed. Thirdly, and ultimately relevant as to whether an analysis can be properly conducted at all, it is important whether the respective data can be systematically accessed and extracted and used for further analysis in a feasible way relevant for the research question at hand. There are large differences between these five databases – not just in coverage and metadata quality, but also in how the data can be extracted. These differences are highly important to the issue of whether and in which way the sources are useful for a comprehensive bibliometric analysis, specifically one that tackles the research question of the connection between business cycles, economic crises and the relevant economics literature on these. With these considerations in mind, the following subsections therefore also point out why the analysis in this book primarily uses data from JSTOR (for content analysis) and the WoS (for citation analysis).

2.3.1 EconLit

The AEA's EconLit (<<https://www.aeaweb.org/econlit/>>) is a large digital database focused on scholarly publications in economics and related subjects. Institutional subscribers can access EconLit via Ebsco's EBSCOhost Service (which, through the University of Hohenheim's subscription, was used for the work in this book), ProQuest or the Ovid|SP platform. Overall, the database covers more than a million entries dating back to 1886, for which it documents a wide array of metadata ranging from authors, publications and publication years to keywords, JEL codes (i.e. a set of standardized classifiers to label individual items), etc. However, despite this broad coverage of not only entries, but also their related metadata, previous bibliometric work on economics has used EconLit only relatively rarely – but see, for example, Cardoso et al. (2010) or more recently Pitt et al. (2016). Indeed, there are various factors which unfortunately render the database unsuitable for many large-scale bibliometric purposes, as the following paragraphs illustrate.

Overall, EconLit indexes six types of documents:[14] (1) well over one million entries from over 1000 mostly English-language journals,[15] which are selected on the basis of their peer-reviewed economics content; (2) book reviews from the *Journal of Economic Literature* (*JEL*); (3) abstracts of economics books with more than 60 pages, mirroring the *JEL*'s "Annotated List of New Books" section and starting in 1987; (4) articles in collective volumes; (5) a list of dissertations (primarily from American universities) since 1987; and finally (6) about 200 000 working papers which are indexed in collaboration with the RePEc archives (see footnote 13 on page 52). EconLit indexes primarily and mostly English texts; foreign-language contributions are indexed only if an English abstract is available.

The majority of the around 1.3 million items on EconLit are journal articles. Given this comprehensive sample size, EconLit covers a very large fraction of the (English) economics literature in peer-reviewed journals. All entries can be searched by the different categories of metadata which are listed on the database: authors, their affiliation, the publication source (titles of journals, books or working paper series), the document type (journal article, book review, etc.), ISSNs or ISBNs, keywords for articles published since 1991, JEL codes, as well as a person and a geographical descriptor category which refer to the contents of an item, e.g. in the case of biographical papers or analyses of a particular country.[16] Furthermore, a full-text search for a given string can be conducted via the access to PDF scans of the documents provided by third parties such as Ebsco. Results can then further be refined by item types (i.e. the six kinds listed in the previous paragraph), sources (i.e. the source of the publication, which can also further be refined by different journals, publishers, etc.), years, subjects (where the JEL codes feature) and language (although the vast majority of items are in English).

JEL codes seem like an ideal starting point to identify texts concerned with a specific topic. However, practically implementing this idea for a bibliometric analysis of work on business cycles and economic crises is far from straightforward, and, ultimately, not really possible. First, JEL codes can hardly be used for a long-term analysis: JEL codes were developed for use in the *JEL* which first appeared in 1969, but had already been preceded by earlier classification systems of the AEA which were first presented in 1911 (see Cherrier 2017). However, the now familiar letters and corresponding overarching main categories were only introduced with the 1991 version of the JEL codes and replaced earlier and different three-digit categories. Indeed, over the course of the history of this classification system, it has been changed multiple times, including fundamental changes to the topic identifiers and overarching categories these refer to. In the latest reiteration of the coding table considered for this book (including changes from February 2016), business cycles and economic crises are covered by codes such as "E30 Prices, Business Fluctuations, and Cycles: General (includes Measurement and Data)", "E32 Business Fluctuations; Cycles", "E37 Prices, Business Fluctuations, and Cycles: Forecasting and Simulation: Models and Applications" and "E39 Prices, Business Fluctuations, and Cycles: Other".[17]

Arguably, any paper which deals with business cycles and is classified with JEL codes should likely feature at least one of those four codes. Theoretically, therefore, the codes could be used to identify the whole body of economics literature dealing with business cycles and economic crises (or more precisely, the large sample covered on EconLit) by simply identifying all papers tagged respectively. The actual range of papers assigned and classified by JEL codes, however, severely limits this option. Since JEL codes are not assigned retrospectively, i.e. to older items published before a particular code had been introduced, those items are always indexed without respective (newer) identifiers. This means that the latest classification is only available for items published since 1991. Furthermore, even among newer items, JEL codes are not always available. While, nowadays, many working papers include JEL codes supplied by the authors in order to provide the reader with a quick reference to the topics covered by the paper (or alternatively make it easier for an editor to assign a referee), this has clearly not always been the case, and evidently not every journal started reporting the codes at the same time. Therefore, JEL code coverage tends to become less comprehensive the farther one goes back in time.

This is indeed quite unfortunate, for combining EconLit's JEL code metadata with citation counts could have allowed for an assembly and analysis of time series on both their actual frequencies, and also how often *all* papers (or at least all papers indexed in both databases) on business cycles and economic crises have been cited. Therefore, even though valuable bibliometric work (e.g. Duarte and Giraud 2016) has successfully used JEL codes, their history (mostly not going back farther than 1991 for a uniform category, and in many individual cases even shorter), characterized by frequent and often major revisions, makes them a less than ideal starting point for the content analysis in this book. Indeed, at most two economic crises and subsequent recessions in the United States (March 2001 – November 2001 and December 2007 – June 2009, see Table 2.2 on page 22) could be fully covered. It is thus necessary to devise another way to identify the relevant set of papers dealing with business cycles and economic crises. The method suggested in Subsection 2.4.2.1 is to use specific notions which are important in discussions of business cycles and economic crises, and to consider papers which use these terms in the text or in their titles.

Another more general problem with EconLit is the lack of a feasible interface to export the results to any search query. In general, search queries return a list of all matching items (which can then further be refined). Even though the search results can be arranged differently, and a permanent link to the results (before refining them) is generated, it is not readily possible to export them in any way to another format, e.g. a spreadsheet which could then be imported into other programs and processed further. Items can be stored into an online folder, and this folder can then be exported. However, the exported files are text documents which do contain all the metadata in an ordered list, but not one where, for example, all data of the same kind for a given sample (say, publication dates for a set of articles featuring the word "crisis") are in the same column. In order to actually use these data in a bibliometric analysis, a major amount of post-processing would be required, which is not feasible for the amount of items and data we deal with here (see, for example, the aggregate numbers summarized in Section 3.1), especially when similar data are available from JSTOR. Therefore, while the EconLit interface is great for browsing a huge body of economics literature (and further for finding what one searches therein), it is not – nor was it developed for that purpose – well-suited for bibliometric research as of yet, and is not used for the analysis in Chapter 3.

2.3.2 JSTOR

JSTOR (<<http://www.jstor.org>>) is another major database that contains a full-text archive of economics and neighbouring disciplines. JSTOR archives mostly items in journals, at a total of over nine million items across all disciplines. Concerning economics, there are over 280 000 research articles in about 190 economics periodicals. A better comparison with EconLit can be gained when comparing items in the business and economics categories, for EconLit also archives not only economics, but also content from neighbouring fields. Here, there are nearly 400 000 research articles in over 280 business and economics periodicals on JSTOR. Concerning articles flagged as economics or business and economics independently of the journal (see later paragraphs here, as well as Subsection 2.4.2.1 on the difference), JSTOR lists over 140 000 items as economics, and nearly 640 000 as business and economics as of February 16th, 2017. In terms of absolute numbers, coverage is therefore less comprehensive than on EconLit, although there can be little doubt that JSTOR still provides a very large sample which especially contains most of the major journals in economics and neighbouring fields (some notable exceptions are the *Journal of Monetary Economics* or the *Journal of Financial Economics*; also see Subsection 2.4.1).

While EconLit coverage begins in 1886, JSTOR goes further back in time, with economics coverage dating back to 1844. However, earlier years are characterized by low absolute item counts (naturally, only some journals date back as far), so this does not make much of a difference for the overall distribution of items in both the EconLit and JSTOR populations. A potentially more important difference concerns the more recent coverage. Here, there is what is usually labelled a "rolling wall" on JSTOR: the number of indexed items greatly decreases towards more recent years, because many journals and publishers only make their recent content available on other outlets first before they become accessible via JSTOR. For example, on February 15th, 2017, the latest available *Econometrica* issue was that from November 2014. Therefore, for recent years especially, EconLit coverage is superior. For the long-term analysis in the present book, however, this does not matter as much, although the general problem has to be taken into account when constructing bibliometric time series (see Subsection 2.4.2.1). Another difference in coverage is that, in contrast to EconLit, JSTOR does not cover books, dissertations or working papers. Especially for earlier periods, and well into the first half of the 20th century, this may be problematic when, as in the analysis here, an impression of developments in the general literature is to be gained. However, as long as the general sample is large enough (which is arguably the case with JSTOR), the lack of books should not be expected to skew or bias the results, as long as the topics discussed and terminology used to do so are not systematically different between books and articles. What is more, Stigler and Freidland (1979: 3f.) pointed out that "books have declined relative to journal articles as the form of initial publication of economic work since, one would estimate, roughly 1885". In this case, using a large sample of journal articles seems to be not only akin to using a reasonable sample for the population of journal articles, but of the economics literature in general, and of the 20th and 21st century in particular, indeed.

Whereas EconLit lacks a feasible option to extract data, it is possible to do exactly that with JSTOR's handily usable "Data for Research" (DfR; <<http://dfr.jstor.org>>, respectively <<http://www.jstor.org/dfr/>> after the August 2017 JSTOR update[18]) interface, which can be used to both comprehensively search and identify a body of literature, and then export relevant metadata for that sample. Since JSTOR also contains full-text PDFs, it is possible to search all the documents' contents directly, especially via DfR. Given the combination of broad coverage and good access and exportability of the data,

JSTOR therefore serves as the primary data source for the content analysis in the present book.

The most straightforward way to use the DfR search is to enter a search term, then narrow the results down by selecting categories on the left of the interface. The default option for searches is "anywhere in document", which means that the whole body of text, including authors, titles, abstracts and keywords (where available), references and the main text itself are searched – i.e. a full-text search. However, searches can also be limited to these categories: authors, titles, abstracts, keywords and references. An author's name, for example, can of course be searched for both within author names only, and anywhere in the document. In the latter case, mentions of the name in any part of the document – particularly the references, e.g. if the item cites an author by that name – would also return the item as a search result. Searches are case-insensitive and can be conducted for single terms, or longer strings consisting of multiple words, with the strings indicated by double quotes (" "). Multiple terms or strings can further be connected via "AND", "+", "OR" (which is applied as the default conjunction operator), "NOT" and "–" Boolean operators. Search strings can also contain single or multiple character wildcards ("?" and "*", respectively), except as the first character. By searching references, it is theoretically possible to identify citation links and thus count references to individual papers (by using those papers' authors, titles and journals as search strings). However, this is generally not feasible for larger samples of cited papers due to different citation styles, the risk of false attributions, etc., especially in light of the fact that there are citation databases which provide exactly that information in a systematic manner (see the next two subsections).

Results for a given search string can be further narrowed down by a wide set of different categories (called "facets" on the DfR search help). First, the year of publication can be selected – either one single year, or a continuous period. Secondly, search results may be filtered by their type and related features: the "Content Type" facet distinguishes between journals and pamphlets, and the "Article Type" facet then can be further used to narrow down results to "research articles" and "book reviews" (which together constitute the large majority of nearly 88% of items in journals), as well as "miscellaneous" (which contains list of abstracts and everything else not covered by the other categories), "news" and "editorials". Among book reviews, it is also possible to further refine the sample by "Reviewed Author" and "Reviewed Work", i.e. by author and work that is being reviewed. Similar to a range for the years of publications, a range for the "Page Count" of the sampled items can be selected.

The more important facets for the purpose of the present study, however, are those that refine the sample by "Subject" or "Subject Group", respectively "Discipline" or "Discipline Group". JSTOR lists an "Economics" (E) category that is part of a larger group category, "Business and Economics" (BE), which additionally includes the neighbouring fields of "Business", "Development Studies", "Finance" (F), "Labor & Employment Relations", "Management & Organizational Behavior" and "Marketing & Advertising". In general, it should be noted that all categories – also including the overarching groups – can overlap, and items will frequently have multiple corresponding flags (on the group level, for example, there is a large overlap with "Social Sciences").

On DfR, then, the sample can be narrowed down to E via the "Subject" or "Discipline" facets, and to BE via the "Subject Group" or "Discipline Group" facets, respectively. For future reference, "Discipline" and "Subject" categories (as well as the groups) are indicated by a lower-case "d" or "s" before the category acronym, e.g. "dE" for the E "Discipline" category, or "sBE" for the BE "Subject Group". The "Subject" (and, correspondingly, "Subject Group") filter limits the search to all those items in the result sample which were attributed that subject, algorithmically based on their full texts (e.g. an E text is characterized by some specific terminology, and a BE text can have either E terminology, or business terminology, etc.). In contrast, the "Discipline" and "Discipline Group" facets return those items which were published within a journal which was flagged as a certain discipline by the JSTOR staff (that is, directly by humans, not automated via an algorithm). For example, therefore, all items in the *American Economic Review* (*AER*) are dE. However, not all of these items are sE, for that category is algorithmically determined for each item individually based on its text. An example which also features a term relevant for the analysis in this book (see Subsection 2.4.2.1) would be a paper on depressive people published in the *AER*: since the "Discipline" categorization is adopted from the journal, the paper would be flagged as dE, but might very well *not* be sE. In general, therefore, sE research articles are economics papers, and those in dE are papers published in an economics journal.

Furthermore, results can be narrowed down to only those items within a particular journal, by a specific author, or by a certain publisher (three different facets). There is a facet for the language of the publication. Most items on JSTOR are in English: of the nearly 4.8 million journal research articles, about 87.5% are in English, and roughly 3% each in French, German and Italian. Among both all business and economics journals (dBE) and all business and economics research articles (sBE), over 90% of items are in English, and virtually all economics papers (sE) archived on JSTOR are in English.

Last, but not least, for every result set, DfR also automatically generates around 300 single word key terms based on the contents of that sample. Selecting the "Key term" facet will provide a word cloud of these terms with their size proportional to their weight. Terms in the clouds can then be clicked to narrow down the sample further (but see Subsection 2.4.2.1 on the limitations). All the different facets can be combined to obtain, for example, a set of all research articles within a given journal during a particular time frame which contain a specific term in their title. As King et al. (2012) argue, DfR is therefore particularly useful for historians of thought who wish to trace the development and spread of particular ideas and theories over time – i.e. exactly the aim of this book.

Once the desired set of items has thus been obtained, the resulting list can be exported in two different ways. First, a spreadsheet containing a list of all components of a facet and the corresponding number of items in the result set for that component can be exported. The primary use of this for the analysis in the present book was to export, for each sample, a list of the number of items per year. Secondly, after registering an account with DfR, it is possible to export metadata for a set of documents via the "Dataset Requests" options. There are multiple elements which can be included in this export. First, it always contains as a default a spreadsheet of all exported items with their corresponding bibliographic metadata, i.e. title, authors, year, the publication source, volume, issue, publisher, page numbers, an abstract where available, and IDs and DOIs from JSTOR. Exports can further contain word counts, bi-, tri- or quad-grams (i.e. strings of two, three or four consecutive words) and key terms. Selecting one of these options will generate one spreadsheet per option and item (i.e. 500 individual word count list files for 500 articles). Word count lists contain a ranked column of the most frequent words and their corresponding frequencies. The *n*-gram lists of two-, three- and four-word strings similarly produce one spreadsheet per article, with the difference that these lists now do not contain single terms, but the respective strings. All of these spreadsheets contain an exhaustive list of *n*-grams (including single words), i.e. a potentially long lists of strings. The key term lists similarly contain spreadsheets for each item, with about 25 key terms automatically generated by JSTOR and their corresponding weights. As of yet, it is unfortunately not possible to directly combine and aggregate the individual result spreadsheets, especially directly before exporting them into individual documents, which is why this option is not feasible for large sets of articles. Despite the large amount of potentially useful data which can be extracted via JSTOR, therefore, the actual applicability of these results seems to be rather limited. Otherwise, these could serve as a great starting point, for example, for a semantic analysis which examines how the usage (and corresponding occurrence) of terms may have shifted between different years, etc. Be that as it may, JSTOR nonetheless provides a very rich source for the content analysis that is the backbone of the empirical approach to assessing this book's PPT research question (see Subsection 2.4.2.1).

2.3.3 Web of Science

The Web of Science (WoS; <<http://wokinfo.com/>>) is the current iteration of the first original database of citation data (see Subsection 2.1.1), and has also long and frequently been considered the standard, go-to reference (see Harzing and Alakangas 2016: 791). Indeed, until 2004 it had even been the only such source. With Scopus (see Subsection 2.3.4) and Google Scholar (see Subsection 2.3.5), two major competitors have entered the market since, but the WoS still serves as an important point of reference and source for bibliometric analyses.

There are multiple citation indexes on the WoS, including the original – albeit now, of course, digitalized – Science Citation Index. Economics items are archived within the Social Science Citation Index (SSCI), which indexes over 1950 journals from over 50 different research fields and disciplines in the social sciences. Furthermore, the SSCI also includes relevant items from over

3300 leading journals in other fields which were individually selected. Access to the WoS is subscription-based. For the work on this book, the authors could access the SSCI while one of the authors was a visiting researcher at the University of Helsinki. The University of Helsinki's subscription then covered all the years since and including 1956. While this unfortunately does not include periods of interest to the research question at hand, such as the Great Depression, it still allows for over five and a half decades of comprehensive and reliable citation data.

Corresponding to the different indexes on the WoS, there are also multiple research fields into which articles are categorized. Specifically, there is an "Economics" category which included 235 journals when the data were extracted, and also still in February 2017.[19] Once again, in addition to not indexing books, this is a smaller list than on EconLit, although especially most major journals are indexed. Similarly, although of a comparable size and with a large intersection, the sample is not identical with that of JSTOR. This means that citation data from the SSCI for all economics articles are derived from a somewhat different population than content analyses based on JSTOR data, so, even independently of the particular methods employed in the content and citation analyses, respectively, results cannot be directly compared. There are also some other categories capturing neighbouring fields of economics (e.g. "Business"), but there is, for example, no correspondingly labelled counterpart to finance (instead there is "Business Finance"), so the focus with SSCI data will be only on the economics category. As in the other databases, WoS categories can overlap.

In general, there are two ways to search for and identify citation links between items on the WoS. The first and most straightforward one is to find a particular item by using a "Basic Search" to identify an article, and then following the links to "cited" or "citing references" on the item's page. This provides a list of all respectively linked items within the index being searched. The "cited" list shows all indexed items cited by the one that was searched for; and "citing references", as the name implies, are other items on the index which cite the article at hand. It is also possible (although less straightforward) to compile a list of several items and then identify all items citing at least one from the list. Citation counts and references obtained this way via a basic search only include citations from items actually indexed on the SSCI, respectively WoS. This means that citations from books as well as from working papers, journals, etc. which are not catalogued are not included. However, it is possible to get citation counts to items not indexed – including books. This is because, within the items indexed on the SSCI, all their citations, even those to items which are not on the SSCI, are recognized (but clearly not curated in the same way as references between two items which are both indexed). Those can be searched via the "Cited Reference Search" option.

Whatever the search method, search results are a set of citing (or cited) items, which can then be exported with their metadata. Before the export, it is also possible to narrow down the result list further, e.g. to only items from a particular research field, year, etc. In general, there are two main options concerning which data to extract and how they will be arranged in the spreadsheet returned by the data export. When exporting a list of citing items (e.g. those items which cite a selected article, or cite at least one in a set of articles), the result is a spreadsheet that contains a short (but not complete) summary of the search that led to this result list and also some aggregate data, namely the overall number of results, overall number of citations to all citing items, and the *h*-index of the list of citing items. More importantly, the spreadsheet contains an ordered list (e.g. by date of publication or number of citations, as can also be selected before the export) of all the citing items, with all kinds of relevant metadata: author, year, title, publication source, journal volume and issue, page numbers and a DOI. What is more, annual total citation counts are also included for each item individually. It should be noted, however, that if the list was generated as one that samples items citing a set of other items, there is no distinct information on how often, and by which citing item, cited items were referenced. For this additional information, it would once again be necessary to take a step back to the individual level of single papers. Also note that citation counts derived from these data exports are total counts on the WoS, respectively the selected index (e.g. the SSCI), i.e. including subjects other than economics and not just research articles.

Alternatively, it is also possible to export a set of items directly, before getting to its corresponding list of citing articles. This list contains even more metadata where available. In addition to those data also obtainable from the previous method for data extraction, there are identifiers for the publication and document type (primarily journal and article), language, and there is information on the publisher, their address, author contact details, and WoS and subject categories. Furthermore, especially more recent items may also contain an abstract as well as keywords provided by the author and automatically generated key terms. These so-called "KeyWords Plus" are compiled for each paper from the titles of its references.[20] A notable downside, however, is that citation counts are not available per year via this export, but only for the total time period covered by the respective WoS subscription. The number of cited references indexed on the respective database (e.g. on the SSCI) is also included for each article on the list, and short identifiers can additionally be extracted to link the items. Data exports of this kind are, therefore, less suitable for citation analysis, but can be used very well for supplementary and complementary content analyses, e.g. of term frequencies in titles, in addition to what can be done with JSTOR (see Subsections 2.4.2.1 and 2.4.2.2). In general, a maximum of 500 items can be exported at once, so multiple requests followed by a subsequent combining of the individual files are necessary to extract longer lists.

2.3.4 Scopus

Elsevier's Scopus (<<https://www.scopus.com/>>) was launched in 2004 as a competitor, and has quickly advanced to become the primary alternative to the WoS, since it provides the same kind of data, i.e. primarily citation links between different publications. Scopus's overall coverage of journals is now higher than that of the WoS. According to the *Scopus Content Coverage Guide* from January 2016, "[i]t is the largest abstract and citation database of peer-reviewed literature" (Elsevier 2016: 3), which features over 21 500 peer-reviewed journals, over 530 book series, well over 100 000 books and over 7.2 million conference papers. Scopus therefore now constitutes a well-established alternative to the WoS which is frequently referenced, e.g. in international university rankings (see Harzing and Alakangas 2016: 791). As with the WoS, access is subscription-based. For the present book, the authors were able to access Scopus via the University of Hohenheim's subscription.

About two-thirds of Scopus's over 60 000 000 items are post-1995, and their absolute number has more than doubled over the past ten years, whereas the number of around 20 000 000 pre-1996 items increased far less between 2008 and 2015 (see Elsevier 2016: 4). The largest part of Scopus's coverage, therefore, is in more recent items, and this is also where most additions have been made over the past few years (of course, this is a natural byproduct of all the new publications, especially those in sources already indexed on the database, and similarly holds for other databases). Economics is classified as part of category "2000 Economics, Econometrics and Finance". Similar to other databases discussed before, categories can overlap, and many economics journals are also part of the category "1400 Business, Management, and Accounting". When the Scopus Source List[21] from October 2016 was last accessed on February 22nd, 2017, there were 992 entries in the "2000" category, 900 of which are journals. Coverage in terms of the number of periodicals is thus nearly as comprehensive as on EconLit (see Subsection 2.3.1). Generally, therefore, Scopus seems like a very reasonable alternative source to the WoS, especially when economics or related fields such as business are concerned (also see Levine-Clark and Gil 2009: 45).

However, despite its broad coverage, Scopus lacks depth in terms of indexed years when compared to the WoS. Even many renowned journals with a long history are not fully covered on Scopus. For example, *Econometrica*, which was first published in 1933, is only available continuously since 1994, and the only additionally available older vintages are 1974, 1977–1984 and 1990. Similarly, the first listed *AER* issue dates from 1978 – even though the journal has a much longer history of over a century. Indeed, Scopus covers the large majority of journals (namely 780) in the "2000" category non-stop since only the 1990s. The longest continuous coverage is provided for the *Oxford Economic Papers*, beginning in 1949. This introduces major inconsistencies into the creation of long historical time series, since journal contents and their metadata are unavailable even for years where the journal had in fact already been published. Therefore, more recent years feature more entries not just because of more journals and absolute publication counts, but also because of incomplete coverage of indexed journals in earlier time periods. For a long-term analysis aiming at a large dataset that is as coherent as possible, both the short and frequently non-continuous coverage are two considerable problems which make the use of

Scopus for the purpose of the present book much less promising than sticking with the less broad, but more in-depth, data from the WoS.

Another major issue concerns the general availability of citation data, which is what made Scopus a source of interest for the present study in the first place. Like the WoS, Scopus provides all kinds of metadata. However, for pre-1996 items, no references are available (see Elsevier 2016: 9). In recent years, Elsevier has greatly expanded Scopus in this respect and especially added cited references to pre-1996 articles published since 1970 into the metadata of post-1995 items (i.e. if a later item cited an older one, it is then indexed). However, since references of pre-1996 items are not indexed, it is impossible to generate a comprehensive and especially uniform citation time series which goes back further than two decades. What is more, due to the limited coverage of pre-1990 entries in economics journals on Scopus, even the additional indexing of citations from newer works to older publications does not solve the problem, for as long as the economics articles are not indexed in the first place, no citation links can be added to them either. Since the research interest of the present book primarily lies in a long-term analysis, this is too short of a time frame, for a period starting in 1996 would at most cover two recession periods.

Overall, therefore, the citation time series which can be obtained from the WoS may be less comprehensive for those years where Scopus also provides continuous coverage (i.e. post-1995). However, the WoS access available for the work on this book covers in a coherent manner four more decades than would have been possible with data from Scopus, and thus spans a time period about three times as long. Also, WoS journal coverage – for the smaller number of periodicals which is available – seems to be more consistent and continuous. Therefore, ultimately, despite its constant improvements not only in breadth but also in depth of coverage, Scopus is not used in the analysis here, and citation data are instead taken from the WoS.

2.3.5 Google Scholar

Google Scholar (GS; <<http://scholar.google.com>>) provides the largest database of scientific literature, spanning the whole breadth of different subjects and topics, and featuring not just journal articles, but also all kinds of other publication types, including books, working papers, and even blog posts and similar outlets which are usually not necessarily considered forms of scholarly publication, and correspondingly do not feature in the other databases at all. More recently, GS has also started to provide coverage on patents. Individual items on GS can include (but do not always necessarily do so) metadata on the online source of the publication, its publication date, publisher (including most importantly, in the case of articles, the corresponding journals, volume and issue numbers), fields of study (although only indirectly, and to a very limited degree) and also citation counts. All of these are automatically generated by an algorithm adding items to the database. Compared with the WoS or Scopus, the broad coverage of GS allows not only for a better assessment of the overall spread and discussion of an individual contribution, but also, due to the inclusion of working papers, etc., for a more readily available (due to the lower publication delay) quantitative assessment of the reception of especially junior scholars' works at an early stage in their career (see Hamermesh 2015: 4). What is more, GS has one significant advantage over both the WoS and Scopus: GS access is free of charge.

In general, as Harzing and Alakangas (2016) point out, coverage of WoS and Scopus (especially on an absolute level of items, and across all disciplines) is fairly similar, whereas that of GS is clearly the largest and considerably higher. Despite the differences in coverage, Hamermesh (2015) shows that, for economics, GS and WoS citation counts are highly correlated with each other, so that results for relative citation analyses (e.g. to compare authors' metrics) are rather similar as long as comparisons are made within the same database. To assess the impact of individual items in business and economics, Levine-Clark and Gil (2009) recommend to use the three databases alongside one another.

However, for the purpose of the present study there are a number of problems with GS – both practical, in how the data can be handled, and concerning the data quality itself. First of all, ever since it was originally introduced, GS has frequently been criticized for its low-quality metadata and citation links as a consequence of the algorithms sifting through the web and generating them, which would consequently make it unsuitable for bibliometric analyses – especially see Jacsó (2010), and also Harzing and Alakangas (2016: 791). Owing to the way the metadata were obtained from publishers' websites for scholarly outlets, especially the authors of a listed item would often be misrepresented, which of course greatly influences an actual author's citation counts. While there have been many improvements in response to the criticisms ever since, and while the WoS and Scopus, which are often directly compared to GS, also contain such errors (see Franceschini et al. 2016), this is probably still more of an issue for GS than for the other two sources, since both WoS and Scopus data are manually curated. For example, searching GS for author names containing "policy" (inspired by Jacsó's (2010) demonstration of errors in GS, searched on February 8th, 2017) still returns thousands of items, many of which on the first result page already did not actually have an author by the surname "policy".

Be that as it may, the way the data can be exported and assembled is in fact more relevant and a bigger problem when working with GS. Indeed, GS's native interface is not very suitable at all for bibliometric analyses. Using the advanced search in GS, search queries can be refined to papers containing (or not containing) a set of words in the text, or in their titles, and authors, publications and years can be searched as well. However, the return to any query cannot readily be exported via the website. For purposes of citation analysis, in particular, there is a handy tool, though – Harzing's (2007) "Publish or Perish" (PoP) software. But even using PoP, metadata (including especially citations) on only a limited number of at most 1000 items per search query can be taken and extracted from GS and subsequently imported into PoP. For example, since there were nearly 20 000 items on GS which were returned to a search for "business cycle theory" on February 8th, 2017, the export can thus at best cover a small fraction of just about 5% of the results, and it is likely skewed towards the most cited, "most relevant" (as determined by an algorithm listing GS results, similar to that used for Google searches) or most recent contributions, and not a cross-section of all results. What is more, overall results cannot be properly organized by field of study, so it is not possible to identify reference categories, e.g. all papers (or, for GS, items) in economics in a certain year. Thus, relative citation frequencies cannot readily be calculated, so that long-term relative comparisons which are not skewed by the much greater number of items in recent years (even more so in GS, which covers much more than articles and books) are impossible. Owing to the limited number of items which can be exported in general, and the fact that even those (or the underlying search results) cannot be readily classified into their respective subject categories, an analysis of the frequencies of particular notions or key terms is not really possible, either. PoP allows the user to trace citation frequencies for limited samples of items, but concerning the research question tackled in the present book – a long-term analysis of developments in economics research articles – not even PoP renders GS a feasible data source. Therefore, GS is not used in the analysis in Chapter 3.

2.4 Method and procedure

In order to perform a bibliometric assessment of PPT, proxy measures for the relevant variables – the spread and discussion of work on business cycles and economic crises – need to be identified. Using records from the databases presented in Section 2.3, we construct time series of frequencies of papers containing particular terms (Subsection 2.4.2.1), trace citation frequencies (Subsection 2.4.2.2), and discuss issues of semantics with respect to the context in which particular terms (such as 'crisis') are set (Subsection 2.4.3). In order to compare not only developments in economics and neighbouring disciplines, but also within economics – specifically, economics as a whole on the one hand, and its premier, most influential outlets on the other – Subsection 2.4.1 first describes the sample of premier journals. Identifying bibliometric proxies of the spread of business cycle and crises theory is, however, only half of the work needed to tackle PPT (also see Subsection 2.1.3): it still lacks the first half, the "panics", i.e. the actual economic development. The combination of economic and bibliometric data is achieved via various econometric methods, which are laid out in Subsection 2.4.4.

Counting term frequencies is certainly an approximation to a comprehensive answer to our research question, but it is also a rather superficial approach, of course. In a way, it can be seen as the extreme to one end of the trade-off sketched in Subsection 2.1.3, where previous research which referred to PPT (see Chapter 1) occupies the other end. A careful, qualitative reading of selected papers, or the highlighting of particular landmarks (Keynes's *General Theory*, Fisher's *Booms and Depressions*, etc.), provides valuable and compelling examples – but it is not enough to assess overall, broad developments in the literature. Our bibliometric method does aim at painting this overall picture, but it lacks the qualitative aspect. For example, the analysis does not discriminate between how often a term is used within a paper, and, more importantly, in what context. Therefore, it cannot distinguish between papers which concern business cycle theory or economic policy advice related to economic crises, on the one hand, and those which merely refer to recent events, on the other. We discuss this problem, among other issues, in Section 3.3, which relates the results not only to previously published research, but also to particular historical episodes and individual items.

2.4.1 *Identification of top journals*

Identifying the most relevant and important journals in economics has been a frequent topic in bibliometric and scientometric articles on economics (e.g. see Quandt 1976; Laband and Piette 1994; Burton and Phimister 1995; Stigler et al. 1995; Beckmann and Persson 1998). In a paper on flows of knowledge between economics and neighbouring disciplines, Pieters and Baumgartner (2002) named the *American Economic Review* (*AER*), *Econometrica*, the *Journal of Political Economy* (*JPE*), the *Quarterly Journal of Economics* (*QJE*) and the *Review of Economic Studies* (*REStud*) as the top five journals. Indeed, these five are a standard reference for the top journals in economics, both for recent years as well as for longer-term comparisons.[22] Cardoso et al. (2010) classify the same five plus the *Journal of Economic Theory* as top journals, and Hamermesh (2015: 6), quoting Pieters and Baumgartner (2002), uses the same sample and even argues that the *REStud* may be considered as an outlier, so that the other four constitute the actual "elite" group of economic journals (see Hamermesh 2015: 25). Repeated identifications of a similar set of journals are especially important because the body of journals available and actually covered in the databases of course changes over time (see Section 2.3), and it is not necessarily convincing to assume *ex ante* that every journal has had the same relevance in every year, especially over a long time span. However, for those select few it is probably safe to argue that they were both very relevant historically, and are also highly relevant today.

The simplest measure to assess a journal's relative relevance is to compare IFs (as discussed in Subsection 2.1.1). Using, for example, the SJR2 indicator from the SCImago Journal Ranking (<<http://www.scimagojr.com/>>), the ten highest ranked journals among the 836 periodicals in the "Economics, Econometrics and Finance" category on March 6th, 2016[23] were (in descending order): *QJE*, the *Journal of Finance* (*JF*), *Econometrica*, *JPE*, *Journal of Economic Literature* (*JEL*), *REStud*, *Review of Financial Studies* (*RFStud*), *Journal of Financial Economics* (*JFE*), *AER* and *American Economic Journal: Applied Economics* (*AEJ: AE*). Perhaps unsurprisingly, this list contains all the journals from the top five list by Pieters and Baumgartner (2002). Additionally, it features three prominent finance journals (*JF*, *RFStud*, *JFE*), one of them even among the top five. Furthermore, the SJR2 top five also includes the *JEL*. While there is little doubt about the *JEL*'s prestige and status, studies such as the one previously mentioned that not only base their rankings on simple numbers, but also contain a qualitative discussion of their procedure, often do not include the *JEL*. This may be related to its special nature of mostly containing book reviews and only a small number of research articles, which are usually literature reviews. Rank 10 is occupied by the *AEJ: AE*, a very new journal, the first issue of which was published in 2009. As a comparison, the same ten journals made the top ten in February 2017, with only some changes in their order among these top spots, but not the first three.

The RePEc Aggregate Ranking is another easily accessible ordered list of economics journals (<<http://ideas.repec.org/top/top.journals.all.html>>). This ranking is calculated based on data from the CitEc project (<<http://citec.repec.org/>>) which uses RePEc citation records. Several bibliometric measures are calculated for each journal: simple IFs and three versions thereof, the *h*-index, as well as abstract views and file downloads on RePEc. Journals are ranked for each of the seven measures individually. The overall rank is then obtained by removing the worst and the best ranking factor for each journal individually, and then taking a harmonic mean of the remaining factors' positions. When the RePEc ranking was accessed in March 2016, the top ten were, in descending order: *JPE*, *AER*, *QJE*, *Econometrica*, *JEL*, *JFE*, *Journal of Economic Growth*, *JF*, *Journal of Monetary Economics* and *REStud*. For comparison, just like with the SJR2 ranking, the same ten journals constituted the top ten in February 2017, and only some changed their ranks (e.g. the *JEL* made way in the top five for the *JFE*). Given the relative stability in both rankings over the period of a year as well as their general congruence with bibliometric work on the most important journals in economics, journals from these lists, especially those present in both, thus seem to be reliable candidates for being considered a top economics journal.

Building on this, two top journal groups are used in the following analysis. The first one, TJ5, comprises the top four that Hamermesh (2015) highlighted (the five of Pieters and Baumgartner 2002 minus *REStud*), i.e. *AER*, *Econometrica*, *JPE* and *QJE*, plus the *JEL*. The latter is included due to its overall relevance in the rankings and its established status. However, since only research articles are considered and the *JEL* is also the newest of those five, it contributes only a small fraction of the total articles in all five journals overall, and for every single year. For example, in the ten years between 2000 and 2009, 4873 research articles in the TJ5 are archived on JSTOR, and only 154 of these (less than 3.2%) are from the *JEL*. Therefore, even if review articles had very different citation profiles (see e.g. Ho et al. 2017) or writing styles as regards the terms they employ, this is unlikely to bias the overall results for the TJ5 category, especially since the econometric analysis in Section 3.2 does not aim to identify a citation network or the like, but instead employs other methods. What is more, the top journal categories primarily feature in the descriptive analysis anyway. The second category contains journals which were among the top ten of both the SJR2 and the RePEc ranking in March 2016. This list

Table 2.3 Journals in the two top journal categories from JSTOR data

Title	*Abbrev.*	*Period*	*TJ5*	*TJ7*
American Economic Review	*AER*	1911–2012	✓	✓
Econometrica		1933–2012	✓	✓
Journal of Political Economy	*JPE*	1892–2012	✓	✓
Quarterly Journal of Economics	*QJE*	1886–2012	✓	✓
Journal of Economic Literature	*JEL*	1969–2011	✓	✓
Review of Economic Studies	*REStud*	1933–2012		✓
Journal of Finance	*JF*	1946–2012		✓

Note: In each case, the first year of the period is when the journal was first published, and the latest year is either the year of the last available issue on JSTOR when the data were assembled, or 2012 as the generally last year of JSTOR data in this study.

includes eight periodicals, namely *AER*, *Econometrica*, *JPE*, *QJE*, *JEL*, *JFE*, *JF* and *REStud*. The *JFE*, however, is not archived on JSTOR, so when working with JSTOR data, the second top journal group – TJ7 – will contain a sample of seven journals. By including the *JF*, this larger top journal category naturally has a relatively bigger emphasis on finance as compared with the more narrowly economics-focused TJ5 category.

When identifying and counting research articles in TJ5 and TJ7, the JSTOR search was not further restricted by subject or discipline so that the numbers for TJ5 and TJ7 represent all research articles within these journals, independent of the specific subject in particular. Consequently, since the journals contain articles flagged as all kinds of subjects, most but not all articles in the journals are in one of the subject categories which constitute sBE (especially sE and sF). Therefore, neither TJ5 nor TJ7 is a subset of any of the subject categories of interest. TJ5, however, is a subset of dE, because all five journals – and thus all articles within them – are attributed to the dE category. Since *JF* is not flagged as dE, TJ7 is not a subset of dE, although, like TJ5, it is a subset of dBE. For both TJ5 and TJ7, Table 2.3 summarizes the journals and their respective periods of availability.

2.4.2 Primary bibliometric time series

2.4.2.1 Content analysis

The main part of this book is a content analysis which extends the empirical study of Kufenko and Geiger (2016). For the bibliometric part of the empirical analysis, we construct time series of frequencies of research articles in JSTOR featuring particular terms related to BCCT at least once in their whole body of text. These series are then compared with economic data by means of econometric methods to quantitatively test PPT. The bibliometric time series are derived from JSTOR searches for papers containing particular search strings, which serve as a means to identify the set of relevant papers, i.e. work which discusses business cycles and economic crises (for which we ideally would have used JEL codes, if these were comprehensively and consistently available). The analysis here uses not only additional and longer economic time series (see Section 2.2), but also further samples of bibliometric data. The bibliometric method and data sources also resemble other bibliometric work on the HET. For example, Hoover (2004) similarly traced the notion of "causality" in economics.

The theoretical core of the analysis and the construction of the relevant sample of bibliometric data remain the same as in Kufenko and Geiger (2016), which also ensures comparability of the results (especially see Subsection 3.3.3). Building on Besomi (2011), 15 search strings are selected to represent proxies for discussions of BCCT, or business cycles and economic crises in general, in the literature. For his own empirical analysis, Besomi (2011) had explicitly identified 11 such terms: glut, distress, embarrassment, stagnation, panic, bubble, depression, crisis, cycle, fluctuations and recession. Besomi's (2011) selection of these terms was based on a comprehensive study of a wide set of different literature on the topic, from over two centuries back up until the late 20th century. Since the term "cycle" can quite obviously be used in contexts other than BCCT (for example, when referencing the life-cycle hypothesis of consumption), the analysis here considers the frequency not only of the term alone, but that of papers featuring either (or both) of the two most frequent specifications in the context relevant here, i.e. the compounds "business cycle" and "trade cycle" (further, BCTC; also see Besomi 2011: 94ff.). In order to include another notion relating to the upswing of business cycles, i.e. to the opposite of what notions such as "distress" refer to (see Besomi 2011: 59ff.), "prosperity" is included as a 13th (including the BCTC compound) term. Among these 13 terms, four are further classified as the most relevant to our analysis, and are considered in most detail in Chapter 3. This includes, first and foremost, BCTC – i.e. the name often attributed to the overall phenomenon itself. Furthermore, since PPT primarily relates to the downswing of a business cycle, the three most prominent notions in this context are also considered as major terms: crisis, recession and depression.

Additionally, two indexes are created to gauge the overall breadth of the relevant literature: a DOWNSWING index, which contains the central terms of crisis, recession and depression, and an OVERALL index, which comprises all 13 terms. Indexes provide frequencies of papers which contain at least one of the terms in the index, so naturally their item sets (and the corresponding time series) are at least as large as their biggest component. Table 2.1 summarizes the 15 notions and also documents the search strings employed in creating them. The table also lists a reference number for each term, which will be used throughout the book in some of the tables to keep potentially cluttering text to a minimum. There are no different spellings between American and British English for the terms; and, with one exception ("crisis" and "crises"), the plural

Table 2.4 Reference table for bibliometric series

#	*Term*	*Search string*
1	BCTC	"business cycle" OR "trade cycle"
2	crisis	"crisis" OR "crises" (crisis crises)
3	depression	"depression"
4	recession	"recession"
5	DOWNSWING	"crisis" OR "crises" OR "recession" OR "depression" (crisis crises recession depression)
6	bubble	"bubble"
7	cycle	"cycle"
8	distress	"distress"
9	embarrassment	"embarrassment"
10	fluctuations	"fluctuations"
11	glut	"glut"
12	panic	"panic"
13	prosperity	"prosperity"
14	stagnation	"stagnation"
15	OVERALL	"crisis" OR "crises" OR "recession" OR "depression" OR "cycle" OR "fluctuations" OR "bubble" OR "distress" OR "embarrassment" OR "glut" OR "panic" OR "prosperity" OR "stagnation" (cycle crisis crises recession depression fluctuations bubble distress embarrassment glut panic prosperity stagnation)

Note: Column 2 lists the terms employed in the analysis, whereas column 1 provides the corresponding reference numbers, and column 3 the respective search strings. For 'crisis' and the two indexes (DOWNSWING and OVERALL), the top string was used for searches anywhere in the documents, and the bottom one for title-only searches.

is simply formed by the addition of an "s", so instances of that are automatically included in the JSTOR search as well.

To create this and other compounded search terms with different elements, the relevant words were put in double quotes and connected via the Boolean "OR" operator. Two remarks are in order. First, for the OVERALL index, it is of course sufficient to use the term "cycle" in the search string, for this also necessarily includes all instances of "business cycle" and "trade cycle". Secondly, JSTOR's DfR search engine handled search requests anywhere in the document somewhat differently from those in titles only. Therefore, search strings for the two indexes were arranged as a series of the individual words within a set of simple parentheses "( )". For BCTC, where the same method would not have properly counted "business cycle" and "trade cycle", all respective instances of "business cycle" and "trade cycle" from two individual searches were added up, and then manually checked for double countings (as it turned out, however, no title in any category featured both expressions).

In their econometric analysis, Kufenko and Geiger (2016) compared time series for the same terms and indexes with economic data.[24] However, they did so only for two JSTOR categories, namely sE and sBE, and only for frequencies anywhere in the documents. The present analysis expands this greatly. First, the finance subject category sF is also included in the descriptive analysis. This is due to the close connection between the two fields. As Pieters and Baumgartner (2002: 499) show through a citation analysis of major journals in both economics and finance (using SSCI data for 1995–1997), the fields are closely related to one another, with a very large proportion of interdisciplinary citations from economics going to finance, and vice versa – also see Borokhovich et al. (1995) and further see Borokhovich et al. (2015). Additionally, to get an impression not just of economics (and related) articles, but also of those in economics (and related) journals, all corresponding discipline categories (dE, dF, dBE) are considered as well. The top journal sets as described in Subsection 2.4.1 are included as the seventh and eighth categories. Additionally, we also compile time series of frequencies within titles of documents in all these categories, which more closely follows Besomi's (2011) original approach.

Overall, this results in a large number of bibliometric time series compiled for the analysis in this book. In addition to the eight reference series listing total items every year in each category (sE, sF, sBE, dE, dF, dBE and the two top journal categories TJ5 and TJ7), 240 bibliometric series were built from JSTOR DfR search requests for the purpose of this study.[25] To do so, the search strings were entered in JSTOR's DfR search, and then subsequently narrowed down to "Journal" in the category "Content Type", "Research article" in "Article Type", and finally to the respective subject or discipline group (sBE and dBE) and additionally the respective subject or discipline (sE, sF, dE, dF). The results were then exported as a spreadsheet containing years in one column, and corresponding absolute frequencies in another. Absolute counts were exported for every single year where they were available, sometimes dating back to the 17th century, and including the latest available data. In presenting the data, however, the time period is limited by both the availability of the economic data used for comparison, and the "rolling wall" of available texts on JSTOR (see Section 2.2 and Subsection 2.3.2).

With respect to the way the bibliometric series were used in the econometric analysis, years without any item from the respective category are treated as empty or missing values before the year in which the first item is listed, and have their value set to zero for all years without any item after the first occurrence. Relative frequencies were calculated by dividing, for every individual time series and of course every year, those absolute counts by those from the respective reference series, e.g. for 'crisis' anywhere in sE, by the total number of journal research articles in sE. The focus on relative frequencies serves the purpose of allowing better comparisons between the different categories and between different points in time, which otherwise would be skewed by the different sizes of the article samples (e.g. when comparing 1860 with 2010). Work on this part of the database by accessing JSTOR's DfR was started in early

April 2016 and completed by early May 2016. A detailed documentation of the search queries, etc., also including direct links to each of the particular search results used for assembling the data, is available from the authors upon request.

In order to allow identification of a particular set or variable, reference groups are indicated by adding an encoded suffix composed of an underscore "_" right after the term and followed by the respective subject and discipline indicators introduced earlier (sBE, sE, sF, dBE, dE, dF). "TJ5" and "TJ7" indicate the corresponding top journal categories (see Subsection 2.4.1). If a time series documents frequencies within titles, an additional "t" is added before the variable identifier. When the detrended version of a time series is concerned, a prefix "c_", to indicate that this filtered series represents cyclical fluctuations, is added. Therefore, for example, tRecession_dBE consists of all journal articles in the JSTOR discipline group "Business and Economics" which contain the term "recession" at least once in their title; and c_tRecession_dBE would be the corresponding detrended relative frequency series. When it is possible to distinguish easily between different sets and their frequency time series without these identifiers, they will be dropped in order to make the text more readable (e.g. in the descriptive statistics of Section 3.1), but when the presentation of results is more formal (e.g. in the econometric Section 3.2), they will be used.

To avoid the convoluted phrase "frequencies of papers featuring a term at least once", unless otherwise noted, "term frequency" further refers to the number (or most of the times relative amount) of papers in which the term appears at least once, i.e. not the overall frequency of that term across the whole body of text of that paper (or all papers). Furthermore, when talking about the frequency of the term, and not the meaning of the term itself, it is put in single quotes, i.e. a statement such as "in more recent years, 'crisis' was annually more frequent than 'recession' had ever been" means that more articles at that time had featured the words "crisis" or "crises" at least once than had ever featured "recession" in any year. Owing to their already specific spelling, BCTC and the indexes are referred to without the quotes.

Another extension to the work of Kufenko and Geiger (2016) is that we similarly construct and include time series from WoS data for the descriptive overview. On the WoS interface, the set of all listed economics research articles was generated by browsing all SSCI items and then limiting the sample to "Article" in the publication type category (thus limiting results to research articles in peer-reviewed journals), and further to the "Economics" subject category. These items were then extracted with all their metadata and rearranged into various spreadsheets for use in the present analysis. From the resulting list, it was then straightforward to generate time series for every term with simple algorithms identifying for each of the terms how often it appeared in the titles[26] of (economics) articles in a given year. Since every term from Table 2.4 is included, this means that, ultimately, 15 bibliometric time series were constructed from WoS data. These are identified by a "WoS" in the suffix, e.g. as tBCTC_WoS. WoS term frequency series are used to provide an additional check and potential validation for the results obtained from the JSTOR series, especially, for example, sE.

Ideally, we would also like to extend the analysis of Kufenko and Geiger (2016) by considering term frequencies in papers' keywords. As indicated in Subsection 2.3.2, it is possible to export a sample's (e.g. all papers in a category, such as dE, in a certain year range) automatically generated keywords from JSTOR. However, when taking, for example, all dBE journal research articles published between 1990 and 2010 which also contain the term "business cycle" anywhere in the text, the five key terms on top of that list are "model", "market", "variable", "price" and "capital". Between 1950 and 1970, the top five had been "income", "investment", "price", "capital" and "market". While there is no doubt that these are all relevant notions to the samples at hand (indeed, they probably are relevant terms of the texts, and the lists exclude, for example, words such as "the", etc.), many are still so general that, at least by taking a small number of the most prevalent terms, they are not very useful in characterizing a set of papers as, for example, "business cycle theory", at least not much more so than a search for the term alone could be. Similarly, in larger samples, the overwhelming majority even of the 301 key terms that can be extracted is still so general that relative importances of notions related to BCCT cannot be reliably traced. For example, taking all dBE and sBE journal research articles published in 1950–1970 (respectively 57 762 and 93 015 total items), both key term lists actually contain none of the terms from Table 2.4. Similarly, the keyword set of all the 4970 dE journal research articles published in 2000 contains only "crisis" (on rank 137). The 1716 sE journal research articles from 2000 produced a keyword set that contained only "crisis" (rank 117) and "cycle" (rank 227). Therefore, this extension is unfortunately not feasible for our analysis of the PPT hypothesis.

2.4.2.2 Citation analysis

Another extension to the previous empirical work of Kufenko and Geiger (2016) is that we also include a citation analysis. With the data available from the WoS, it is in principle possible to create two kinds of citation series for any set of articles. First, all articles citing at least one from the original set can be identified. Secondly, all the annual citation counts for individual items from that original set are available. In the latter case, citation counts are higher, for a paper which cites multiple items from the original set enters the counts with that number. Furthermore, counts from the second method cannot be further refined by subject or document categories.

In our analysis, we track citation counts using both methods for three sets of articles. Mirroring the method for term frequencies, these sets were compiled based on the occurrence of BCTC, DOWNSWING or OVERALL in paper titles. The BCTC set contains all economics research articles published in 1956–2016 which contain BCTC in their title (i.e. tBCTC_WoS), and correspondingly for the other two (tDOWNSWING_WoS and tOVERALL_WoS).

SSCI economics articles which cite at least one from that original set are labelled with a "cit" suffix, so tBCTC_cit contains all economics research articles that cite at least one economics research article on the SSCI that features BCTC in its title (tBCTC_WoS).

To generate the three sets of relevant citable articles and their corresponding lists of citing items, a WoS search within titles indexed on the SSCI was conducted for each of three corresponding search strings: '"business cycle" OR "trade cycle"' (BCTC), 'crisis OR depression OR recession' (DOWNSWING) and 'crisis OR depression OR recession OR bubble OR cycle OR distress OR embarrassment OR fluctuations OR glut OR panic OR prosperity OR stagnation' (OVERALL). The three concatenated search strings are made up of everything within the associated single quotes, but without the quotes themselves. In each case, results were further defined by limiting "Document Types" to only "Article", i.e. research articles in peer-reviewed journals, and selecting only the "Web of Science Category" of "Economics". The resulting sets were each exported twice (using the two different methods described in Subsection 2.3.3) to obtain all relevant metadata on all SSCI economics articles which contain at least one of the respective terms in their titles. For each of these sets of articles, a second step was then performed to obtain detailed records of citing items. Individually for each set, the list of all items on the SSCI which cite at least one of the articles in the original set was accessed via the corresponding link to the "Citing Report" (i.e. list of citing articles) in the WoS interface. The thereby generated lists were then exported with all metadata except citations. These lists of citing items were not limited to economics or research articles in order to be able to assess the full scope of citations in the SSCI. Whenever the analysis in Chapter 3 refers to total citation counts without further qualification, it refers to these data. On the other hand, it is explicitly stated if only citing economics research articles are concerned. Since the metadata contain information on the document type and WoS category, however, it is possible to limit the results to economics articles. All data were originally compiled, extracted and organized between May 2nd and May 9th, 2016.

With the term frequencies, it was fairly easy and straightforward to account for the growing body of literature and its effect on frequency comparisons by taking the size of that body into account. With citation records, however, the problem of normalizing and rescaling the data surfaces multiple times, and is further complicated by the fact that citations often already imply links between different periods. Of course, citations to a set of papers (e.g. tBCTC_WoS) may be rescaled for each year to provide a measure of the percentage of items citing at least one from the original set. However, this original set expands over most years, so the body of citable literature grows. While surely only a small fraction of older texts remain relevant over a long time frame, this does raise another rescaling issue, namely accounting for the absolute number of available items that might have generated a citation in the first place. Furthermore, it begs the question of how to weigh this in either the record for citing papers, or absolute numbers of citations (in the latter case, it is probably more relevant). Anyway, normalization and adequate rescaling of citation data arguably require the consideration of multiple parameters. These may include, for example, the number of citable items every year or until a given year, average counts of references and citations per document, an estimate of the time it usually takes for an average paper to no longer be cited, an estimate of the time it usually takes between a paper's publication and its first citation and especially citation peak (also accounting for differences in papers' life-cycles, as documented, for example, in Costas et al. (2010)), etc.

For an analysis which primarily builds on citation data, these are crucial points. In this book, however, citation records are used to descriptively supplement the main argument which uses term frequency data in an econometric analysis. Therefore, some simple normalizations are used. This particularly includes citing economics papers relative to all economics papers, and the annual numbers of references per citing paper and per every citable paper published until that year (especially see Subsection 3.3.5 on this). Furthermore, we also include an extension of this approach to identify possible differences between contraction and non-contraction years, once again mirroring the methods outlined in the previous subsections. To do so, we construct corresponding cumulative citation distribution functions (CCDFs) for the absolute citation counts of our sets of citable items (tBCTC_WoS, etc.). Specifically, we create arrays of articles' citation frequencies inside and outside of contraction years, as well as within the first, second and third year following a contraction. For each of these sets of years, we can then order citable articles by the number of references to them (from lowest to highest) and thus construct the CCDFs, which indicate the fraction of all citations to that set in the given years received by all those items which have at most a specified number of citations to them. Note that this includes citations from non-economics articles on the WoS.

2.4.3 The potential for and limitations of a semantic analysis

The core of our quantitative analysis is the list of central notions documented in Subsection 2.4.2.1 which is used to identify the relevant set of papers discussing business cycles and economic crises. While these terms are used in referring to the same set of phenomena, it deserves to be noted that they specifically highlight different aspects of it. From a theoretical point of view, for example, "recession", "depression" and "prosperity" refer to different phases of the business cycle, whereas "crisis" is the name traditionally given to a particular point, namely where the upswing turns into the downswing. Additionally, there may be shifts in the terms' specific meanings over time. For example, in the original NBER data (Section 2.2), "recession" is used interchangeably with "contraction" in reference to the whole downswing. However, in older theoretical literature (e.g. Schumpeter 1939), "recession" was usually defined as that part of the downswing between the crisis and the economy's hypothetical equilibrium level, i.e. the phase during which the economy moved towards that level from increased activity. The potential other part of the downswing where the economy would overshoot the equilibrium level towards lower activity was labelled "depression" (see e.g. Geiger 2014).[27] What is more, some of the terms are also prominent in the discussion of other topics in economics or other fields. Generally, therefore, it is arguably somewhat blurry what exactly the terms refer to (even within BCCT), and in contrast to an actual careful reading of the texts, a mere spotting of occurrences clearly cannot distinguish between these differences. Since the aim of this part of the analysis is not to trace the evolution of a specific notion over time, it seems reasonable to put this caveat aside for the empirical analysis.

However, there are three closely related biases when classifying papers by the terms they use. These biases may affect frequencies observed with the methods sketched in Subsection 2.4.2, and the resulting issues will be discussed in Section 3.3:

1. There may be some kind of an "afterglow" if a particular term features in later publications, even though the concept itself is not employed or even referenced, simply because it had featured in the title of a cited work. However, this only biases results to the extent that, even though the referenced paper uses the term in the title, the citing text itself does not discuss the related concept at all. Of course, the more general the notion is, the more likely it is that there will be some bias.
2. A particular term may be used, but in a completely different meaning or context. The odds of this happening are naturally much higher for more common and less specific terms: for example, the term "mathematic" can feature in an article about economics which bears no resemblance to mathematical economics; for example, if that article is an interview in which one person talks of their relative who happens to be a mathematician (see King et al. 2012: 7f.). While some of the notions in our analysis here are sufficiently specific (e.g. BCTC), others are likely to also appear in very different contexts not related to BCCT. "Crisis", for example, can feature in all kinds of other, e.g. political, contexts. Similarly, "depression" is a term and research subject in both psychology and geology.
3. The use of a particular term may be mere lip service or name dropping, i.e. the notion may be mentioned, but not actually discussed. Clearly, not every paper which uses the term "business cycle" actually discusses business cycles, whether from a theoretical or empirical perspective. Indeed, in the context of BCCT, such lip service may be particularly relevant, for, in the years following a crisis or severe recession, authors may just motivate and introduce their paper with a throwaway reference to current or recent events such as "in light of the financial and economic crisis". A purely quantitative analysis of term frequencies alone could not differentiate between an increase in frequencies due to actually increased discussions of business cycles and economic crises, and one that is purely

due to such term dropping, i.e. one could not differentiate whether not just the wording, but also the content of the economics literature actually responds to economic crises.

Overall, therefore, there is an undeniable risk of false positives when identifying relevant papers by the occurrences of specific terms such as those documented in Subsection 2.4.2.1, for some (or potentially many) of the thereby identified articles will not actually contain discussions of business cycles and economic crises. Indeed, this constitutes a fundamental shortcoming of large-scale bibliometric analyses, whether based on term frequencies or citation counts. In contrast, an in-depth reading of the considered texts allows the reader to discern the said text's meaning and thus supply a knowledgeable interpretation of whether a given paper actually falls into a particular category, discusses particular issues, etc. Taken the other way around, these problems could, theoretically, be tackled by actually looking into all of the texts and reading them carefully – which, however, is not feasible given the scope of our analysis.

However, a first and very broad step to approach these shortcomings is already built into our research strategy, namely by narrowing down the field from which items are included. If articles from psychology journals are not included (e.g. by taking dE), the amount of false positives for 'depression' in the sample, for example, should be smaller. An even higher accuracy could potentially be obtained by coupling the search with a semantic analysis that investigates which other words the term in question occurred in conjunction with, and can thus derive inferences about the meaning of the terms. The straightforward next step would thus be to identify all instances of a particular notion and, by analysing its context, infer its meaning. This is a further approximation to the ideal of reading all papers and grasping their meaning through a theoretically founded understanding, and would allow two things: (1) differentiate between false positives and actual hits in the remaining smaller sample, as well as (2) identify changes in meaning over time. Generally speaking, as long as a set of bodies of text (whether full texts or a list of titles) is digitally available, all individual instances of a term can be spotted, and, from these occurrences, lists of words (and their frequencies) which appear in conjunction, before or after the terms of interest, can be compiled. It is then possible, for example, to connect different adjectives to various connotations related to a term, and interpret time series documenting potential changes in frequencies and co-occurrences.

Ideally, therefore, we would like to work with the full texts of all the items in our sample. Unfortunately, data availability severely limits our scope in this direction. JSTOR does archive full texts of the relevant items. Given our sample sizes, this would have required downloading many thousands of PDFs, probably via an automated script. Unfortunately, our correspondence with JSTOR's staff could not settle with sufficient certainty whether we were legally "on the safe side", and we therefore had to decide to leave this aspect of the analysis out. If the issue were to be resolved at a later point, we would gladly supplement this book's research with the new options. While this means that we cannot include a detailed evaluation of issues of semantics as part of and consistent with the empirical analysis, the points raised above will nonetheless feature prominently in the discussion and the validation (Section 3.3) of the empirical results gained from the frequency data.

2.4.4 *Econometric methods*

The core of the econometric analysis are several tests to assess the association between economic and bibliometric variables. The methodology we apply to draw empirical inferences involves tools used for both the short- and the long-run analysis. The goal of the econometric analysis is to derive a causal inference on the interplay between economic and bibliometric variables. In order to focus on predictive causality between fluctuations in economic and bibliometric variables, their long-run exogeneity is also tested. The latter allows us to take advantage of persistence, often observed for bibliometric and also for economic series: large changes with a long duration. In general, since we focus on deviations from trend in both economic and bibliometric time series, and on their interrelations, the methods employed here may be familiar from empirical analyses of business cycles. Primarily, in order to compare economic and bibliometric time series and to statistically assess whether they can be associated with and related to one another, we employ the method of fractionally co-integrated vector autoregression (FCVAR).

Bibliometric variables often exhibit time-series persistence and therefore a separate remark has to be made on the long-memory effects in the context of business cycle empirics. It is often the case that economics as well as econometrics profit from scientific spillovers from other sciences: the concept of long-memory effects migrated to economics from natural sciences and engineering, in particular from hydrology (see Hurst 1951, 1957; Mandelbrot and Wallis 1968). However, the long-memory concept was introduced to the problems of economics, specifically to the analysis of business cycles, with a certain lag. Among the first works of this kind were Mandelbrot and Van Ness (1968) and Mandelbrot (1972). Whereas in the first of these two, a small remark was made on the existence of the long-memory effect in economic series, the latter work was solely focused on applications in economics. A simple illustration of a random walk as in Aimar et al. (2010: 30) and Baillie (1996: 10–14) can serve as an illustration. Consider

$$(1 - L)^d y_t = u_t,$$

where L is the lag operator, d is the fractional difference operator, and u_t is an ergodic and stationary error term. The long-memory effect is present if $0 < d < 0.5$, which means that there is a positive autocorrelation coefficient, decreasing at a hyperbolic rate. If $-0.5 < d < 0$, then short memory is assumed. As Baillie (1996: 22) notes, for $0.5 < d < 1$, the process is not covariance-stationary; however, it is still mean-reverting (does not contain a unit root).

Therefore, a long-memory process of a fractional order is a process neither $I(0)$ nor $I(1)$. A more vivid and intuitive interpretation is provided by Mandelbrot (1972: 259f.). He distinguishes between long-memory effects of two kinds: the "Noah effect", embodied in the extremely large non-Gaussian changes of the series (e.g. shocks and crises of large magnitudes), and the "Joseph effect", embodied in the presence of long cycles – non-periodic developments, with a periodicity compared to the length of the whole sample. Another interesting aspect is the relation between d and the Hurst parameter, a quantitative measure of the long-memory effect: Mandelbrot (1972: 275) notes that, if the Hurst parameter equals $H=0.7$, then this corresponds to the presence of cycles with periodicity of around one-third of the signal length. The long-memory effect is present if $0.5 < H < 1$. If $H=0.5$, then the series are uncorrelated and resemble a standard Brownian motion; and if $0 < H < 0.5$, the process is anti-persistent (see Beran et al. 2013: 35). There is a simple relation between the fractional differencing parameter d and the Hurst parameter H (see Baillie 1996: 16, 34; Beran et al. 2013):

$$d = H - \frac{1}{2}.$$

If such a series had a trend component, they would be non-stationary and the differencing parameter would be between 0.5 and 1, hinting at the presence of a certain persistence. The opposite applies as well: if $d=0$ then $H=0.5$ and therefore the series are uncorrelated. If the process has the property $-0.5 < d < 0.5$, it is stationary. Consequently, if $0.5 < d < 1$, the process is non-stationary, but mean-reverting (see Baillie 1996: 18, 21), and $d=1$ corresponds to a unit-root case (see Phillips 2007: 105).

This framework perfectly suits our research question, since scientific debates tend to exhibit a certain persistence, which we want to abstract from to focus on shorter-run, potentially cyclical fluctuations in the bibliometric data that may originate in response to business cycle fluctuations and economic crises. Similarly, the long-memory properties exhibited by economic variables such as output, income and inflation are a well-established observation (see Abderrezak 1998). Therefore, this approach allows us to focus on the association between short-run fluctuations in economic variables, and similar changes in the bibliometric series.

Another crucial aspect of this methodology is the notion of fractional co-integration and causal inference based on it, namely via FCVAR. Referring to Johansen and Nielsen (2012), a pair of $I(d)$ variables would exhibit fractional co-integration if their combination is $I(d-b)$ with $1 > b > 0$. Appealing to this framework offers crucial advantages to our empirical strategy. First of all, traditional co-integration tests such as those of Engle and Granger (1987) or Johansen (1991) assume the presence of co-integration if a combination of $I(1)$ variables is $I(0)$. Therefore, these tests assume a sharp distinction between $I(1)$ and $I(0)$ processes. Yet, the reality is fuzzy and the combination of the variables of interest may be between $I(0)$ and $I(1)$.

If the variables are fractionally co-integrated, we appeal to the FCVAR framework and the long-run exogeneity test for causal inference:

$$\begin{aligned}
\Delta^d Y_t &= \alpha_i \Delta^{d-b} L_b(\mathcal{E}) + \sum_{k=1}^{K} \Gamma_k^y \Delta^d L_b^k Y_{t-k} + \sum_{k=1}^{K} \Gamma_k^x \Delta^d L_b^k X_{t-k} + \varphi_t, \\
\Delta^d X_t &= \alpha_i \Delta^{d-b} L_b(\mathcal{E}) + \sum_{k=1}^{K} \Phi_k^y \Delta^d L_b^k Y_{t-k} + \sum_{k=1}^{K} \Phi_k^x \Delta^d L_b^k X_{t-k} + \omega_t, \\
\mathcal{E} &= \lambda_i^y Y_{t-1} - \lambda_i^x X_{t-1}.
\end{aligned} \tag{2.1}$$

Here Δ^d is the fractional difference operator; L_b is a lag operator; α are the loading coefficients, involved in the restrictions for the long-run exogeneity testing; λ is the speed of adjustment to long-run equilibria; Γ and Φ are the coefficients for the fractionally differenced part; m is the lag length; and φ and ω are errors. It is important to note that equation (2.1) is expressed in a similar fashion as equation (2.2), and that, in our FCVARs, Y are economic series and X are the bibliometric series. For all fractionally co-integrated pairs, a white noise test (the Portmanteau Q-test, i.e. the multivariate version of a Q-test as in Box and Pierce (1970) and Ljung and Box (1978)) is performed. In the FCVAR analysis, no previous detrending of the time series is necessary, and the long-run exogeneity test is applied to the difference terms of the equations. For six of the economic series presented in Section 2.2 – income per capita, industrial production, investment, bankruptcies, consumer prices and the stock market index – logarithmic transformations are used in both the FCVAR and the vector autoregression (VAR, see below) specification. The logarithmic transformations are indicated by a "ln" prefix just before the variable name, i.e. lnCPI corresponds to the natural logarithms of the original CPI series.

In addition to the main FCVAR framework, we also provide select impulse response functions (IRFs) using the standard VAR framework with the Granger-causality test for causal inference:

$$\begin{aligned}
Y_t^c &= \beta_0 + \sum_{j=1}^{J} a_j Y_{t-j}^c + \sum_{j=1}^{J} b_j X_{t-j}^c + e_t, \\
X_t^c &= \theta_0 + \sum_{j=1}^{J} c_j Y_{t-j}^c + \sum_{j=1}^{J} d_j X_{t-j}^c + \eta_t.
\end{aligned} \tag{2.2}$$

Here Y_t^c denotes cyclical fluctuations in the economic variables; X_t^c denotes cyclical fluctuations in bibliometric variables; β and θ denote constants; a, b, c and d denote coefficients for the respective lags and variables; e_t and η_t are error terms; and $t-j$ is the lag operator.

The optimal lag length, whether K for the FCVARs or J for the VARs, is determined for each case by referring to the Akaike information criterion (Akaike 1974), the Hannan–Quinn information criterion (Hannan and Quinn

1979) and the Schwarz criterion (Schwarz 1978) according to the parsimony principle.[28]

For the series included in the VAR analysis and used to plot the IRFs, detrending is applied. In order to obtain cyclical fluctuations, a dynamic linear first-order model, resembling the Kalman filter, is applied as in Kalman (1960) and Petris (2010). The parameters of the filter, including the initialization point, are calculated by maximum likelihood estimation. The cyclical fluctuations are further used for inference based on equation (2.2). As indicated in Subsection 2.4.2.1, such detrended series are indicated by a "c_" prefix. The general framework for the dynamic linear model is set up in the following way:

$$\begin{cases} r_t = F_t z_t + v_t, & v_t \sim N(0, V_t), \\ z_t = G_t Z_{t-1} + w_t, & w_t \sim N(0, W_t). \end{cases}$$

Here r_t is an observed state of Y or X, whereas z is the unobserved one; F and G are weights; and v and w are errors. In order to detrend the series for the short-run analysis, we apply an ARMA (1, 1) model, which performs better than the (1, 0) specification.

To sum up, therefore, we test for, and potentially establish a relation between, bibliometric and economic variables by running an FCVAR analysis with long-run exogeneity tests for pairs of economic and bibliometric time series. Economic series are the seven (excluding the binary variable representing contraction years) presented in Section 2.2. As bibliometric data for the econometric analysis, we mainly use term frequency data anywhere in texts from the JSTOR categories of primary interest, namely sE, sBE, dE and dBE. Given the 15 search strings as identified in Subsection 2.4.2.1, this results in 105 pairs for each of the relevant categories. Every pair is tested for fractional co-integration and, given fractional co-integration, long-run exogeneity tests are conducted. Since the FCVAR analysis implies a form of detrending and the VAR analysis explicitly employs detrending (as described above), we can focus on cyclical fluctuations, i.e. exactly the main point of interest implied by PPT. It also deserves to be noted that we do not separately check for and remove potential outliers in our series, both economic and bibliometric – the reason being that, in the context of business cycle and especially crises analysis, outliers often are exactly the observations of interest (such as the Great Depression, or more severe contractions in general), so they should not be removed from the sample. The results of the econometric analysis are presented in Section 3.2.

Notes

1 A widely known example of bibliometric research is the power-law probability distribution described by Zipf's law, which holds that the frequency of a word measured as the number of occurrences in a body of text is inversely proportional to its frequency rank, meaning that the most frequent word occurs x times as often as the second most frequent, which in turn features x times as much as the third most frequent (see Zipf 1935, 1949). For an application concerning economics journals, see Sutter and Kochner

(2001). Also see Lotka (1926) for the original statement of Lotka's law on the number of persons with a given number of publications, which likewise constitutes a power law for a scientometric observation.

2 See Garfield (1979, 2007) and Subsection 2.3.3; further see the *Festschrift* for Eugene Garfield edited by Cronin and Atkins (2000) on the history of scientometrics.

3 When comparing different fields of research (which is not done in this book), it is therefore a frequent and recommended procedure to normalize citation counts by average citation counts in the discipline. Interestingly, Radicchi et al. (2008) find that, when doing so, adjusted citation distributions across a wide range of scientific disciplines are virtually identical. However, normalizing citation counts can affect index numbers, which are built in some way or another on rank orders (such as the *h*-index), as the discussion at the end of this subsection shows.

4 For example, consider the *European Journal of the History of Economic Thought*, *History of Political Economy* and the *Journal of the History of Economic Thought*. In recent years, these three journals taken together have annually published 15 issues, which of course contained many more articles, whereas the overall number of bibliometric works published in these three journals since 2010 is in the single digits.

5 <<https://fred.stlouisfed.org/series/A229RX0A048NBEA>>

6 <<https://fred.stlouisfed.org/series/UNRATE>>

7 <<https://fred.stlouisfed.org/series/INDPRO>>

8 <<https://fred.stlouisfed.org/series/A006RA3A086NBEA>>

9 From the website <<https://www.measuringworth.com/uscpi/>>.

10 <<http://irrationalexuberance.com/>>

11 <<http://www.nber.org/cycles/recessions.html>>

12 <<http://www.nber.org/cycles/cyclesmain.html>>

13 While certainly covering the most prominent sources used in bibliometric analyses of the scientific and especially economics literature, this list of five databases is obviously not exhaustive. For example, the RePEc archive of economics and finance research, accessible via IDEAS (<<https://ideas.repec.org/>>), indexes over 2200 000 items, including close to 1.4 million journal articles in over 2600 periodicals, over 750 000 working papers, and also several tens of thousands of books and chapters in books (statistics on the front page, accessed on February 22nd, 2017). Close to 30% of journal articles and well over 50% of working papers have (part of) their citations indexed. However, RePEc does not provide full historical records for many of the journals it lists: for example, the *American Economic Review* is only indexed since the 1969 issues, and *Econometrica* dates back no further than 1950 on RePEc. In general, more recent years are more likely to be covered, which skews the distribution of records similar to those on Scopus (see Subsection 2.3.4). At the time of writing this book, full metadata coverage seems to be available only for about half of the journals (as indicated by a rough impression of scrolling through the list at <<https://ideas.repec.org/i/a.html>>). The more problematic issue, however, is that there is no feasible way to select sets of items of interest, e.g. a set of papers identified to be research on business cycles and economic crises, and extract their metadata. While RePEc is thus a great source of finding specific economics research on any topic of interest, it is not very suitable for accessing or using the search with a large-scale bibliometric analysis in mind, even though the site also documents some bibliometric statistics for its items.

Another digital library which also contains many economics entries can be found with the HathiTrust (<<https://www.hathitrust.org/>>) which indexes not only many journal articles, but also millions of books (across all subjects) and provides PDFs to many. While some general core metadata on the database's contents are available (see <<https://www.hathitrust.org/hathifiles>>), it is not possible to extract metadata or the list of items from a search result (or for more than 20 items at once in general), e.g. for the almost 13 000 items in the "Subject: Economics" category found when doing a simple search for "business cycle".

14 See the overview on <<https://www.aeaweb.org/econlit/content>>, accessed on February 8th, 2017.

15 A full list is available at <<https://www.aeaweb.org/econlit/journal_list.php>>, accessed on February 8th, 2017.

16 See the documentation on <<https://www.aeaweb.org/econlit/search-hints>>, accessed on February 8th, 2017.

17 In the old three-digit classification system which preceded the present iteration, "fluctuations" featured in categories "100 Economic Growth; Development; Planning; Fluctuations" and "130 Economic fluctuations; forecasting; stabilization, inflation". This highlights the problem of getting a long time series for a uniform sample. While there clearly is an overlap between the various categories captured by the different identifier codes, it can hardly be argued that either of the old categories is a perfect match for E30, E32, E37 and E39. In general, of course, how to actually classify – and correspondingly define – the different categories to which the codes refer is far from a trivial task (see Cherrier 2017): it is highly dependent on what is actually researched in, and of interest to, economics, and therefore necessarily subject to changes. However, a bibliometric analysis that aims both to gauge trends over longer time frames, and at the same time to identify short-term fluctuations which are not due to changes in the classification system, requires a rather consistent set of categories and identifiers. Unfortunately, this is not available with the JEL codes (and preceding classifications) for longer time periods, especially when reaching back farther than 1991.

18 Unfortunately, this update has also changed DfR, which now only provides greatly reduced search options as compared with the previous iteration which was used for this book (e.g. many of the facets to organize search results have been removed, including the differentiation between subjects and disciplines). In order to make the way the datasets in this book were accessed and compiled as transparent as possible, the following description naturally relates to the old layout and options.

19 See <<http://science.thomsonreuters.com/cgi-bin/jrnlst/jlresults.cgi?PC=J&SC=GY>>, accessed on February 21st, 2017.

20 Even though they provide a classification system of the papers, these keywords, similar to JEL codes, are not very useful to the analysis in this book. Of the 398 921 economics research articles published 1956–2015 that are indexed on the SSCI, 150 108 (37.6%) contained key terms provided by the respective authors, and just over half of all items (203 403) featured automatically generated key terms. However, their distribution over time is highly uneven. Except for eight earlier items with automatically generated key terms, both those provided by authors as well as the automatically generated key terms only become available for publications beginning in 1990. This leaves a period of 26 years, 1990–2015, for the analysis, which hardly covers enough crises and recession periods to draw well-founded econometric conclusions.

21 Available from <<https://www.elsevier.com/solutions/scopus/content>>.

22 The list also matches the "Top Five" from a recent AEA panel discussion, see <<https://www.aeaweb.org/webcasts/2017/curse.php>>.

23 That is, before the bibliometric data were extracted and arranged from the respective databases. The rankings were accessed before that in order to know which journals were

identified as top journals, and therefore were to be included in the search and extraction procedures.

24 That is, with one exception: Kufenko and Geiger (2016) also documented the frequency of "business cycle" separately, whereas, here, only BCTC is reported.

25 There are 15 search strings which are used for two kinds of searches (only in titles, and anywhere in the documents), and for each of the eight different categories.

26 Since full-text searches are not possible via the WoS, respective frequencies cannot be generated. It could be done for abstracts, but they are not generally available for all articles over the whole period included here (which is very similar to the availability of keywords). Whereas in the 2010s, more than 95% of all items featured an indexed abstract and even in the 1990s, around two-thirds of articles came with an abstract, the first abstract dates from 1988.

27 Therefore, and in order to avoid confusion with the terms included in the bibliometric analysis, we use only the label "contraction" in referring to the NBER downswing periods (as documented in Table 2.2 on page 22).

28 A detailed documentation of the individual steps and the selection procedure for each variable pair is available from the authors upon request.

3 Empirical results

The following sections present descriptive results (Section 3.1), econometric results (Section 3.2), and a detailed discussion concerning the robustness and validity of the different findings (Section 3.3). In general, the amount of both economic and especially bibliometric data assembled for this book is too large to present everything in full detail even within the scope and framework of a book. Therefore, specific categories are highlighted, and others are used primarily as validation and reference for the discussion. For example, concerning the major terms and their frequencies, the focus is put on the most central notions to BCCT, i.e. BCTC, 'crisis', 'depression' and 'recession'. Concerning categories, results for economics, and, where available, overarching categories (e.g. business and economics) are always provided (for JSTOR data, both sE and dE, respectively sBE and dBE) and presented and discussed in more detail, whereas details on finance research as well as the top journal categories are primarily used as the aforementioned references.

3.1 Descriptive statistics

Before the econometric analysis, some descriptive statistics can provide an overview of the scope and nature of the bibliometric data and, very broadly, how they relate to business cycles and economic crises. Subsection 3.1.1 summarizes overall frequencies of papers featuring the relevant terms identified in Subsection 2.4.2.1. Subsection 3.1.2 then documents relative frequencies of these terms inside and outside of contraction years and provides figures with historical time series for the central terms and indexes. Time series for citation records are presented in Subsection 3.1.3.

3.1.1 General overview

Table 3.1 documents the overall numbers of journal articles from JSTOR in the eight categories of interest (sE, sF, dBE, dE, dF, dBE, TJ5, TJ7). It also lists the respective numbers of items featuring the terms relevant for discussions of business cycles and economic crises (see Subsection 2.4.2.1). Numbers in

Table 3.1 Bibliometric reference numbers, JSTOR, 1855–2012

	sE		*sF*		*sBE*		*TJ5*	
total	140669		204365		634095		31684	
BCTC	11728	(535)	17139	(893)	23113	(988)	3338	(216)
crisis	22565	(943)	27005	(1431)	97518	(3431)	3517	(108)
depression	21307	(413)	17924	(336)	49824	(690)	4222	(86)
recession	13421	(261)	17231	(329)	32144	(457)	1883	(32)
DOWNSWING	42342	(1544)	46814	(2059)	144593	(4495)	7343	(222)
bubble	1275	(20)	3416	(163)	5828	(184)	315	(31)
cycle	21446	(913)	36823	(1678)	82636	(2349)	5997	(368)
distress	4921	(20)	6554	(108)	19261	(219)	889	(5)
embarrassment	1633	(9)	1760	(10)	7055	(16)	405	(0)
fluctuations	22817	(306)	33725	(520)	60055	(668)	5773	(120)
glut	1015	(7)	858	(5)	2780	(20)	125	(0)
panic	3476	(103)	3956	(121)	9071	(157)	776	(23)
prosperity	16215	(216)	11183	(133)	40947	(266)	2858	(17)
stagnation	6151	(110)	4986	(73)	18176	(179)	979	(18)
OVERALL	67107	(3043)	88146	(4692)	249662	(8333)	14083	(779)
	dE		*dF*		*dBE*		*TJ7*	
total	279026		32094		395489		40377	
BCTC	16934	(852)	2361	(107)	19244	(910)	4118	(245)
crisis	45164	(1831)	3655	(154)	58628	(2127)	4172	(131)
depression	24257	(352)	2327	(42)	30228	(392)	4731	(92)
recession	17509	(303)	2238	(18)	21328	(332)	2356	(37)
DOWNSWING	68892	(2459)	6500	(210)	88862	(2823)	8652	(256)
bubble	2745	(122)	744	(37)	4199	(161)	487	(45)
cycle	39776	(1656)	4740	(170)	57996	(1978)	7434	(432)
distress	7720	(88)	1564	(44)	11594	(156)	1326	(25)
embarrassment	2690	(11)	323	(0)	4057	(12)	447	(0)
fluctuations	34820	(526)	5392	(77)	42812	(565)	7268	(151)
glut	1383	(13)	90	(1)	1702	(15)	139	(0)
panic	4602	(108)	572	(6)	5743	(111)	876	(26)
prosperity	19024	(127)	1321	(12)	24565	(152)	3068	(21)
stagnation	10915	(127)	496	(6)	12198	(129)	1054	(20)
OVERALL	117595	(5080)	13250	(536)	161355	(5937)	17423	(953)

Note: Cells indicate the absolute number of research articles listed in the respective JSTOR categories, and frequencies of papers from that category which feature a particular term anywhere in the text (or the title, in brackets).

brackets are frequencies in titles. The time frame is 1855–2012: it begins with the first year for which the contraction periods series is available (see Subsection 2.2.8), and ends in 2012 due to JSTOR's "rolling wall" of available records (see Subsection 2.3.2). To also provide an impression of aggregate trends and developments over time, Figure 3.1 plots the timelines of total papers published

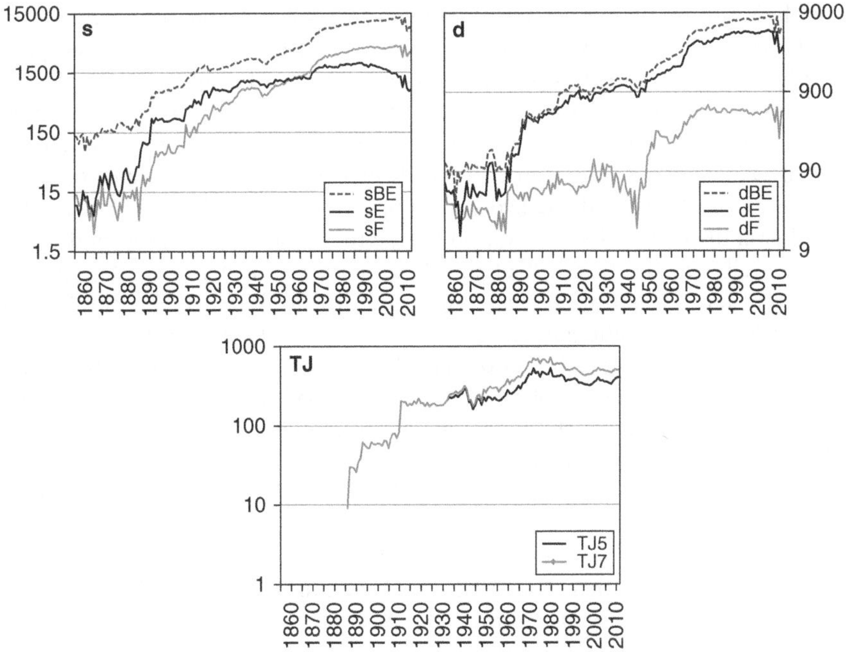

Figure 3.1 Time series of JSTOR papers per category, 1855–2012.

Note: Top left panel: subject categories. Top right panel: discipline categories. Bottom panel: top journal categories. Logarithmic scales.

per year, with the subject categories in the top left, discipline categories in the top right, and top journals in the bottom panel.

As Table 3.1 shows, there are 634 095 journal articles in sBE between 1855 and 2012, and 395 489 in dBE. The respective economics categories list 140 669 items for sE, and almost twice as many, 279 026, for dE. The table further shows which terms have been featured in the greatest number of articles overall. This includes the primary notions of interest 'crisis', 'depression', 'recession' and BCTC (in all categories, over 90% of BCTC matches feature "business cycle"), as well as 'fluctuations', 'prosperity' and, naturally, 'cycle'. This is true both for appearances anywhere in the documents as well as in titles. However, in titles, 'crisis' and BCTC appear relatively more often than the other frequent terms, across all categories. It should also be noted that frequencies of the two indexes – DOWNSWING and OVERALL – amount to only a fraction of the sum of their individual components' frequencies: anywhere in documents, that fraction is between 74% and 81% for DOWNSWING, and between 49% and 59% for OVERALL (with both indexes, it is only slightly higher for titles). This indicates that many papers which feature one of the relevant terms also feature at least one additional other term. Naturally, as they consist of only a few words, this occurs less often in titles. The final column of Table 3.1 shows research article counts in the two top journal categories (see Subsection 2.4.1). Here, the increased relative frequency of BCTC compared with the other major terms is quite noteworthy: within top journals, BCTC features in almost as many papers as 'crisis', and more often than, for example, 'recession' (which is only the case in one of the six other categories, namely dF).

As is evident from the top two panels of Figure 3.1, the number of papers published each year and indexed in the respective six JSTOR categories is much higher at the end of the observation period than near its beginning, and indeed until well into the first half of the 20th century. Furthermore, despite their different levels, the time series for sBE and dBE look remarkably similar. The logarithmic scale highlights that the annual number of papers in both categories began to grow considerably in the late 19th century, at a trend of about 2.5% to 3% per year. Annual publication numbers in both categories increased about a hundredfold between the beginning and the end of the observation period, from just about a 100 in the 1850s to well over 10 000 in the 2000s (sBE), respectively from around 75 to 7500 (dBE). Between 1985 and 2007, there were continuously more than 10 000 sBE and well over 6500 dBE items every year, whereas 1907 was the first year with more than 1000 sBE, and 1913 the first year with more than 1000 dBE items. Within the 1855–2012 observation period, 85% of sBE items are from the post-war years (1946–2012), and over 41% of these (35 percentage points) are from the latest two decades (1993–2012) alone. The respective numbers for dBE are almost identical and even slightly higher (almost 87% and near 42% or 36 percentage points, respectively).[1]

For the most part, the trends of sE and dE are nearly parallel to those of sBE and dBE, respectively, implying an almost identical growth rate – and consequently share – of the E subcategories within the overarching BE categories. However, sE noticeably diverges from this pattern due to a decreasing number of new items since the 1990s. A similar contrast can be observed between sF and dF: whereas sF mostly follows a similar trend to sBE, the trends of dF and dBE are very different. Overall, the number of sF papers has grown faster than those of sE and sBE, with sF also overtaking the absolute frequencies of sE in the 1960s and generally increasing its relative share within sBE throughout. In contrast, dF has grown neither steadily nor faster than dE and dBE, and thus the relative share of dF within dBE has diminished.

The uneven distribution of items over time and across categories raises several issues for the quantitative analysis. First, when comparing a term's frequency within a category, but over time, absolute numbers can be expected to be much higher in more recent years than earlier in the observation period, owing to the fact that the total number of items is that much higher. Similarly, when comparing frequencies between categories, differences in their volumes may contribute to differences in term frequencies, etc., as well. Furthermore, time series of term frequencies are more volatile in early years of the observation period due to the lower number of items. These difficulties can be tackled and partly smoothed by working with relative frequencies, as most of the analysis in this book does (see Section 2.4), but those too are, of course, more volatile for low overall item counts. This especially holds for frequencies in titles, which are considerably lower in general. The following Subsection 3.1.2 further illustrates some of the problems this causes. These issues will be taken up again and discussed where they are relevant for results and their interpretation.

The bottom panel of Figure 3.1 depicts the number of research articles in the two top journal categories. Albeit to a lesser degree, the time series have also increased over the long run. Whereas especially early movements, such as the shift in 1911, can often be attributed to composition changes like the first issue of the *AER*, the number of papers published per journal in a year has also undergone some changes over the observation period. The *AER*, for example, has increased the number of items per year from about 120 in the 1910s to near 200 in the 2000s (and indeed already in the 1960s). Meanwhile, the *JF*, *Econometrica* and the *JPE* (and to a lesser degree, even the *QJE* and *REStud*) had increases in the annual number of items with peaks in the 1960s and 1970s, followed by decreases towards earlier levels (but slightly higher). In the 1910s and 1920s (when only the *AER*, *JPE* and *QJE* were published), there were about 200 items per year; in the 1970s, the series peaked around 700 (TJ7) and 500 (TJ5); and in the 2010s, numbers were close to 500 (TJ7), respectively 400 (TJ5). The difference between the levels in the 2010s and the 1900s is thus a result of composition changes, large increases in the *AER*, and minor overall increases in all other journals. As depicted in Table 2.3, the difference between the two categories is the introduction of the *REStud* in 1933 and the *JF* in 1946. Ever since then, numbers for TJ7 have naturally been bigger, but the series have mostly followed a similar path, as the annual number of items in the *REStud* and *JF* were not characterized by a very different pattern from the other journals.

3.1.2 Downswings and term frequencies

3.1.2.1 Frequencies inside and outside of contraction years

Tables 3.2 and 3.3 display relative term frequencies between 1855 (1901 for BCTC) and 2012, anywhere in the documents (Table 3.2) and just in their titles (Table 3.3). The columns, starting from the second one, show frequencies across all years, in non-contraction years, contraction years (as defined in Subsection 2.2.8), and the first, second and third year following a contraction. Each cell contains four values: frequencies in sE on top and in dE on bottom; annual averages (i.e. the sum of all annual values divided by the respective number of years) outside of parentheses; and the total weighted average (i.e. the total absolute frequency across all years divided by the total number of items in these years) in parentheses. In order to keep the tables manageable, only sE and dE, the most important categories to represent economics, are displayed. The two averages allow for a differentiation between the actual average frequency, on the one hand, and annual averages irrespective of the total number of items

Table 3.2 Term frequencies, 1855–2012, in %

	Overall	*Outside*	*During*	*Contraction + 1*	*Contraction + 2*	*Contraction + 3*
BCTC (starts 1901)	7.69 (8.55)	8.50 (9)	6.04 (7.33)	6.56 (7.85)	6.99 (8.04)	7.01 (8.1)
	5.61 (6.21)	6.10 (6.46)	4.63 (5.42)	5.07 (5.98)	5.33 (6.23)	5.30 (6.24)
crisis	14.39 (16.04)	14.78 (16.65)	13.83 (14.49)	14.14 (15.19)	13.61 (15.25)	13.65 (15.44)
	10.50 (16.19)	12.38 (16.91)	7.73 (14)	8.33 (14.73)	8.29 (14.43)	8.43 (14.61)
depression	15.72 (15.15)	14.92 (14.26)	16.90 (17.41)	17.51 (18.43)	17.88 (18.55)	17.18 (18.33)
	9.90 (8.69)	10.41 (8.23)	9.16 (10.09)	9.65 (10.6)	10.07 (11)	9.81 (10.52)
recession	5.72 (9.54)	7.18 (10.29)	3.58 (7.63)	4.19 (8.76)	4.21 (8.8)	4.08 (8.45)
	3.51 (6.28)	4.36 (6.68)	2.25 (5.04)	2.58 (5.83)	2.67 (6.07)	2.49 (5.87)
DOWNSWING	27.44 (30.1)	28.10 (30.29)	26.45 (29.62)	27.28 (31.12)	26.92 (31.29)	27.10 (31.25)
	18.99 (24.69)	21.54 (25.19)	15.24 (23.19)	16.23 (24.34)	16.41 (24.33)	16.36 (24.24)
bubble	1.40 (0.91)	1.33 (0.97)	1.52 (0.74)	1.23 (0.84)	1.27 (0.85)	1.61 (0.83)
	0.70 (0.98)	0.74 (1.03)	0.63 (0.84)	0.62 (0.88)	0.70 (0.93)	0.69 (0.9)
cycle	10.03 (15.25)	12.43 (16.4)	6.50 (12.29)	6.90 (13.06)	7.33 (13.09)	7.20 (13.05)
	8.30 (14.26)	10.33 (15.12)	5.31 (11.64)	5.76 (12.23)	5.99 (12.52)	6.00 (12.63)
distress	6.54 (3.5)	5.31 (3.23)	8.36 (4.19)	8.80 (4.4)	7.65 (4.6)	7.31 (4.55)
	3.02 (2.77)	2.95 (2.71)	3.13 (2.95)	3.05 (2.97)	3.08 (2.96)	3.09 (2.96)
embarrassment	2.13 (1.16)	1.64 (1.01)	2.86 (1.54)	2.50 (1.46)	2.59 (1.46)	2.23 (1.56)
	1.33 (0.96)	1.30 (0.93)	1.39 (1.07)	1.48 (1.06)	1.23 (1.02)	1.24 (1.05)
fluctuations	15.33 (16.22)	15.74 (16.33)	14.72 (15.95)	14.74 (16.38)	14.51 (16.28)	14.03 (16)
	10.43 (12.48)	11.41 (12.68)	8.98 (11.88)	9.17 (12.3)	9.53 (12.6)	9.39 (12.39)
glut	0.91 (0.72)	0.93 (0.7)	0.89 (0.77)	1.11 (0.78)	0.76 (0.72)	0.75 (0.76)
	0.41 (0.5)	0.44 (0.49)	0.37 (0.53)	0.36 (0.54)	0.38 (0.53)	0.40 (0.55)
panic	4.75 (2.47)	3.53 (2.09)	6.53 (3.46)	6.88 (3.42)	6.05 (3.34)	5.61 (3.36)
	2.02 (1.65)	1.75 (1.52)	2.42 (2.04)	2.27 (2)	2.30 (2.01)	2.34 (1.96)

(*Continued*)

Table 3.2 continued

	Overall	*Outside*	*During*	*Contraction + 1*	*Contraction + 2*	*Contraction + 3*
prosperity	17.96 (11.53)	14.72 (10.37)	22.72 (14.5)	22.41 (14.62)	21.77 (14.81)	21.50 (14.55)
	8.66 (6.82)	8.49 (6.41)	8.92 (8.06)	9.26 (8.14)	9.29 (8.42)	9.38 (8.12)
stagnation	3.57 (4.37)	3.77 (4.61)	3.27 (3.77)	3.37 (4.06)	3.41 (3.99)	3.43 (4.04)
	3.03 (3.91)	3.52 (4.07)	2.32 (3.42)	2.53 (3.63)	2.68 (3.66)	2.64 (3.72)
OVERALL	47.07 (47.71)	46.53 (47.83)	47.87 (47.39)	47.46 (48.55)	47.36 (48.91)	46.71 (48.8)
	33.23 (42.14)	36.93 (43.03)	27.79 (39.47)	28.99 (40.59)	29.69 (40.92)	29.43 (40.82)

Note: Each cell contains relative frequencies anywhere in documents during and outside of contraction years, in sE (top) and dE (bottom). Values outside of brackets are annual averages; those within brackets are the total averages.

Table 3.3 Term frequencies, in titles, 1855–2012, in %

	Overall	*Outside*	*During*	*Contraction + 1*	*Contraction + 2*	*Contraction + 3*
BCTC (starts 1901)	0.37 (0.39)	0.39 (0.41)	0.31 (0.33)	0.34 (0.39)	0.36 (0.38)	0.35 (0.38)
	0.30 (0.31)	0.32 (0.34)	0.25 (0.22)	0.28 (0.27)	0.31 (0.31)	0.30 (0.32)
crisis	0.56 (0.67)	0.64 (0.71)	0.45 (0.56)	0.61 (0.68)	0.59 (0.66)	0.56 (0.64)
	0.35 (0.66)	0.42 (0.68)	0.25 (0.59)	0.29 (0.66)	0.26 (0.58)	0.26 (0.57)
depression	0.27 (0.29)	0.24 (0.26)	0.30 (0.38)	0.32 (0.38)	0.37 (0.44)	0.32 (0.37)
	0.11 (0.13)	0.12 (0.12)	0.10 (0.14)	0.12 (0.16)	0.11 (0.17)	0.11 (0.13)
recession	0.12 (0.19)	0.15 (0.2)	0.06 (0.14)	0.11 (0.23)	0.10 (0.18)	0.10 (0.2)
	0.06 (0.11)	0.07 (0.12)	0.04 (0.09)	0.05 (0.13)	0.04 (0.11)	0.05 (0.15)
DOWNSWING	0.91 (1.1)	1.00 (1.14)	0.77 (0.99)	1.00 (1.25)	1.00 (1.21)	0.95 (1.14)
	0.51 (0.88)	0.60 (0.9)	0.38 (0.81)	0.45 (0.93)	0.41 (0.85)	0.41 (0.84)
bubble	0.01 (0.01)	0.01 (0.02)	0 (0.01)	0 (0.01)	0 (0.01)	0 (0)
	0.02 (0.04)	0.02 (0.05)	0.01 (0.03)	0.01 (0.03)	0.01 (0.03)	0.01 (0.03)
cycle	0.42 (0.65)	0.52 (0.71)	0.26 (0.5)	0.30 (0.59)	0.31 (0.57)	0.30 (0.54)
	0.37 (0.59)	0.45 (0.65)	0.24 (0.43)	0.25 (0.49)	0.29 (0.53)	0.29 (0.54)
distress	0.01 (0.01)	0.01 (0.02)	0 (0.01)	0.01 (0.02)	0.01 (0.02)	0.01 (0.02)
	0.02 (0.03)	0.02 (0.03)	0.02 (0.02)	0.02 (0.03)	0.02 (0.02)	0.02 (0.03)
embarrassment	0 (0.01)	0 (0.01)	0 (0.01)	0 (0)	0 (0.01)	0.01 (0.01)
	0 (0)	0 (0.01)	0 (0)	0 (0)	0 (0)	0 (0)
fluctuations	0.16 (0.22)	0.17 (0.21)	0.15 (0.25)	0.15 (0.24)	0.14 (0.21)	0.12 (0.18)
	0.14 (0.19)	0.15 (0.2)	0.12 (0.17)	0.12 (0.16)	0.10 (0.16)	0.12 (0.2)
glut	0 (0)	0 (0)	0 (0.01)	0 (0)	0 (0)	0 (0.01)
	0 (0)	0 (0)	0 (0)	0 (0)	0 (0)	0 (0.01)
panic	0.08 (0.07)	0.07 (0.07)	0.09 (0.08)	0.11 (0.1)	0.05 (0.08)	0.07 (0.09)
	0.05 (0.04)	0.05 (0.04)	0.05 (0.05)	0.06 (0.06)	0.04 (0.05)	0.04 (0.04)

(Continued)

Table 3.3 continued

	Overall	*Outside*	*During*	*Contraction + 1*	*Contraction + 2*	*Contraction + 3*
prosperity	0.26 (0.15)	0.13 (0.13)	0.45 (0.21)	0.43 (0.19)	0.47 (0.2)	0.43 (0.17)
	0.05 (0.05)	0.05 (0.04)	0.05 (0.06)	0.05 (0.06)	0.06 (0.07)	0.04 (0.04)
stagnation	0.07 (0.08)	0.08 (0.08)	0.05 (0.08)	0.08 (0.06)	0.07 (0.06)	0.08 (0.07)
	0.03 (0.05)	0.03 (0.05)	0.01 (0.04)	0.02 (0.04)	0.02 (0.04)	0.02 (0.04)
OVERALL	1.85 (2.16)	1.95 (2.23)	1.69 (1.98)	1.99 (2.28)	2.02 (2.21)	1.99 (2.08)
	1.14 (1.82)	1.33 (1.91)	0.85 (1.56)	0.94 (1.73)	0.90 (1.69)	0.91 (1.71)

Note: Each cell contains relative frequencies in titles during and outside of contraction years, in sE (top) and dE (bottom). Values outside of brackets are annual averages; those within brackets are the total averages.

within a given set of years, on the other (the latter avoids overweighting of more recent years with higher publication counts). Figure 3.2 offers a more illustrative overview by plotting the numbers for columns three to seven from Table 3.2, with annual averages in the left panel, and total averages in the right panel.

By comparing the third and fourth columns (respectively, the black and white bars in Figure 3.2), frequencies outside of and during contractions can be contrasted. Interestingly, for the majority of terms, both for frequencies anywhere as well as those in titles only, and irrespective of the average used, numbers are higher outside of contraction years. For example, BCTC featured in 8.5% (respectively 9%) of all sE articles published outside of contraction years in 1901–2012, and only in 6.04% (7.33%) of those published in contraction years. Data for 'crisis' and 'recession' show the same pattern. This is surprising, because PPT implies the opposite, namely that frequencies of these terms – as a proxy for discussions of business cycles and economic crises – are higher during contractions, not outside of them. However, as in the case of BCTC, the pattern for many terms is not just in the reverse order, but the differences between contraction and non-contraction years are also considerable, meaning frequencies outside of contraction years are much higher (for example, note 'crisis' in dE).

One of the few terms which follows the expected pattern is 'depression'. With the exception of annual averages anywhere in dE, 'depression' featured more frequently during contractions than outside of them. Also similarly, and quite uniformly across categories and averages, 'distress', 'embarrassment' and 'panic' display higher frequencies during contraction years than outside of them. Another term which shows this pattern – in almost every dimension across frequencies both anywhere in documents and only in titles – is 'prosperity'. This, however, seems almost paradoxical in light of PPT, for it implies that the term 'prosperity', which, for example, is used to describe the upswing of a business cycle, is employed more frequently during downswings.

An intuitive potential explanation for these observations considers publication lag. If an economic crisis sparks respective discussions, then the articles responding to these events need to be written first and then pass through the peer-review and publication process, which can easily take more than a year. Therefore, the fifth, sixth and seventh columns of Tables 3.2 and 3.3 list frequencies in the three years following a contraction year (the respective values from Table 3.2 correspond to the shaded grey bars in Figure 3.2). In the overwhelming majority of cases, average term frequencies – whether annual or total – in both sE and dE are higher one year after than during a contraction. However, two and three years after contractions, the picture is less clear, with many terms still becoming more frequent, but by a smaller margin, and some even becoming less frequent than in the year right after a contraction. Overall, there is hardly a uniform trend where a term's frequencies across both categories and both averages rises throughout the three years following a contraction year – both 'crisis' and 'recession' illustrate this very well.

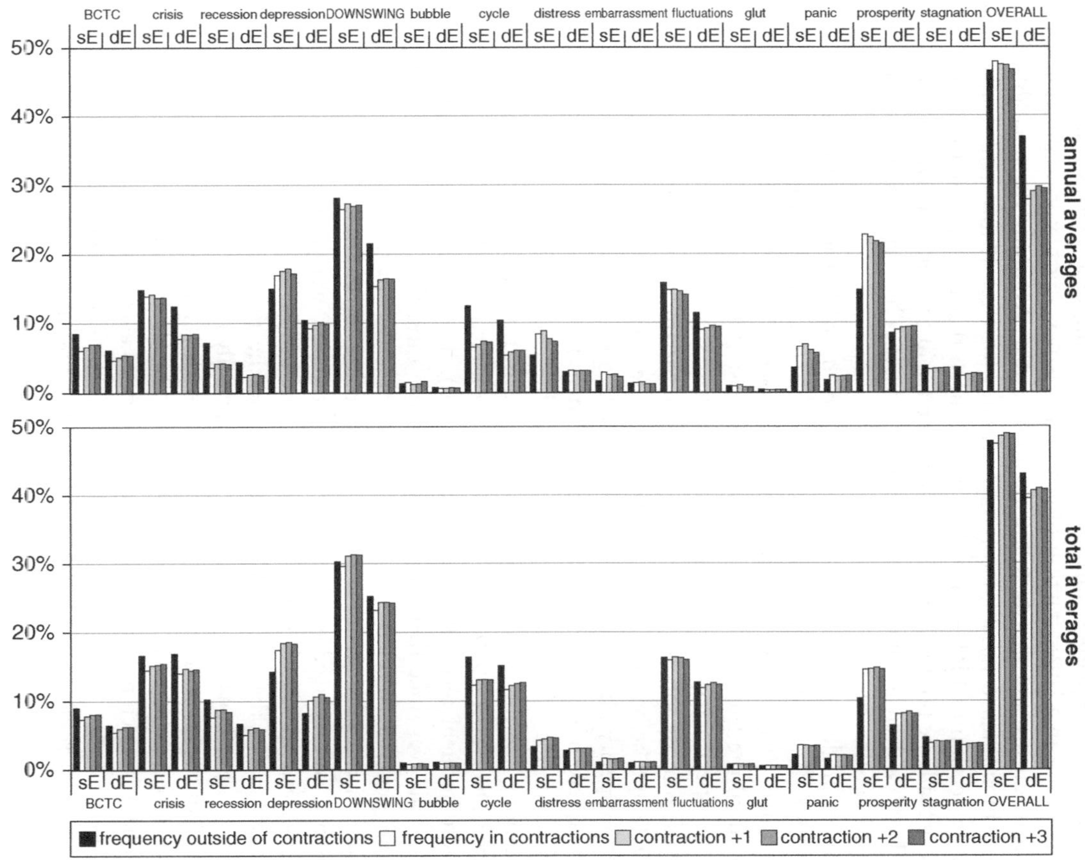

Figure 3.2 Relative frequencies of terms anywhere in documents, sE and dE, 1855–2012.

Note: Differently shaded bars correspond to years outside of, during and after contraction periods. The upper panel displays annual averages; the lower panel shows total averages. See columns three to seven from Table 3.2 for the corresponding numbers.

What is more, for most terms, frequencies one year after a contraction are still considerably lower than those outside of contractions (the most prominent exceptions, once more, are 'depression' and 'prosperity'). Since frequencies in the second and third year after a contraction are only slightly higher, this means that publication lag can hardly explain the main observation derived from Tables 3.2 and 3.3 – namely that, on average, many important terms related to BCCT feature in a larger fraction of economics papers outside of contraction years than during and shortly following a downturn. Assuming the reliability of these bibliometric variables as proxy measures for BCCT, this result could imply a rejection of PPT – indeed, it would mean that the supposed relation would actually be positive, meaning that a decrease in economic activity is correlated with a decrease in talk about economic crises. This surprising finding is discussed in Subsection 3.3.2.

Another angle on the terms is to identify which one featured in the largest number of sE and dE items during any specific contraction period (and the up to three years following that).[2] From the beginning of the observation period until the late 1910s (specifically the August 1918 – March 1919 recession), 'prosperity' had been the predominant term – even in contraction years and those directly following. Over the course of the three contractions during the 1920s and before the Great Depression, 'depression' gained in importance, while 'prosperity', however, still featured very frequently and often still as the most frequent notion. This shifted with the Great Depression, when 'depression' became the most frequent term used during contractions. In the 1960s, 'fluctuations' was the most frequent term for a short time. However, beginning with the December 1969 – November 1970 contraction, 'crisis' has become the most frequent term (first in dE, then in sE). The second most frequent term overall ever since then, sometimes even the most frequent in individual years and generally very close to the frequency of 'crisis', has been 'cycle'. The first shift in the most frequent terms thus occurred during the 1920s, when 'prosperity' was replaced by 'depression'. After the post-war years, 'depression' then gave way to 'crisis', which has been featured most frequently ever since the beginning of the 1970s. When considering the theoretical notions used in describing and analysing business cycles, especially the second development may be considered a shift away from dealing with a phase of the cycle, but towards a particular event within it. However, the descriptive overview presented here is much too coarse, in many respects, to allow for any far-reaching implications derived from it alone at this point. The discussion of Section 3.3 will revisit this result in combination with similar findings.

3.1.2.2 Time series of term frequencies

Figures 3.3–3.8 illustrate term frequencies within full texts and titles in six JSTOR categories (sBE, sE, sF, dBE, dE, dF) as well as the two top journal categories TJ5 and TJ7 between 1855 and 2012. Figure 3.9 similarly shows WoS frequencies in titles (1956–2015). As was documented in Figure 3.1 on page 57, the absolute number of items increased greatly especially over the

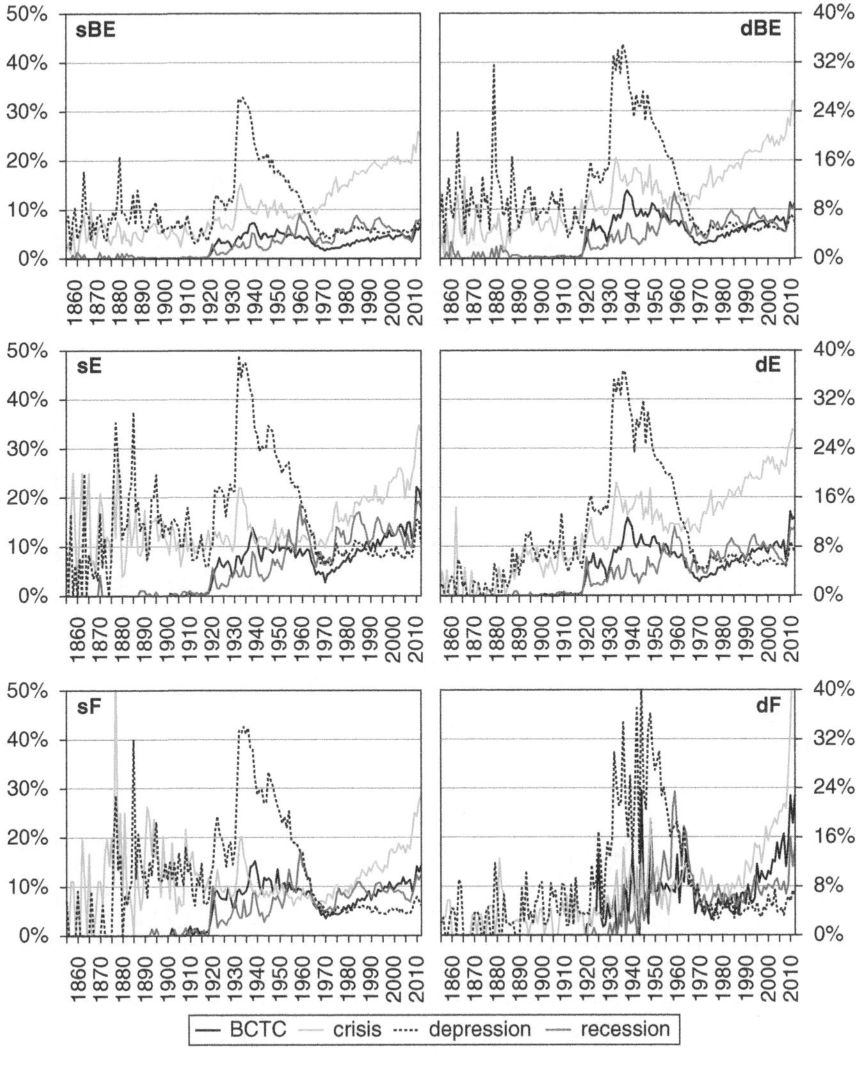

Figure 3.3 Relative frequencies of central terms, 1855–2012.

Note: Each panel shows the respective timelines for relative frequencies of the four central terms when searching anywhere in documents, all six JSTOR categories. Left column: subject categories. Right column: discipline categories.

course of the 20th century. Therefore, both absolute and relative frequencies of occurrences of individual terms (which naturally do not feature in every single item) are more volatile earlier in the observation period. This especially holds with respect to frequencies within titles, which is why the corresponding JSTOR series in Figures 3.4–3.8 have been smoothed by five-year moving

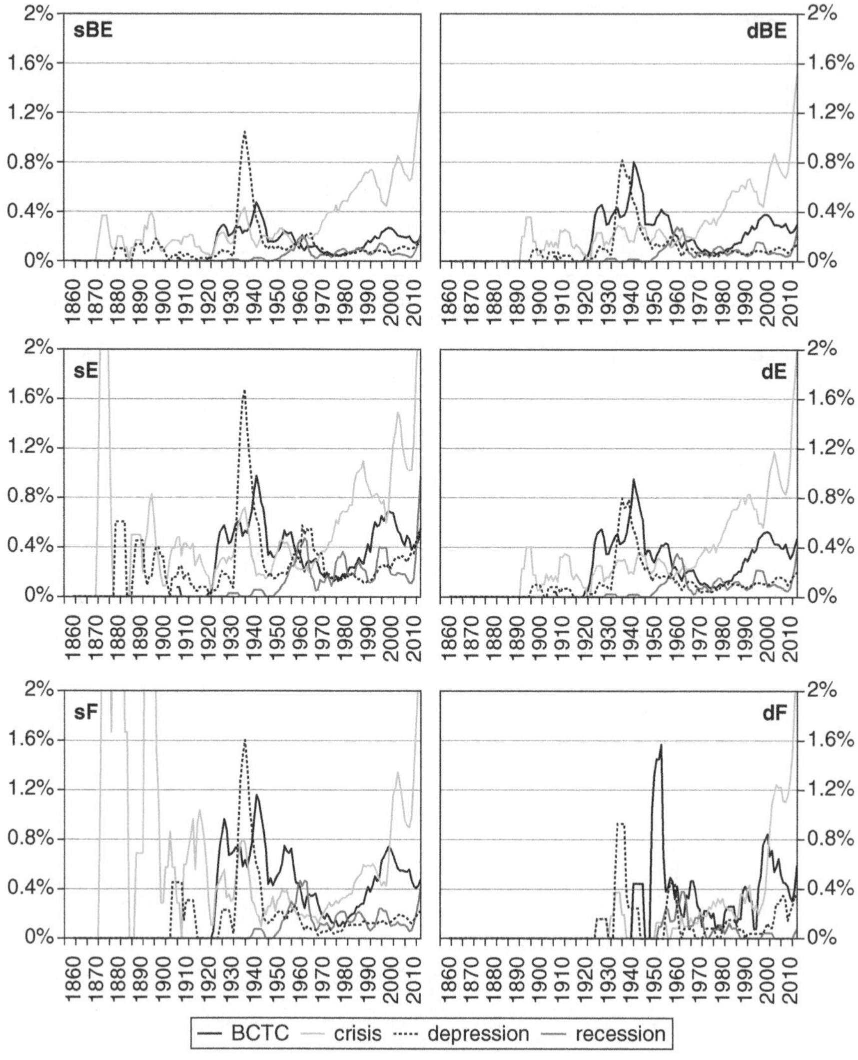

Figure 3.4 Relative frequencies of central terms, in titles, 1855–2012.

Note: Each panel shows the respective timelines of five-year moving averages for relative frequencies of the four central terms when searching document titles, all six JSTOR categories. Left column: subject categories. Right column: discipline categories.

averages. This reflects common practice to allow for less convoluted figures of time series subject to such variations.[3]

Figure 3.3 displays time series for relative annual frequencies of papers featuring BCTC (black), 'crisis' (light grey), 'depression' (dotted black) and 'recession' (dark grey) anywhere in the text. Each panel represents a different JSTOR

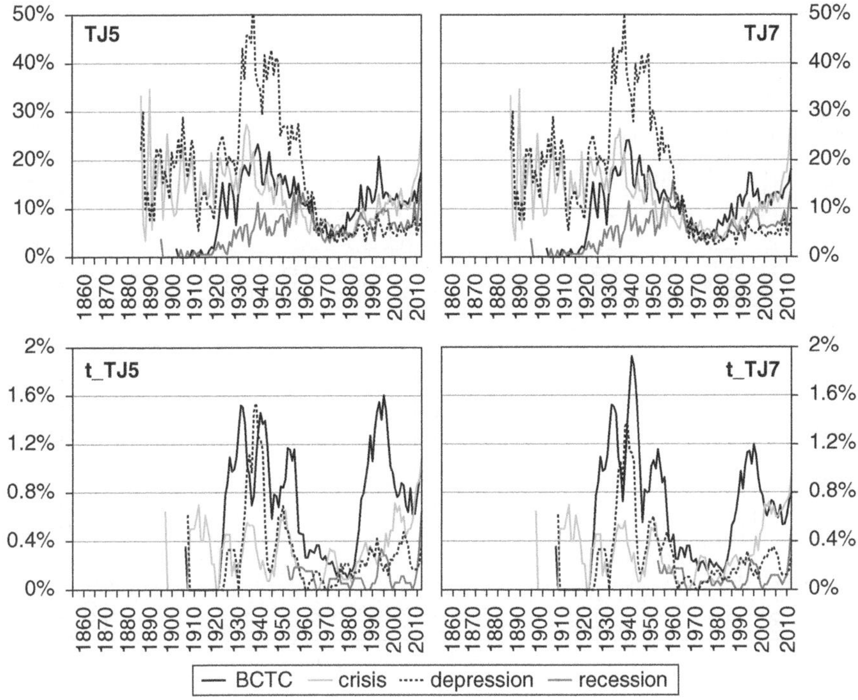

Figure 3.5 Relative frequencies of central terms, in top journals, 1855–2012.

Note: Each panel shows timelines for relative frequencies of the four central terms. Top left panel: TJ5 category, anywhere in documents. Top right: TJ7, anywhere. Bottom left: TJ5, only in titles. Bottom right: TJ7, titles. Title series are five-year moving averages.

category: sBE (top left), sE (middle left), sF (bottom left), dBE (top right), dE (middle right) and dF (bottom right). Generally, the timelines for all four terms are similar across all six panels (respectively categories). This implies somewhat robust results for whatever trends or fluctuations can be identified, irrespective of the precise sample. Throughout all panels, the highest frequencies observed over a couple of subsequent years are for 'depression' in the 1930s. Indeed, in the first half of the 1930s, almost half of all articles in sE, and well over 30% in dE, contained the word 'depression'. The frequency of 'depression' has subsequently decreased, and, in more recent decades, the other three terms have generally been in broader use throughout all categories. This holds for 'crisis' in particular, which has recently featured in two to three times as many articles as the other terms (with the exception of dF, where the difference is considerably smaller).

Concerning BCTC and 'recession', the close proximity of the timelines since the early 20th century is noticeable. Before the 1950s, BCTC was generally the more frequent term, although this order has somewhat reversed afterwards (more so for the subject than the discipline categories). BCTC appeared in the

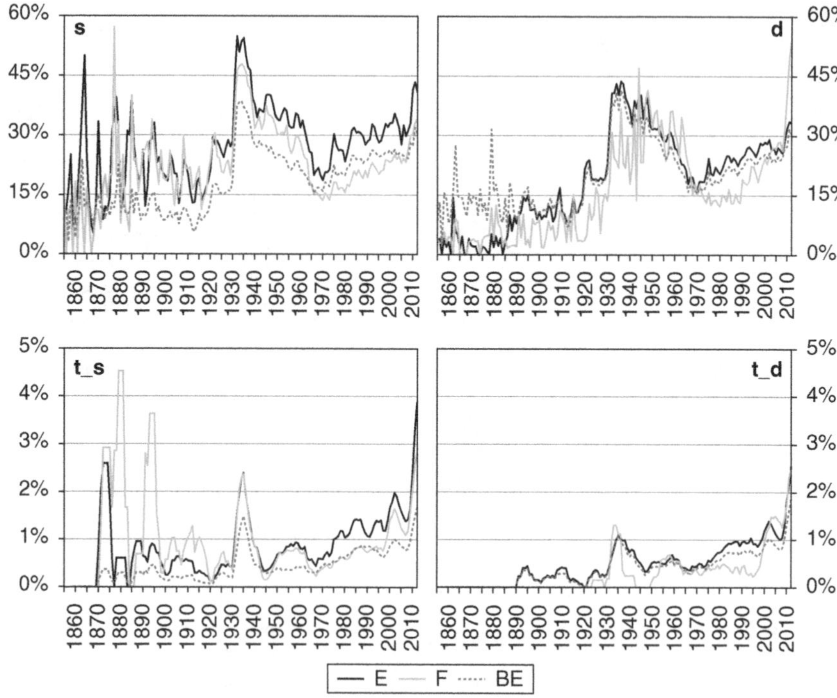

Figure 3.6 Relative frequencies of the DOWNSWING index, 1855–2012.

Note: Top row: occurrences anywhere in document. Bottom row: titles only (five-year moving averages).

relatively largest number of items first in the 1930s, when the timelines peaked a few years after the series of 'depression' and 'crisis', and reached similar levels, of around and over 10% in sE and dE, again in the second half of the 2000s. In between, the 1960s and 1970s constitute a period where the relative frequency of BCTC had reached a trough of comparatively low levels. What is more, it is quite evident from Figure 3.3 that, even though in the last five years of the observation period, the 'recession' series did see a considerable rise in frequency – towards the levels of the 1950s and 1960s – this increase, when looking across the different categories displayed in Figure 3.3, was not much larger than previous increases had been, and most notably not nearly as large as the burst in frequency of 'depression' during the 1930s. This may be taken to imply that, in contrast to the "Great Depression" of the 1930s, either the term, or talk about it (or both) of the "Great Recession" of more recent years is not nearly as prevalent.

Figure 3.4 mirrors Figure 3.3, except that the time series here display frequencies within titles of articles. For the subject categories on the left of

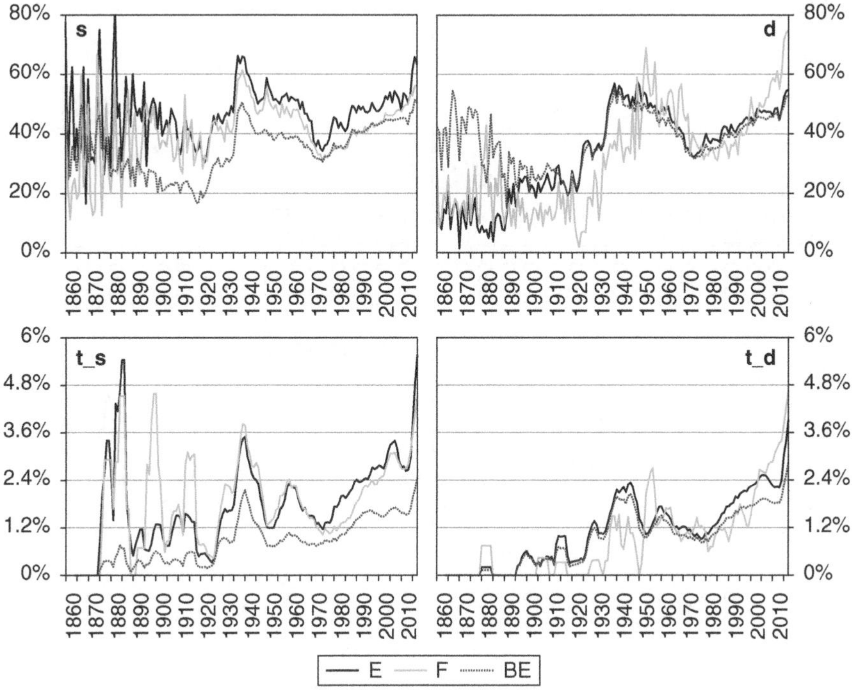

Figure 3.7 Relative frequencies of the OVERALL index, 1855–2012.

Note: Top row: occurrences anywhere in document. Bottom row: titles only (five-year moving averages).

Figure 3.4, the impression is broadly the same as that gained from Figure 3.3. 'Depression' was the most frequent term in the 1930s, and its frequency subsequently declined – much faster than in the series depicted in Figure 3.3 – to a level very close to that of 'recession'. Interestingly, here, 'recession' only ever really started to become featured in titles once the decline in 'depression' frequencies had set in (which makes sense, given the limited number of words in a title, and the fact that both terms refer to the downswing of a business cycle). At the same time, while also peaking in the 1930s, 'crisis' has continuously climbed ever since the 1960s, to its highest levels in the new millennium. The overall trends of BCTC look largely similar to those observed in Figure 3.3, although, throughout most of the observation period, the levels are relatively higher compared to the other terms. In more recent decades, the peak frequency of BCTC had already been reached around 2000, even shortly surpassing 'crisis' in sE and sF, but levels a decade later were lower again. 'Crisis' then continued to rise in frequency whereas BCTC dropped (down to the levels of 'recession and 'depression' in the 2010s in sBE and sE).

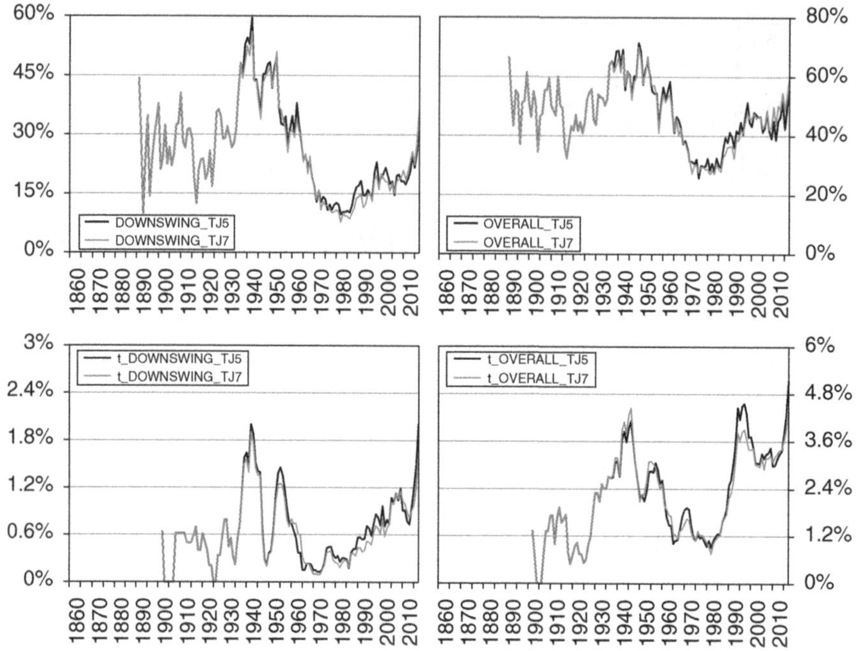

Figure 3.8 Relative frequencies of the indexes, in top journals, 1855–2012.

Note: Each panel shows timelines for relative frequencies of an index in both the TJ5 and TJ7 categories. Top left panel: DOWNSWING, anywhere in documents. Top right: OVERALL, anywhere. Bottom left: DOWNSWING, only in titles. Bottom right: OVERALL, titles. Title series are five-year moving averages.

The discipline categories on the right of Figure 3.4 show a slightly different picture. As in the other panels, including those in Figure 3.3, the 'depression' series peaked in the early 1930s. However, shortly afterwards, there are even larger peaks in dE and dF, and a similarly large peak in dBE, for the BCTC series. The most frequent of the major terms featured in dE, dF and dBE paper titles during and after the Great Depression was thus, at first, 'depression' – but as this frequency declined, BCTC came to be used even more often for a short period of time. The largest peak came in 1940, where 1.54% of all articles in an economics journal indexed on JSTOR (dE) featured BCTC in their title (for comparison, the highest level of 'depression' was 1.06% in 1934). In the subsequent decades and until the end of the observation period, the development of BCTC in the discipline categories was largely similar to that in the subject categories (including the peaks around 2000), and indeed this also holds for the other three terms. In both the subject and discipline categories taken together, and similar to what was observed for Figure 3.3, 'recession' did not feature nearly as frequently in titles during the "Great Recession" as 'depression' had during the "Great Depression" about eight decades earlier.

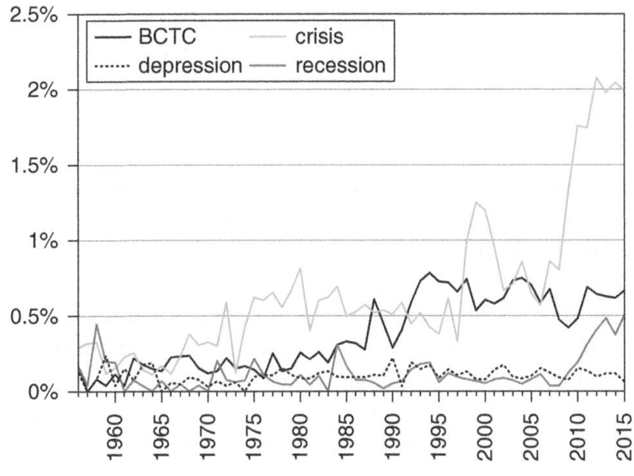

Figure 3.9 Term frequencies in the SSCI records, 1956–2015.

Note: Timelines for relative frequencies of SSCI economics article featuring the major terms in titles.

The graphical illustrations of Figures 3.3 and 3.4 can likewise be repeated for the two top journal categories TJ5 and TJ7 (see Subsection 2.4.1), as in Figure 3.5. Even though the first item in both categories is from 1886 (see Table 2.3 on page 38), Figure 3.5 depicts the same 1855–2012 time period, in order to allow an easier connection of relevant points in time between the figures. The top two panels show frequencies anywhere in documents, the bottom two frequencies in titles. The left column shows frequencies within the TJ5 category, while those in the TJ7 category are on the right. Owing to the major overlap between the TJ5 and TJ7 categories (since TJ7 is the five journals from TJ5 plus two more), the panels on the left and right of each row look highly similar, especially with regards to the general trends of movements.

It is interesting to compare the time series depicted in Figure 3.5 with those of Figures 3.3 and 3.4 in order to identify similarities and differences between the literature at large, and the premier journals. There are considerable similarities indeed. The most discernible peaks in any of the series are with 'depression' in the 1930s, followed by declines to relatively low levels until the 1970s, where the series have remained fairly stable ever since. The BCTC series also show peaks and subsequent declines in the 1930s. However, whereas the BCTC series in Figure 3.3 since the 1970s were characterized by a relatively steady upward trend in all panels, Figure 3.5 sketches a somewhat different picture. There is a second peak of the BCTC series in the 1990s, followed by a decline and then, finally, another rise towards the very end of the observation period. The 'crisis' pattern in the top two panels of Figure 3.5 also shows differences from what was seen in Figure 3.3. Relatively high levels until the 1930s were followed by a subsequent decline, which made way for a rising trend again only in the 1970s.

Meanwhile, the 'recession' series peaked in the 1950s and early 1960s. Overall, the largest overall difference between the top two panels of Figure 3.5 on the one hand, and Figure 3.3 on the other, is probably that 'crisis' is much closer to the other series and that BCTC, as well as showing two clearly identifiable peaks, is also considerably larger in the top journal categories as displayed in Figure 3.5.

The comparison highlights similar points when putting the bottom two panels of Figure 3.5 next to Figure 3.4. The title series from top journals also display a second peak in the BCTC series, which, interestingly, also showed a second peak just a few years later in all panels of Figure 3.4. What is more, the title series in Figure 3.5 further attest to the prominence of the BCTC series here, with peaks of the same or even higher magnitude than 'depression' even during the 1930s, and with 'crisis' not being an outlier among term frequencies in top journal titles as well (especially as compared with the series in Figure 3.4, the more so the closer to the end of the observation period one looks). This is demonstrated even more by the magnitudes of the frequencies: the scale in all these two (bottom two in Figure 3.5), respectively six (Figure 3.4), panels is the same, so that it is easily possible to identify, in general and over much of the observation period, the much higher relative frequency of BCTC in titles of top journals especially when compared with sBE and dBE, but also with sE and dE.

Figure 3.6 shows time series for the DOWNSWING index across all categories, with subject categories on the left, and discipline categories on the right. The two panels on top display relative frequencies of the index anywhere in documents, whereas the two on the bottom do the same for frequencies in titles. The latter have been smoothed with a five-year moving average. Different from Figures 3.3 and 3.4, the panels in Figure 3.6 contain time series for the same term, but within different categories. This other way of organization highlights the remarkable similarity across a term's timelines within different categories. Indeed, not only general, overall trends across decades, but also short-term fluctuations and ephemeral peaks and troughs, are largely mirrored between categories. This broadly holds for both subject and discipline categories, as well as for frequencies anywhere in the documents and only in titles. This implies that term frequencies of the notions related to business cycles and economic crises (or specifically of the DOWNSWING index, as depicted here) are fairly generally similar within economics and neighbouring subjects, respectively disciplines, such as finance, and the overall category including economics, namely BE.

Since, in addition to 'recession', the DOWNSWING index contains two terms – 'crisis' and 'depression' – which show large frequencies at different points in time, the historical development of the DOWNSWING index naturally follows a shape along the upper lines of what could be identified in Figures 3.3 and 3.4. In the 1930s, DOWNSWING ranged between around 33% (sBE) and up to about 47% (sE) of all articles (about 36% in dBE, and near 39% in dE). For sE, the average difference between the frequency of 'depression' alone, and the DOWNSWING index, is just about 6 percentage points in the 1930s, even though 'recession' featured in around 5%, and 'crisis' in over 10% of all articles in the same period – at the same time, however, 'depression' featured in about 87% of the DOWNSWING items. In dE, numbers are lower, with the average annual frequency of 'depression' at about 32% in the 1930s, over 7 percentage points lower than the index (i.e. 'depression' alone appeared in more than 81% of the papers in the index). This implies that many papers speaking of a 'recession' or 'crisis' in the 1930s also mentioned 'depression', further highlighting 'depression' as the standard term to refer to current events then. Starting in the 1970s, the rise of the index closely mirrors that of 'crisis', which was already observable in Figure 3.3. In the 2000s, the DOWNSWING index in sE was at about 33%, or 8.2 percentage points higher than the average frequency of 'crisis'. Here, then, a quarter of the index is exclusively due to the other two terms, implying that, in sE, 'crisis' has become less of a default notion than 'depression' had been in the 1930s. In dE, this difference is smaller: about 27.6% of papers in the 2000s feature the DOWNSWING index, and 5.7 percentage points (about a fifth) of these are not due to 'crisis'.

The bottom panels for frequencies within titles compare to those of Figure 3.4 just like the two on top had compared to Figure 3.3. They follow a similar course to the respective most frequent term of the index ('depression' in the 1930s, 'crisis' beginning in the 1940s). Similar to frequencies anywhere in the documents, the timelines for dE and dBE are closer to one another than those for sE and sBE, on the other hand (which is not surprising, because dE is a much larger fraction of dBE than sE is of sBE). A final interesting observation from Figure 3.6 is that in the bottom right panel, which displays frequencies within titles of the discipline categories, the DOWNSWING index climbed towards higher values in the 2000s than in the 1930s – especially in dE – even though the peaks in the terms' individual time series (see Figure 3.4) had been on similar levels. This is a byproduct of the smoothing in combination with the fact that the high frequency of 'depression' within 1930s titles was a flash-in-the-pan kind of event, with a sudden upward burst and a quick drop back to lower values a few years later, whereas the relatively high (and rising) levels of 'crisis' in the 2000s result from a continuous upward trend.

Figure 3.7 has the same structure as Figure 3.6, but displays time series for the OVERALL instead of the DOWNSWING index. Panels are organized in the same way, with frequencies anywhere on top, those in titles on the bottom, and subject categories on the left, whereas discipline categories are on the right of the figure. Interestingly, although this index contains ten additional notions – especially including BCTC and, for example, 'prosperity', a term referring to a business cycle's upswing – the OVERALL index of frequencies anywhere in the documents moves largely similar to the DOWNSWING index in Figure 3.6. This holds for both subject and discipline categories. In the 20th century, the first major peak of the series can be found in the 1930s. Following subsequent declines until the 1960s, the timelines climbed upwards again beginning in the 1970s, and continued to do so over the rest of the observation period. In the case of the OVERALL index anywhere in documents, the levels of the

1930s were reached by 2012, whereas the DOWNSWING index anywhere in documents had climbed to just about four-fifths of the 1930s levels in 2012. This implies that the prevalence of "negative" terms in discussions of business cycles – i.e. specifically those major terms captured in the DOWNSWING index – was noticeably higher during and following the Great Depression than during and following the Great Recession, especially when compared with frequencies of all terms related to BCCT. Another similarity between the OVERALL and DOWNSWING indexes is that, in both cases, the time series of sE are considerably higher than those of sBE in the top left panels of both Figures 3.6 and 3.7, whereas those of dE and dBE are very close to one another. This further holds independently of whether one looks at frequencies anywhere in the documents, or just within titles, as the respective panels on the bottom show.

To also document frequencies of the two indexes in top journals, Figure 3.8 plots the corresponding time series. Each panel shows two timelines, which are the frequencies for one index, either anywhere in documents or only in titles (depending on the respective panel), in both the TJ5 and TJ7 categories: DOWNSWING_TJ5 and DOWNSWING_TJ7 (top left); OVERALL_TJ5 and OVERALL_TJ7 (top right); t_DOWNSWING_TJ5 and t_DOWNSWING_TJ7 (bottom left); and t_OVERALL_TJ5 and t_OVERALL_TJ7 (bottom right). Putting the two related time series on top of each other in all of the four panels highlights the major overlap and similarity between the two top journal categories even more than Figure 3.5 had (also see the bottom panel in Figure 3.1 on page 57, as well as the corresponding description there). The two panels on the right of Figure 3.8 with the series for the OVERALL index can be compared with Figure 3.7. There is not much to be said here, except that the series are fairly similar both in magnitude and in their overall shape. For example, there are peaks in the 1930s, the 1970s see the lowest points, and near the end of the observation period, there are fairly high frequencies again. Interestingly, frequencies of OVERALL in top journals did not rise to the level of the 1930s in the late 2000s and 2010s (which they did in all the subject and discipline categories), but title frequencies in the late 1980s, early 1990s and 2010s were nearly as high as or higher than in the 1930s (which more closely resembles the respective panels in Figure 3.7). The DOWNSWING series in Figure 3.8 seem even closer to those from Figure 3.6, especially when looking at the subject categories. The series for the indexes in top journals compared with one another also resemble those in the other categories in the sense that DOWNSWING moves across a comparatively broader band – at least relative to its average over the whole observation period – than OVERALL.

As explained in Subsection 2.3.3, paper lists can be extracted from the WoS in a similar fashion to JSTOR. Therefore, even though full-text searches are not possible, the frequencies of terms within titles can similarly be used to construct bibliometric time series. To supplement the results for JSTOR data, Figure 3.9 mirrors the previous illustration of Figure 3.3 by displaying four time series which trace the relative frequencies in titles of BCTC, 'crisis', 'depression' and 'recession' among all economics articles indexed on the SSCI. Over the whole observation period 1956–2015, 'depression' was very rare, which was also the case for 'recession' until the most recent episode following the global financial and economic crisis of 2007–08. Despite some differences in magnitude, the similarity to the respective parts in several panels of Figure 3.4, especially for sE and dE, is quite apparent. The observed trends and patterns for frequencies in titles therefore seem quite robust. It is also interesting to note that the frequency levels of BCTC and 'crisis' are rather close to each other in the keywords (not in the figure): in fact, BCTC was considerably more frequent in the 1990s. This might be taken as a hint that mentions of 'crisis' anywhere in an article's text are more often "lip service" (see Subsection 2.4.3) than those of BCTC, so that the respective time series built on JSTOR data underestimate the spread of BCTC relative to 'crisis'. This is another aspect which warrants some theoretical reflection and will thus be discussed (in a wider context) in Section 3.3.

3.1.2.3 Graphical comparison of economic and bibliometric data

It is tempting to draw a connection between economic crises or contraction periods with short-term changes in the series depicted in Figures 3.3–3.9. In Figure 3.3, Recession_sE and Recession_dE after World War II are two particularly illustrative examples which show an upward trend spotted with alternating peaks and troughs. Figure 3.10 allows for a closer descriptive assessment of the connection by displaying two panels which each plot one bibliometric and one economic variable. Naturally, this constitutes a very small sample. There are 15 different terms (including the indexes) in eight categories (including top journals) which can be combined with up to seven, respectively eight, economic variables. This results in 840, respectively 960, combinations that could be depicted – and twice as many once frequencies within titles are considered. The econometric analysis takes these combinations into account and thoroughly assesses their potential association. However, the following two examples already illustrate the general idea and issue at hand.

The left panel of Figure 3.10 displays the time series for BCTC_dE and INCPC, and the right panel shows the aforementioned Recession_dE combined with UNEMP. INCPC data are on an inverted logarithmic scale on the right axis, i.e. a downward movement represents an increase. In the 1930s, there seems to be some co-movement in the direction implied by PPT: the drop in INCPC correlated with a major increase in the frequency of BCTC_dE, and the recovery of INCPC was accompanied by decreases in BCTC_dE. However, for the remainder of the series, especially after the 1940s, the rising trend of INCPC catches the eye much more than do shorter variations, such as a decline in 1974. Therefore, no uniform relation between the two series seems to be apparent from the graph alone.

The right panel in Figure 3.10 provides a different impression. The Recession_dE series (black) lacks a strong and clearly discernible trend, but there are frequent up- and downswings over the course of just a few years. Interestingly, these are often mirrored in the UNEMP series (grey). Indeed, Recession_dE

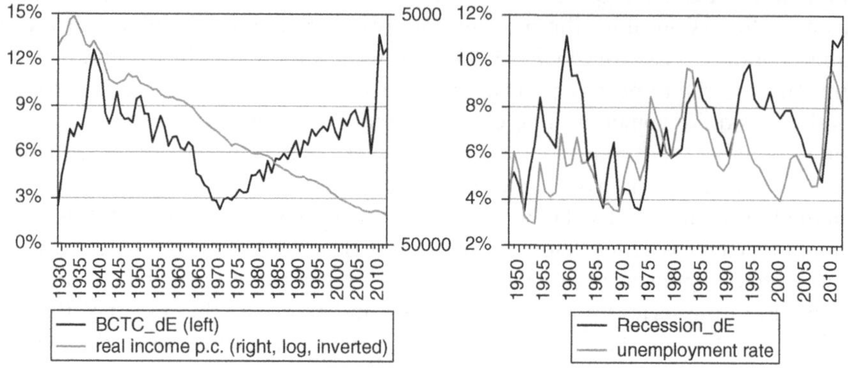

Figure 3.10 Two examples comparing bibliometric and economic time series.

Note: Left panel: BCTC_dE vs. income per capita (right axis, inverted logarithmic scale), 1929–2012. Right panel: Recession_dE vs. unemployment rate, 1948–2012.

frequently shows readily identifiable peaks in the same or the following year as UNEMP. This observation is clearly in line with a literature response as suggested by PPT.

However, two caveats are in order. First, as already pointed out, this chart reading can at best be an introduction to a rigorous statistical analysis of potential connections between the time series. Secondly, even if Recession_dE and UNEMP were statistically closely related, it may well be that this is just an exception among the wide array of possible combinations between economic and bibliometric variables. Indeed, if it turned out to be the only one, this would be very little affirmative evidence for a PPT argument. The left panel in Figure 3.10 has already provided an impression of how the relations between two variables which, following the PPT logic, might plausibly be connected quite closely may not be so clear-cut in the actual data. Therefore, it is necessary to consider the whole range of potential connections between economic and bibliometric variables, as the econometric analysis in Section 3.2 will. This analysis also further highlights the caveat regarding the number of positive findings, which will then be discussed in detail in Section 3.3.

3.1.3 Economic crises and citation frequencies

As pointed out in Subsection 2.4.2.2, identifying the relevant set for the citation analysis, and then scaling the resulting data appropriately for useful historical comparisons, is far from trivial. Nonetheless, some descriptive statistics for the 1956–2015 observation period can be summarized to complement the analysis of relevant terms. The *h*-index is 73 for tBCTC_WoS, 79 for tDOWNSWING_WoS and 152 for tOVERALL_WoS. The three most cited papers in tBCTC_WoS are Hamilton (1989), Nordhaus (1975) and Hansen (1985) with 2162, 871 and 696 citations, respectively. In tDOWNSWING_WoS, Kaminsky and Reinhart (1999), Baumol (1967) and Krugman (1979) were cited 812, 800 and 715 times; and the top three of tOVERALL_WoS are Hamilton (1989), Vernon (1966) and Kydland and Prescott (1982) at 2162, 1972 and 1422 citations. In tBCTC_WoS, the top three most cited papers contribute 14.93% of the 24 978 citations to that set. In tDOWNSWING_WoS and tOVERALL_WoS, the numbers are 5.45% of 42 720, and 3.69% of 150 619, respectively. This short list also illustrates the inaccuracy of categorizing papers by specific terms in their titles. While there is little doubt that almost all items are concerned with economic fluctuations and crises in some way or another (the potential exception being Vernon 1966), clearly multiple items (Baumol 1967; Krugman 1979; Kaminsky and Reinhart 1999) do not primarily deal with business cycles. PPT does not directly refer to this literature, but, as these examples show, this literature nonetheless influences the samples and data used here.

Moving further, Figure 3.11 depicts several time series of interest. The top left panel (a) shows the absolute annual numbers of citable economics papers in each of the underlying sets. The other panels display: (b) absolute citation counts to the respective series; (c,d) absolute numbers of (c) citing economics papers and (d) all citing SSCI items; (e) the relative frequency of citing economics papers among all economics papers; and (f) the annual average number of citations to the citable set for every citing item. The series in panels (a)–(d) are on a logarithmic scale. The BCTC series are black lines; DOWNSWING is light grey with squares; and OVERALL is dark grey with diamonds.

At first glance, remarkable similarities among the absolute citations series (panels (b)–(d)) and the relative frequency of citing economics papers (e) are apparent. At least since the 1980s, absolute frequencies of citations and citing items to the BCTC and DOWNSWING sets were very similar and on the same rising trend (a virtually equal rate of growth of annual citations) until about 2005 (b,d), respectively 2010 (c), when references to DOWNSWING started to increase much faster and thus moved ahead of BCTC. This is mirrored in the relative frequencies of citing economics papers (e), too. This result becomes more interesting when taking into account the frequencies from panel (a), which clearly show that the underlying DOWNSWING series contains more items in almost every single year, and that the annual number of new DOWNSWING items has greatly increased since the mid-2000s. It may be suspected, therefore, that the increase in frequencies of citations to the DOWNSWING papers is largely due to the greater number of available items which can be cited, and further scrutiny (not depicted in Figure 3.11) confirms this. The average number of citations per citable paper published until and including the same year has been greatest, and for the most part considerably larger than DOWNSWING, for the BCTC series since the late 1970s and until 2015. For example, over the 1990s, there was more than one citation per year for every BCTC paper published between 1956 and that year. The same factor for DOWNSWING papers was only at about 0.25. However,

Figure 3.11 Citation frequencies, 1956–2015.

Note: The time series show: (a) citable economics papers in each of the underlying sets (BCTC, DOWNSWING, OVERALL); (b) absolute citation counts to those respective series; (c) absolute numbers of citing economics papers; (d) absolute numbers of all citing SSCI items; (e) the relative frequency of citing economics papers among all economics papers; and (f) the annual average number of relevant citations for every citing item. Panels (a)–(d) are on a logarithmic scale.

the DOWNSWING number greatly increased from the late 1990s onwards, getting very close to BCTC levels by 2015. Therefore, the recent discrepancy in papers citing, respectively citations to, BCTC and DOWNSWING is not only due to the greater frequency of DOWNSWING papers, but also due to them becoming relatively more cited on average over the past 15–20 years.

Furthermore, for a large part of the observation period, not just trends of BCTC and DOWNSWING, but also those of OVERALL were similar, albeit on a higher level (a)–(d). This is more apparent for the citation (b)–(d) than for the underlying (a) series due to the relatively smaller short-term variations in the former. Although far less pronounced than in the DOWNSWING series, and even less so when looking not at citing papers, but at citation counts, the OVERALL series also saw a rapid increase of citations over the course of the most recent 10–15 years. For all three series, it can therefore be concluded that, for most of the observation period, the numbers of citable items as well as those of citing items and citation counts increased at a fairly constant rate on average, but that, more recently, frequencies of the OVERALL and especially DOWNSWING series increased much faster than those of BCTC. Concerning the absolute number of citations (b), this effect is due both to the increasing number of available citable items (both for DOWNSWING and OVERALL) and to an increase in average citations per citable item over the same recent period in both series. This trend shift is furthermore apparent in panel (e), which shows that relative frequencies of economics papers citing at least one from the underlying series have almost doubled for OVERALL, and more than doubled for the DOWNSWING series, over the past decade. Interestingly, here, too, all three series display a rising trend since at least the mid-1960s (OVERALL) and mid-1970s (DOWNSWING and BCTC), which implies that the frequency of papers citing at least one from the underlying series has increased faster than the total body of economics literature. For OVERALL and DOWNSWING, this trend has further accelerated recently.

The series in panel (f) display the average number of citations to the underlying sets for all those papers which cited at least one from the citable set. That is, if no citations to the underlying set were recorded in any given year, the number is 0, and if at least one citation was identified, the number is at least 1. Any number greater than 1 means that one or multiple citing papers were referencing multiple articles from the citable set. Interestingly, the three series mostly follow a similar pattern. They are close to 1 and frequently 0 (especially BCTC) throughout the 1970s, and then, starting in the early 1980s, follow upward trends which become flatter and, in the case of BCTC, even slightly negative, around 2000. The DOWNSWING and OVERALL series also show an early peak in the 1960s. Every paper published in 2000 which cited a BCTC item contained about 1.71 BCTC references on average, and the corresponding figures for DOWNSWING and OVERALL are 1.48 and 1.86, respectively. Next to these general trends, there are clearly recognizable short-term fluctuations in each of the three series. In general, it should be pointed out that many of the positively sloped lines displayed in Figure 3.11 do not necessarily imply increased interest in the source material, but can instead be linked with changing trends in metadata such as the average number of references per paper. Subsection 3.3.5 provides a detailed discussion of this issue.

Another way to arrange the citation data with the aim to identify potential linkages to business cycles and economic crises is to construct citation

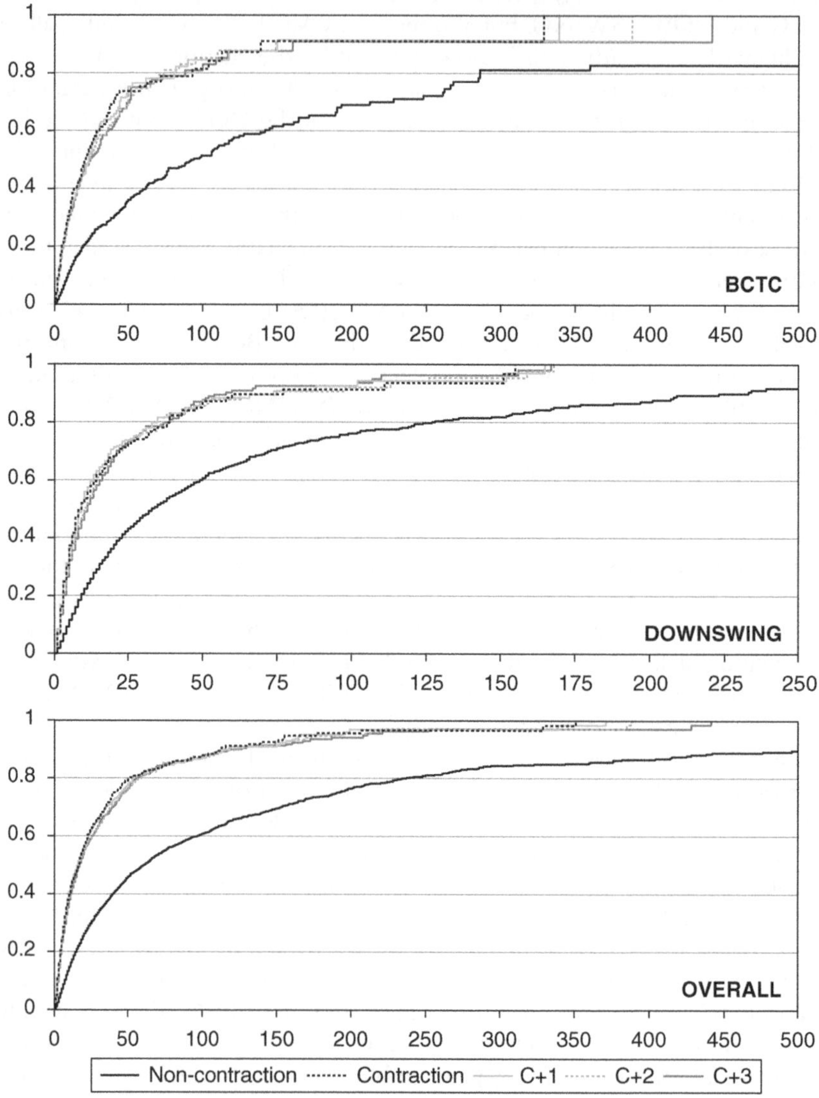

Figure 3.12 Cumulative citation distribution functions, 1956–2015.

Note: CCDFs of citations to all papers containing BCTC (top), DOWNSWING (middle) and OVERALL (bottom) in their titles. Each panel contains CCDFs for non-contraction and contraction years as well as the first, second and third year after a contraction (C+1, etc.).

profiles inside and outside of contraction years, mirroring the method used in Subsection 3.1.1 for term frequencies. To this end, Figure 3.12 displays cumulative citation distribution functions (CCDFs) for tBCTC_WoS (top), tDOWNSWING_WoS (middle) and tOVERALL_WoS (bottom). Each panel contains five CCDFs representing the respective sets' citation counts from within non-contraction years (NC), contraction years (C), and within the first, second and third year following a contraction (C+1, C+2, C+3). The panels were scaled so as to gain a more detailed picture of the C, C+1, C+2 and C+3 series, at the expense of plotting the full NC series. However, the major difference between the latter and the four former is still evident. In each of the three panels, the respective CCDFs show the same two clearly identifiable features. First, the NC CCDFs lie far to the right of the respective other four, which reflects the much higher total citation counts to most papers outside of contraction years. However, since these are non-normalized absolute numbers, and only 12 of the 60 years between 1956 and 2015 were contraction years, this result by itself does not imply much with regards to PPT. Even a considerable increase in citation frequencies during contraction years could result in a much smaller absolute number of citations in these years due to the low number of years (one contraction year per four non-contraction years). Indeed, normalized (divided by the number of years in the category) citation counts in non-contraction years are very close to those in the other years, and the CCDFs are sometimes even to the left, but also still sometimes to the right, of the C, C+1, C+2 and C+3 CCDFs (since the corresponding depiction would make the graphs even more cluttered in the relevant areas, Figure 3.12 does not display normalized values). There is no uniform pattern though. The picture most in line with PPT can be gained from the DOWNSWING CCDFs, where the normalized NC CCDF is mostly to the left (although not far) of the others. On the other hand, average normalized citation counts of NC are higher than those of C for BCTC, DOWNSWING and OVERALL. This quite clearly allows for the interpretation that average citation counts to the BCTC, DOWNSWING and OVERALL sets do not greatly increase during and following contraction years as compared with non-contraction years.

The second observation regarding the other four series (i.e. not NC) is more interesting and potentially telling, namely that all of them are very close to one another, with no overall order of any one being continually to the left or right of another. This is interesting because a version of PPT which takes publication lags into account might suggest higher citation counts in the first, second or third year following a contraction as compared with the original contraction year. This is not observable in Figure 3.12 on the whole (i.e. when considering all parts of the CCDFs). However, a closer look at the data and figures shows that, for papers with citation counts of up to about 50 (BCTC), 25 (DOWNSWING) and 75 (OVERALL), CCDFs of C+1 and especially C+2 and C+3 are fairly consistently, albeit not much, to the right of those of C. Given a quite stable rank order among papers,[4] this implies that, for a majority of BCTC, DOWNSWING and OVERALL articles, citation counts do indeed increase following a contraction, at least after the original contraction year (but frequently not as compared with non-contraction years). Admittedly, though, the descriptive evidence is not very comprehensive.

3.2 Econometric analysis

As was already evident from the presentation of the economic time series back in Section 2.2, the periods covered differ quite substantially between variables. On the other hand, most of the relevant bibliometric time series date back well into the 19th century. However, coverage in terms of absolute items gets ever thinner the further back in history one goes, and the descriptive overview in Section 3.1 has also shown that the majority of items in the bibliometric series are actually fairly recent, especially from the past six to seven decades. This is why 1855, the starting year for the reference series of NBER contraction years, was chosen as an overall benchmark and as the cut-off year onwards from which the bibliometric series are considered. The uneven distribution of bibliometric records over time also means that even a shorter economic series may potentially be compared with the largest part of the bibliometric series in terms of the number of items. Table 3.4 demonstrates this by showing sizes of any combination of economic series and bibliometric sets used in the econometric analysis.

A few notes on how to read Table 3.4 are in order. The absolute numbers and percentages documented in a particular cell are determined based on a comparison in which the full available bibliometric sample in the given category is taken (see Table 3.1 on page 56 for reference numbers), and then compared with the part of that series for which economic data are available in the same years. The period considered for the econometric analysis is thus the intersection of years covered in both series. In the case of per capita income and sE, 121 891 is the absolute number of sE items published between 1929 and 2012 (the years covered by the INCPC series for which there are items in the bibliometric set), and 86.65% is that absolute number divided by the total number of items in the sE category published between 1855 and 2012. In cases where the bibliometric series has the same or a shorter historical record than the economic series (e.g. SPC with TJ5 and TJ7; any combination with CPI; or due to the 2012 cut-off date for JSTOR data), the absolute numbers are, of course, still limited by the available bibliometric series, and naturally these cases will have 100% coverage.

Table 3.4 shows quite clearly that, even with the shortest economic time series (UNEMP), a large absolute number of items is part of the bibliometric sets, and a large percentage of at least 70% and often more than 80% of the respective items is included. Nonetheless, despite the relatively comprehensive bibliometric sample size of the shorter series, their major shortcoming still remains, namely that they only cover a considerably lower number of business cycles and economic crises, and therefore less observations of fluctuations in both economic and consequently bibliometric variables. While the sample of items in each bibliometric set is large, the number of observations on intertemporal changes in relative frequencies – the relevant aspect for the statistical analysis of co-movements between economic and bibliometric time series – is nonetheless directly limited by the available years. WoS data coverage is not explicitly documented in Table 3.4, because only the bankruptcies series

Table 3.4 Coverage of bibliometric series by economic variables

	sE (*1855–2012*)	*sF* (*1855–2012*)	*sBE* (*1855–2012*)	*dE* (*1855–2012*)	*dF* (*1855–2012*)	*dBE* (*1855–2012*)	*TJ5* (*1886–2012*)	*TJ7* (*1886–2012*)
INCPC (1929–2016)	121 891 (86.65%)	196 234 (96.02%)	577 737 (91.11%)	252 884 (90.63%)	28 576 (89.04%)	362 502 (91.66%)	26 913 (84.94%)	35 606 (88.18%)
UNEMP (1948–2016)	103 095 (73.29%)	182 700 (89.4%)	532 393 (83.96%)	234 245 (83.95%)	27 353 (85.23%)	339 783 (85.91%)	22 744 (71.78%)	31 147 (77.14%)
INDP (1919–2016)	129 498 (92.06%)	200 317 (98.02%)	595 869 (93.97%)	260 978 (93.53%)	29 375 (91.53%)	372 075 (94.08%)	28 801 (90.9%)	37 494 (92.86%)
INV (1929–2016)	121 891 (86.65%)	196 234 (96.02%)	577 737 (91.11%)	252 884 (90.63%)	28 576 (89.04%)	362 502 (91.66%)	26 913 (84.94%)	35 606 (88.18%)
BANKR (1900–2005)	130 337 (92.66%)	178 313 (87.25%)	548 976 (86.58%)	244 587 (87.66%)	27 184 (84.7%)	342 053 (86.49%)	28 479 (89.88%)	36 327 (89.97%)
CPI (1774–2016)	140 669 (100%)	204 365 (100%)	634 095 (100%)	279 026 (100%)	32 094 (100%)	395 489 (100%)	31 684 (100%)	40 377 (100%)
SPC (1871–2016)	140 443 (99.84%)	204 206 (99.92%)	632 015 (99.67%)	278 289 (99.74%)	31 605 (98.48%)	393 976 (99.62%)	31 684 (100%)	40 377 (100%)
CON (1855–2012)	140 669 (100%)	204 365 (100%)	634 095 (100%)	279 026 (100%)	32 094 (100%)	395 489 (100%)	31 684 (100%)	40 377 (100%)

Note: Numbers and percentages indicate how many items from the bibliometric series (period indicated in the second row) fall within the period of the economic series (period indicated in the first column).

does not cover the full year range of WoS records (1956–2015). Therefore, economic data cover 100% of the bibliometric records from the WoS, except for the bankruptcies series, which covers about 61.3%.

The following two subsections provide a detailed summary of our econometric results derived from the analysis on the combinations of bibliometric and economic series. The FCVAR analysis in Subsection 3.2.1 constitutes the major part by presenting results of the tests on the association between economic and bibliometric variables across the four JSTOR categories of primary interest (sE, sBE, dE, dBE). For a more illustrative picture of the results, Subsection 3.2.2 further provides IRFs of selected pairs of economic and bibliometric variables across the same four categories of interest, which allows for an impression of when and where potential effects are the largest, in which direction they point, and of just how large they actually are.

3.2.1 Fractionally co-integrated vector autoregressions

Tables 3.5–3.8 document results of the FCVAR analysis between seven economic variables (see Table 2.1 on page 16 for references) and the bibliometric series (see Table 2.4 on page 40 for references) of term frequencies anywhere in documents. There is one table each for the primary JSTOR categories of interest: sE, sBE, dE and dBE. Table 3.9 exemplarily summarizes sBE results for the additional FCVAR tests of title frequencies. In order to keep the tables compact, variables are referred to by their short identifiers. The specific variables used are, however, evident from the tables' captions (naming the JSTOR category) and the method (the FCVAR analysis does not require prior detrending of the data). Therefore, for example, "BCTC" in Table 3.5 refers to BCTC_sE.

An empty cell in columns A–G of Tables 3.5–3.9 means that the respective economic and bibliometric variables were not fractionally co-integrated. Therefore, no further testing on the specific relation between the two variables was appropriate. On the other hand, each non-empty cell contains results of the long-run exogeneity tests that were run, given fractional co-integration, on the part capturing differences in equation (2.1). The first number in each cell is the test statistic result for an effect of economic variables on the literature; the second for testing the reverse direction, i.e. bibliometric variables affecting economic data. A small number in the cell means that the given data are unlikely to be observed if the null hypothesis which states that the variable in question is exogenous in the long run (i.e. independent of the other variable) were true. Therefore, for example, cell A4 of Table 3.5 implies that the null hypothesis of Recession_sE being exogenous given INCPC can be rejected, whereas the null hypothesis concerning the opposite direction – INCPC being exogenous given Recession_sE – would not be rejected. This suggests that Recession_sE is likely to be affected by INCPC, while, at the same time, Recession_sE probably has no similar effect on INCPC. To make comparisons more feasible, column, row and cell identifiers are the same throughout all five tables (e.g. A1 always

Table 3.5 FCVAR results, sE category

		A) INCPC		*B) UNEMP*		*C) INDP*		*D) INV*		*E) BANKR*		*F) CPI*		*G) SPC*	
	long-run ex.	*bib*	*econ*	*bib*	*econ*	*bib*	*econ*	*bib*	*econ*	*bib*	*econ*	*bib*	*econ*	*bib*	*econ*
1	BCTC							**0.000***	0.44						
2	crisis											**0.000***	0.74	**0.000***	**0.000***
3	depression														
4	recession	**0.02***	1			0.556	**0.01***					**0.000***	0.645		
5	DOWNSWING														
6	bubble							**0.000***	**0.000***						
7	cycle	0.062	**0.02***			**0.009***	0.215							**0.001***	**0.000***
8	distress							**0.036***	**0.019***			0.802	**0.000***	0.259	0.134
9	embarrassment	**0.009***	0.08			**0.004***	0.645					0.11	0.483		
10	fluctuations					**0.000***	**0.005***								
11	glut					0.116	0.065			**0.000***	0.395	**0.000***	0.571		
12	panic											**0.000***	0.104	**0.000***	**0.001***
13	prosperity			0.311	**0.000***							0.46	**0.000***		
14	stagnation					**0.021***	**0.016***					**0.000***	0.73		
15	OVERALL					**0.002***	**0.000***					**0.000***	0.918	0.386	0.051

Note: * 5% benchmark is used; the H_0 of the test is that the given bibliometric or economic variable is exogenous in the FCVAR model. Significant results are in bold.

Table 3.6 FCVAR results, sBE category

		A) INCPC		B) UNEMP		C) INDP		D) INV		E) BANKR		F) CPI		G) SPC	
	long-run ex.	*bib*	*econ*	*bib*	*econ*	*bib*	*econ*	*bib*	*econ*	*bib*	*econ*	*bib*	*econ*	*bib*	*econ*
1	BCTC							**0.001***	0.317						
2	crisis			1	1							**0.000***	0.067		
3	depression														
4	recession	**0.000***	**0.008***			**0.000***	0.304					**0.000***	0.698		
5	DOWNSWING													**0.043***	0.178
6	bubble			**0.000***	**0.02***	**0.000***	0.241								
7	cycle	0.163	**0.002***	**0.000***	0.292										
8	distress							**0.003***	0.09			0.901	**0.000***		
9	embarrassment											**0.000***	0.138		
10	fluctuations														
11	glut											**0.000***	0.369		
12	panic														
13	prosperity					**0.05***	0.095								
14	stagnation											**0.000***	**0.018***		
15	OVERALL			0.358	0.322										

Note: * 5% benchmark is used; the H_0 of the test is that the given bibliometric or economic variable is exogenous in the FCVAR model. Significant results are in bold.

Table 3.7 FCVAR results, dE category

		A) INCPC		B) UNEMP		C) INDP		D) INV		E) BANKR		F) CPI		G) SPC	
	long-run ex.	*bib*	*econ*	*bib*	*econ*	*bib*	*econ*	*bib*	*econ*	*bib*	*econ*	*bib*	*econ*	*bib*	*econ*
1	BCTC														
2	crisis							**0.041***	**0.01***					0.466	**0.001***
3	depression	0.149	**0.000***					0.145	**0.003***						
4	recession	**0.000***	**0.012***			**0.015***	**0.009***							0.665	**0.000***
5	DOWNSWING													0.211	1
6	bubble					**0.000***	**0.000***	**0.003***	**0.002***	0.461	0.234	**0.013***	**0.008***		
7	cycle													**0.018***	**0.003***
8	distress														
9	embarrassment											**0.000***	0.687	0.15	**0.001***
10	fluctuations														
11	glut	**0.022***	**0.003***			0.109	0.363			**0.000***	0.508				
12	panic														
13	prosperity														
14	stagnation					**0.000***	**0.000***	0.193	**0.000***						
15	OVERALL					0.943	**0.016***								

Note: * 5% benchmark is used; the H_0 of the test is that the given bibliometric or economic variable is exogenous in the FCVAR model. Significant results are in bold.

Table 3.8 FCVAR results, dBE category

		A) INCPC		B) UNEMP		C) INDP		D) INV		E) BANKR		F) CPI		G) SPC	
	long-run ex.	*bib*	*econ*	*bib*	*econ*	*bib*	*econ*	*bib*	*econ*	*bib*	*econ*	*bib*	*econ*	*bib*	*econ*
1	BCTC														
2	crisis							0.135	**0.011***					**0.000***	**0.028***
3	depression	0.213	**0.000***												
4	recession	0.902	**0.001***											0.825	**0.003***
5	DOWNSWING														
6	bubble					**0.000***	0.494					0.794	**0.000***		
7	cycle														
8	distress											0.835	**0.000***		
9	embarrassment													**0.004***	0.633
10	fluctuations	0.072	**0.000***					**0.003***	**0.000***						
11	glut	0.070	**0.000***							**0.000***	0.18	**0.000***	**0.042***	**0.000***	**0.045***
12	panic											**0.000***	**0.014***	0.906	**0.000***
13	prosperity					**0.000***	**0.000***					0.541	**0.000***		
14	stagnation											**0.000***	**0.024***		
15	OVERALL							**0.006***	**0.012***						

Note: * 5% benchmark is used; the H_0 of the test is that the given bibliometric or economic variable is exogenous in the FCVAR model. Significant results are in bold.

Table 3.9 FCVAR results, sBE category, titles

		A) INCPC		*B) UNEMP*		*C) INDP*		*D) INV*		*E) BANKR*		*F) CPI*		*G) SPC*	
	long-run ex.	*bib*	*econ*	*bib*	*econ*	*bib*	*econ*	*bib*	*econ*	*bib*	*econ*	*bib*	*econ*	*bib*	*econ*
1	BCTC	0.066	**0.04***			**0.012***	**0.001***			**0.003***	0.559	0.082	0.167		
2	crisis	**0.006***	**0.03***									**0.001***	0.841	**0.001***	0.356
3	depression							**0.001***	**0.001***			**0.001***	0.668	**0.001***	0.312
4	recession									**0.001***	0.841				
5	DOWNSWING									**0.001***	0.433	**0.001***	0.565	**0.001***	0.082
6	bubble													**0.005***	0.278
7	cycle					0.952	**0.001***								
8	distress	**0.001***	0.382							**0.001***	0.121			**0.01***	0.2
9	embarrassment	**0.001***	0.615					**0.003***	0.373	**0.001***	0.304				
10	fluctuations	**0.001***	0.262			**0.013***	**0.043***					**0.001***	0.228	0.11	0.076
11	glut	**0.005***	0.878					0.265	0.203	0.144	0.054	**0.001***	**0.028***	0.71	**0.001***
12	panic					0.831	0.582	**0.033***	**0.001***	**0.001***	0.445	**0.001***	0.641	0.831	0.582
13	prosperity	0.475	0.402	**0.013***	0.067	1	**0.024***			**0.001***	0.637				
14	stagnation			0.25	0.666										
15	OVERALL											**0.001***	0.734	**0.001***	0.091

Note: * 5% benchmark is used; the H_0 of the test is that the given bibliometric or economic variable is exogenous in the FCVAR model. Significant results are in bold.

contains the results for the tests between income per capita and the BCTC series of the respective category).

In general, the primary results of interest are those among the fractionally co-integrated pairs of economic and bibliometric variables with long-run exogeneity test results significant at the 5% level. These cases for which the test suggests a causal relation are set in bold and marked by an asterisk. For each such cell and corresponding pair, three combinations of causality directions are possible:

1. The first result (testing long-run exogeneity of the bibliometric variable) is significant, whereas the second is not. Those cases are very much in line with and support PPT, statistically suggesting a causal effect running from the economic to the bibliometric variable.
2. However, there are also cases where the first result is not significant, but the second is. With these pairs, not only is there no confirmation for PPT, but indeed there is evidence of an effect running in the opposite direction, namely from bibliometric variables to economic data.
3. Finally, two significant results mean that both variables are likely to affect each other simultaneously. It is not exactly clear how to interpret this combination, especially with regards to supporting or rejecting PPT. The discussion in Section 3.3 will return to this issue. For now, the different (types of) results are merely documented and pointed out.[5]

3.2.1.1 Term frequencies anywhere in documents

Tables 3.5–3.8 summarize the results of the FCVAR and long-run exogeneity tests for the relations between seven economic (columns A–G) and 15 bibliometric (rows 1–15) variables (105 each). Each table contains the bibliometric series for one of four JSTOR categories: sE (Table 3.5), sBE (Table 3.6), dE (Table 3.7) and dBE (Table 3.8).

Of the 105 pairs documented in Table 3.5, 29 are fractionally co-integrated. Among these, the long-run exogeneity test returned results in the direction predicted by PPT 12 times: income per capita with Recession_sE (A4) and Embarrassment_sE (A9); industrial production with Cycle_sE (C7) and Embarrassment_sE (C9); investment with BCTC_sE (D1); bankruptcy rates with Glut_sE (E11); as well as consumer prices with Crisis_sE (F2), Recession_sE (F4), Glut_sE (F11), Panic_sE (F12), Stagnation_sE (F14) and OVERALL_sE (F15). On the other hand, five pairs indicate an effect in the opposite direction: income per capita with Cycle_sE (A7); the unemployment rate with Prosperity_sE (B13); industrial production with Recession_sE (C4); and consumer prices with Distress_sE (F8) and Prosperity_sE (F13). Furthermore, in eight cases, the results suggest long-run causality simultaneously running in both directions: industrial production with Fluctuations_sE (C10), Stagnation_sE (C14) and OVERALL_sE (C15); investment with Bubble_sE (D6) and Distress_sE (D8); and the S&P stock market index with Crisis_sE (G2), Cycle_sE (G7) and Panic_sE (G12). Finally, four of the fractionally co-integrated pairs showed no significant results in either direction for the long-run exogeneity test (C11, F9, G8, G15).

Overall, therefore, for the sE category documented in Table 3.5, just over a quarter of all pairs are fractionally co-integrated, and less than half of these suggest causality running in the same direction as PPT. What is more, even when the positive results in line with that original hypothesis are considered in isolation, the findings are not uniform either, neither for causing economic nor for caused bibliometric variables. For example, the results indicate that Recession_sE is caused by per capita income; but, on the other hand, per capita income seems to be caused by Cycle_sE. Similarly, Recession_sE, while caused by per capita income, seems to cause industrial production. What is more, nine of the fractionally co-integrated pairs further need to be interpreted with care, since they did not pass the white noise test (further: WN). This applies to five pairs where causality runs both ways (C10, C14, C15, G2, G12), one where suggested causality is from bibliometric to economic data (C4), two cases of causality in line with PPT (F2, F12), and C11, where the long-run exogeneity test did not return any significant result.

Table 3.6 documents results from the same tests for the sBE category of bibliometric variables. There are 19 fractionally co-integrated pairs, 11 of which suggest a causality in line with PPT: the unemployment rate with Cycle_sBE (B7); industrial production with Recession_sBE (C4), Bubble_sBE (C6) and Prosperity_sBE (C13); investment with BCTC_sBE (D1) and Distress_sBE (D8); CPI with Crisis_sBE (F2), Recession_sBE (F4), Embarrassment_sBE (F9) and Glut_sBE (F11); and SPC with DOWNSWING_sBE (G5). Two pairs suggest causality in the opposite direction: per capita income with Cycle_sBE (A7); and CPI with Distress_sBE (F8). Another three suggest causality running both ways: per capita income with Recession_sE (A4); the unemployment rate with Bubble_sBE (B6); and CPI with Stagnation_sBE (F14). Two fractionally co-integrated pairs did not return any significant results in the long-run exogeneity test (B2, B15).

Overall, less than one-fifth of the pairs documented in Table 3.6 are fractionally co-integrated. While the majority of these suggest causality in the direction in line with PPT, no uniform results for individual economic or bibliometric variables are evident. What is more, results differ considerably between the sE and sBE categories. Concerning causality running from economic to bibliometric variables, only four out of the 11, respectively 12, cells – D1, F2, F4 and F11 – show the same pattern in both Tables 3.6 and 3.5, even though sE is a subset of sBE (see Subsection 3.1.1). Overlaps and differences between categories are further illustrated and compared in Subsection 3.2.1.3.

Results from the FCVAR analysis for frequencies anywhere in documents from the dE category are given in Table 3.7. There are 21 fractionally co-integrated pairs, but only two of those (bankruptcy rates with Glut_dE in E11; and CPI with Embarrassment_dE in F9) also suggest causality in line with PPT. On the other hand, seven pairs suggest causality running in the opposite direction: per capita income with Depression_dE (A3); industrial production with

OVERALL_dE (C15); investment with Depression_dE (D3, not passing WN) and Stagnation_dE (D14); and SPC with Crisis_dE (G2, not passing WN), Recession_dE (G4) and Embarrassment_dE (G9). For another nine pairs, the long-run exogeneity test suggests that both variables simultaneously affect one another: per capita income with Recession_dE (A4) and Glut_dE (A11); industrial production with Recession_dE (C4, not passing WN), Bubble_dE (C6, not passing WN) and Stagnation_dE (C14); investment with Crisis_dE (D2) and Bubble_dE (D6, not passing WN); CPI with Bubble_dE (F6); and SPC with Cycle_dE (G7). The remaining three fractionally co-integrated pairs (C11, E6, G5) do not suggest any causal relation.

Whereas one-fifth of all pairs are fractionally co-integrated, less than 2% of all pairs in Table 3.7 support PPT. If anything, the evidence of an effect running in the opposite direction – from bibliometric to economic data – is stronger. The results are therefore considerably different from those for the sE and sBE categories. It is also worth noting that neither of the two pairs between economic and bibliometric variables exemplarily depicted in Figure 3.10 on page 78 – income per capita vs. BCTC (A1), and unemployment vs. 'recession' (B4) – are fractionally co-integrated, despite the fact that the graph for unemployment and Recession_dE (the right-hand panel of Figure 3.10) appeared to show some remarkable co-movements. This highlights the necessity of taking a statistically sound approach to the analysis, which provides a more founded impression than a simple reading of descriptive charts.

In Table 3.8, there are 20 fractionally co-integrated pairs with bibliometric variables from dBE, only three of which (industrial production with Bubble_dBE in C6; bankruptcy rates with Glut_dBE in E11; and SPC with Embarrassment_dBE in G9) suggest causality in line with PPT. On the other hand, half of these 20 pairs suggest causality in the opposite direction: per capita income with Depression_dBE (A3), Recession_dBE (A4), Fluctuations_dBE (A10) and Glut_dBE (A11); investment with Crisis_dBE (D2); CPI with Bubble_dBE (F6), Distress_dBE (F8) and Prosperity_dBE (F13); and SPC with Recession_dBE (G4) and Panic_dBE (G12). The remaining seven fractionally co-integrated pairs suggest causality running both ways: industrial production with Prosperity_dBE (C13, not passing WN); investment with Fluctuations_dBE (D10) and OVERALL_dBE (D15, not passing WN); CPI with Glut_dBE (F11), Panic_dBE (F12, not passing WN) and Stagnation_dBE (F14); and SPC with Crisis_dBE (G2) and Glut_dBE (G11).

Results for the two discipline categories are fairly similar, with only a small number (two for dE and three for dBE) of results supporting PPT and many more pointing at the opposite direction. However, with the exception of three cells (A3, E11, G4), individual cases are different in both tables despite the fact that dE is a large subset of dBE. In many cases, different pairs are fractionally co-integrated, and even among those which meet the first requirement in both tables, not all show the same results in the long-run exogeneity test. On the level of the variables, no clear patterns emerge either. For example, in Table 3.7, there are five fractionally co-integrated pairs for combinations of industrial production and bibliometric variables, and only two in column F for the CPI. However, in Table 3.8, only two pairs involving industrial production are fractionally co-integrated, whereas six of those involving the CPI are. Therefore, between the two, the results for dE and dBE are similar to those for sE and sBE in that no clear overall patterns emerge – however, subject and discipline categories are very different still, with more findings supporting PPT in the subject categories. After repeating the same analysis for bibliometric series representing frequencies of titles (Subsection 3.2.1.2), Subsection 3.2.1.3 revisits the issue of comparing the different findings in the summary and general overview of the FCVAR results.

3.2.1.2 Term frequencies in titles

Overall, the general result that can be obtained from the FCVAR tests for term frequencies in titles is comparable to those for frequencies anywhere in the documents, which is why we do not provide all of them in detail here, but only exemplarily show the biggest category, sBE in Table 3.9, to illustrate the case. The general finding is, once more, that, across the various categories, it is usually different pairs of economic and bibliometric variables that are both fractionally co-integrated and display causality test results in line with PPT. For bibliometric series based on frequencies within titles, the results are even more diverse in that respect. In sBE, there are 43 fractionally co-integrated pairs – much more than with bibliometric series for frequencies anywhere in documents, as listed in the previous subsection. Eight of these did not return any significant results in the long-run exogeneity test (A13, B14, C12, D11, E11, F1, G10, G12), whereas 25 returned results in line with PPT (A8, A9, A10, A11, B13, D10, E1, E4, E5, E8, E9, E12, E13, F2, F3, F5, F10, F12, F15, G2, G3, G5, G6, G8, G15), four indicated causality in the opposite direction (A1, C7, C13, G11), and six causality running both ways (A2, C1, C10, D3, D12, F11). It is interesting to see that the number of positive findings is so high here, even after taking into account that three of them (A8, A9, G2) did not pass WN. However, major qualifications can be raised due to the very uneven distribution of findings across the different economic variables, and these are brought forward in Subsection 3.3.2.1 of the discussion.

3.2.1.3 Summary and overview

Table 3.10 summarizes the findings from Tables 3.5–3.8 by showing how many pairs between economic and bibliometric variables across all categories were not fractionally co-integrated, and what kind of causality result was found for the fractionally co-integrated cases. If there are any fractionally co-integrated pairs that did not pass WN, their number is indicated in square brackets. Once more, Table 3.10 highlights the large differences in findings between the different categories. While between just under one-fifth (sBE) and up to just over one-quarter (sE) of all pairs were fractionally co-integrated, the distribution of findings across the different cases of causality is very different. Taking all four

Table 3.10 Summary of FCVAR results

Type of result	*sE*	*sBE*	*dE*	*dBE*
not co-integrated	76	87	84	85
not significant	4 [1]	2	3	0
econ→bib	12 [2]	11	2	3
bib→econ	5 [1]	2	7 [2]	10
econ↔bib	8 [5]	3	9 [3]	7 [3]

Note: Based on the findings from Tables 3.5–3.8. Cells indicate how many of the 105 pairs per JSTOR category were not fractionally co-integrated; fractionally co-integrated without positive results in the long-run exogeneity test; suggesting causality in line with PPT (economic affecting bibliometric variables); causality in the opposite direction; and causality running both ways. Numbers in square brackets (if any) indicate how many of these findings did not pass the white noise test (WN) for fractional co-integration.

categories together, there were 88 fractionally co-integrated pairs, among which 28 (26 when accounting for WN) instances of causality in the direction suggested by PPT were found. This number is not that different from the 24 (21) cases with causality running from bibliometric to economic variables, or the 27 (16) where the test results suggest causality running both ways. Given these nearly equal frequencies, an assessment of the findings without any prior theoretical hypothesis (such as PPT) would hardly conclude that there are any notable causal effects in one and only one direction in particular.

The same data for the 28 cases where causality was found to run from economic to bibliometric variables are arranged in a different manner in Table 3.11, where each cell corresponds to the same coordinates as in Tables 3.5–3.8, and contains the identifiers of categories where a respective positive association in line with PPT was found. If the corresponding pair did not pass WN, this is indicated by square brackets. This allows for a different perspective on the findings. While there is only a relatively small number of positive findings in the aggregate, it might very well be that they cluster in certain cells or in the lines and columns corresponding to certain variables. However, Table 3.11 shows that this is hardly the case as well. Overall, there are 20 cells for which there was a positive finding in at least one category. Among these, six (five when accounting for WN) contain results that were repeated in one other category, and one cell (E11) contained a positive finding in three of the four categories. This comparison also shows that only four (three when accounting for WN) of the positive findings from the sE and sBE categories are present in both, despite the fact that sE is a subset of sBE.

What is more, this fairly weak clustering of results can also be found when comparing occurrences by the row they appear in. Only two of the 15 terms do not feature any positive finding in line with PPT ('depression' and 'fluctuations'). On the other hand, 'embarrassment' and 'glut' were each caused five times by economic variables, and 'recession' four times. Regarding the columns, the variance is higher: 11 (nine when accounting for WN) of the 28

Table 3.11 FCVAR results in line with "panics produce texts" (PPT)

			A) INCPC [2]	*B) UNEMP [1]*	*C) INDP [6]*	*D) INV [3]*	*E) BANKR [3]*	*F) CPI [11]*	*G) SPC [2]*
1	BCTC	[2]				sE, sBE			
2	crisis	[2]						[sE], sBE	
3	depression	[0]							
4	recession	[4]	sE		sBE			sE, sBE	
5	DOWNSWING	[1]							sBE
6	bubble	[2]			sBE, dBE				
7	cycle	[2]		sBE	sE				
8	distress	[1]				sBE			
9	embarrassment	[5]	sE		sE			sBE, dE	dBE
10	fluctuations	[0]							
11	glut	[5]					sE, dE, dBE	sE, sBE	
12	panic	[1]						[sE]	
13	prosperity	[1]			sBE				
14	stagnation	[1]						sE	
15	OVERALL	[1]						sE	

Note: Summary table showing how many of the compared pairs across the four categories (sE, sBE, dE, dBE) were both fractionally co-integrated and displayed long-run exogeneity test results in line with PPT (i.e. long-run exogeneity of only the bibliometric variable was rejected) for frequencies anywhere in documents. Category identifiers in cells indicate the category for which an association between the economic and the respective bibliometric variable was found; square brackets around these indicate that the white noise test for the FCVAR result was not passed. Total numbers of all positive results per (causing) economic and (caused) bibliometric variable are shown next to the column and row headers in square brackets.

(26) instances correspond to bibliometric variables statistically caused by CPI, and this column features both the highest number of cells with at least one item per column (seven, respectively six), as well as four, respectively three, instances of repeated results. The discussion in Section 3.3 revisits these summarized results and reflects on the relevance of some of the repeated findings.

3.2.2 Impulse response functions

In order to provide not just an impression of whether or not select economic and bibliometric variables are statistically associated, but also of the strengths and directions of measured effects, Figures 3.13 and 3.14 contain impulse response functions (IRFs) of four combinations of the central BCCT terms (BCTC, 'crisis', 'depression', 'recession') with an economic variable across the four JSTOR categories of primary interest (sE, sBE, dE, dBE), resulting in 16 IRFs and corresponding panels. Since the FCVAR analysis is a better test of the association between the two variables in our specification than the VAR approach, no detailed VAR and Granger-causality tests for all combinations in every category are reported. Nonetheless, on the four pairs singled out for Figures 3.13 and 3.14 – i.e. CPI and BCTC (F1), SPC and 'crisis' (G2), INV and 'depression' (D3), and UNEMP and 'recession' (B4) – Table 3.12 documents results from the Granger-causality tests. Identifiers correspond to the columns and rows where the FCVAR results for these pairs were documented in Tables 3.5–3.8. Prefixes on the variables further indicate that, as outlined in Subsection 2.4.4, the analysis was performed on cyclical deviations of the series (respectively, cyclical deviations of natural logarithms of the series in the case of all the economic variables except for UNEMP). The pairs were selected so as to represent four different economic variables and were further based on both the economic variable's relevance in theoretical contexts as well as on how strong the respective associations between economic and bibliometric variables were in other parts of the analysis, both descriptive (e.g. see Figure 3.10 on page 78) and econometric (including previous research; also see Subsection 3.3.3.1).

In Table 3.12, each cell for a pair in a respective category contains two numbers which represent the results of the Granger-causality tests for a given direction, in the same way as FCVAR results were documented in Tables 3.5–3.9. Of the 16 combinations presented here, seven are characterized by Granger-causality tests in the direction expected by PPT, namely that the bibliometric variable is Granger-caused by the economic variable, but does not Granger-cause the economic variable (there is a significant result on the left of the cell, and no significant result on the right). On the other hand, no pair displays significant results which would indicate another case. The select sample and resulting IRFs should therefore provide a good impression of what the reaction of bibliometric variables Granger-caused by economic variables looks like. These IRFs are plotted in Figures 3.13 and 3.14 as black lines, with dashed lines representing those pairs where the corresponding Granger-causality test

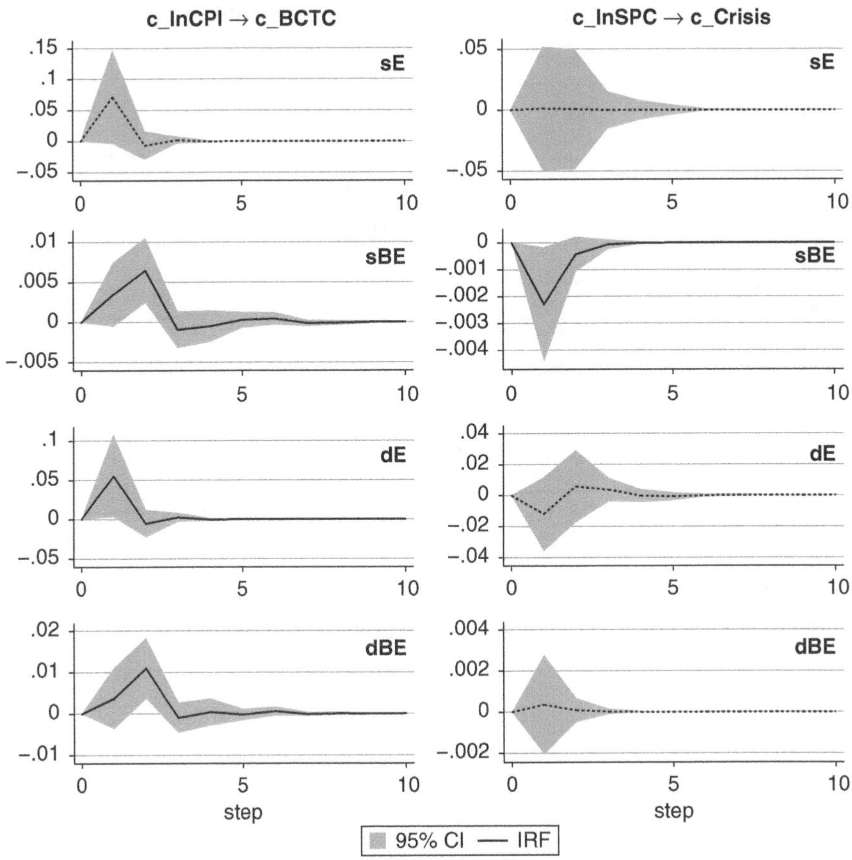

Figure 3.13 IRFs for CPI vs. BCTC and SPC vs. 'crisis'.

Note: Impulse response functions for the effects of economic on bibliometric variables for frequencies anywhere in documents over ten estimation periods. Left column: relative cyclical variations of the consumer price index (c_lnCPI) on changes in cyclical variations of BCTC (c_BCTC). Right column: relative cyclical variations of the S&P composite index (c_lnSPC) on changes in cyclical variations of 'crisis' (c_Crisis). Top row: sE; second row: sBE; third row: dE; fourth row: dBE. Dashed IRFs indicate that the Granger-causality test results for the respective pair of economic and bibliometric variables were not in line with PPT.

results are not in line with PPT. Since the matrix of residuals yielded negligible correlation coefficients close to zero for the investigated pairs of variables, orthogonalization was not crucial. Therefore, instead of orthogonalized IRFs (OIRFs) we report IRFs which allow for a more straightforward interpretation of the effect strengths. What is more, the OIRFs looked largely similar in shape to the IRFs shown here, anyway. The shaded grey areas around the black lines delineate the 95% confidence intervals, which only rarely do not contain zero. The vertical axes on all IRFs indicate the percentage points change in the

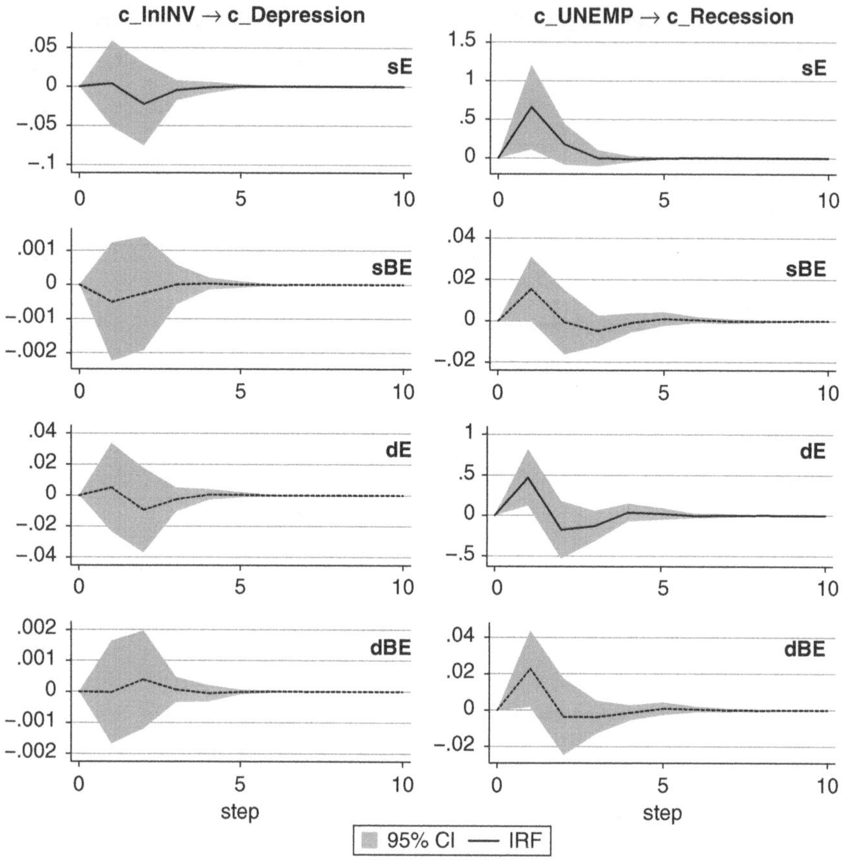

Figure 3.14 IRFs for INV vs. 'depression' and UNEMP vs. 'recession'.

Note: Impulse response functions for the effects of economic on bibliometric variables for frequencies anywhere in documents over ten estimation periods. Left column: relative cyclical variations of investment activity (c_lnINV) on changes in cyclical variations of 'depression' (c_Depression). Right column: cyclical variations of the unemployment rate (c_UNEMP) on changes in cyclical variations of 'recession' (c_Recession). Top row: sE; second row: sBE; third row: dE; fourth row: dBE. Dashed IRFs indicate that the Granger-causality test results for the respective pair of economic and bibliometric variables were not in line with PPT.

bibliometric series (in terms of deviations from trend), i.e. the response, following an impulse of a 1% (or 1 percentage point in the case of UNEMP, which was not logarithmized) deviation from trend in the economic series.

In general, the estimated IRFs therefore document in which direction, how strongly and for how long the literature responds to isolated changes in the associated economic data. The left column of Figure 3.13 shows that changes in c_lnCPI (specifically a 1% deviation from trend) can lead to subsequent changes in c_BCTC. The strongest effect can be seen in the first (sE, dE), respectively

Table 3.12 Granger-causality test results for selected pairs

	F1 *c_lnCPI ↔ c_BCTC*		*G2* *c_lnSPC ↔ c_Crisis*	
Granger-causality	*to lit.*	*to econ.*	*to lit.*	*to econ.*
sE	0.0661	0.4269	0.9986	0.5993
sBE	**0.0023***	0.1375	**0.0359***	0.28
dE	**0.0415***	0.1732	0.5483	0.3478
dBE	**0.0091***	0.1767	0.7729	0.3252

	D3 *c_lnINV ↔ c_Depression*		*B4* *c_UNEMP ↔ c_Recession*	
Granger-causality	*to lit.*	*to econ.*	*to lit.*	*to econ.*
sE	**0.0187***	0.2126	**0.0216***	0.0999
sBE	0.9226	0.8467	0.1449	0.7194
dE	0.9048	0.664	**0.0204***	0.3315
dBE	0.8124	0.7156	0.1014	0.5582

Note: 5% benchmark is used; the H_0 of the test is that the economic variable does not Granger-cause the bibliometric variable (left column), respectively that the bibliometric variable does not Granger-cause the economic variable (right column), in the VAR model. Significant results are in bold.

second (sBE, dBE), period after the change in the economic variable, i.e. given the frequency of both our economic and bibliometric data, in the first and second year. The effects are positive, but quickly fade out and return to zero. This means that a change in c_lnCPI leads to a change in c_BCTC in the same direction, i.e. an upward deviation from the trend of CPI (e.g. because of inflation rates above trend) is followed by a higher frequency of papers containing BCTC. However, the response to the impulse fades out after about four (sE, dE) and seven (sBE, dBE) periods. The 95% confidence intervals mostly contain zero, except for the first period after the change in the economic variable for dE, and the second period in both sBE and dBE. For these three pairs, the results from the Granger-causality tests are in line with PPT, which, combined with the observation that the reaction is in the expected direction and the general similarity of the IRFs across the different categories, implies that they provide fairly strong evidence in favour of an effect of economic on bibliometric variables. This claim can be further affirmed by considering the strength of the effects. In dE, where the largest absolute effect can be observed in the first period after the change in the economic variable, a 1% change of CPI above trend roughly leads to a 0.05 percentage points increase in the frequency of c_BCTC_dE (i.e. relative to the trend) one year later. By conducting a simple calculation which relates this absolute magnitude of the marginal change to the overall descriptive statistics for the given category, we obtain approximations of the relative value of the effect. BCTC_dE mostly fluctuated between about 5% and 13% (see Figure 3.3 on page 67), and using this as a proxy of the trend, the 0.05 percentage points increase constitutes a relative change of between 0.4% and 1% in the bibliometric series following a 1% change above trend in CPI. As is also evident from the IRFs, the magnitude of effects in sBE and dBE is smaller.

For the response of c_Crisis to an impulse from c_lnSPC on the right-hand side of Figure 3.13, the picture is less clear-cut. The individual panels are fairly different from one another and generally document only small effects very close to zero. The exception is in sBE, which is also where c_lnSPC Granger-caused c_Crisis. In the first period after a 1% change above trend in SPC, there is a negative – albeit also small – response of Crisis_sBE, with the 95% confidence interval also not containing zero. Specifically, there is a reduction of around 0.023 percentage points below trend. Given the overall average frequency of Crisis_sBE which is around 15%, this implies a 0.15% relative change. The effect is small, but it is in the direction expected from PPT, for the negativity implies that a decrease in SPC below trend, e.g. a crash on the stock market, is followed by an increase in 'crisis'.

The left column in Figure 3.14 shows IRFs for the effect of a 1% change above trend from c_lnINV on c_Depression. Granger-causality was in line with PPT only for the first panel (sE), but for none of the coefficients; the 95% confidence intervals do not contain zero – and there are none in the other IRFs either. Considering the different shapes of the IRFs (especially compare dE and dBE, which almost seem mirrored), where the only overall commonality is that the effects all fade out after five periods, there is no clear indication of a response in line with PPT either. Indeed, the PPT logic would predict a negative relation – decreasing investment activity leading to a higher frequency of 'depression', and vice versa – but, when abstracting from the broad confidence intervals and just taking the point estimates, this is clearly not the case, at least not in a uniform manner.

On the right-hand side of Figure 3.14, the highly similar IRFs provide a more homogeneous picture of how c_Recession responds to an impulse from c_UNEMP. In all four panels, there is a positive response in the first period after the impulse, and, with the exception of sBE, they are far from zero. In sE and dE, where c_UNEMP Granger-causes c_Recession, the effects are also comparatively large (which, however, is also due to the size of the impulse). One period after a 1 percentage point increase above trend of UNEMP, Recession_sE responds by being about 0.6 percentage points higher than trend. This means that – in line with PPT – an increase in the unemployment rate is followed by a higher frequency of 'recession' above trend. In particular, compared with the average frequency of about 9.5% (total average, see Table 3.2 on page 60), this amounts to about a 6% relative increase. The response by Recession_dE is smaller, but so is the total average frequency of Recession_dE, so that the nearly 0.5 percentage points increase in Recession_dE following the impulse from c_UNEMP implies a relative increase of about 7.5%. The subsequent discussion, specifically Subsection 3.3.2.3, embeds and interprets these observations in a broader context.

3.3 Validation and discussion

The previous two sections contained many different findings relevant to the underlying PPT research question. We will now discuss them, and, in doing so, conduct robustness checks and attempt validations in order to assess whether the empirical results indicate any general patterns, and what implications – if any – and interpretations the data allow for. In order to do this comprehensively, it is important to reflect the results not only against the background of the theoretical literature and the research question itself, but also against the specific methods that were used. This way, we can assess whether and how the findings (or a lack thereof) can be attributed to the specific approach and the tools that were employed. Subsection 3.3.1 discusses the fundamental issue of the identification of relevant papers, i.e. how we arrived at our set of papers discussing business cycles and economic crises, and the problems and shortcomings of this particular method. Subsection 3.3.2 then proceeds to elaborate on various general implications of the results, especially considering the overall lack of conclusive findings in support of PPT and notable differences between the various categories. Subsection 3.3.3 compares the findings from the previous two sections with earlier empirical research by Besomi (2011) and Kufenko and Geiger (2016). A very general perspective on the econometric method is presented in Subsection 3.3.4, which discusses the issue of false positives. Whereas the majority of this section is thus concerned with the results from the content analysis, Subsection 3.3.5 reviews the findings from the citation analysis in Subsection 3.1.3.

3.3.1 Identification of relevant papers

In Subsection 2.4.3, several issues related to the semantic content of the words used to identify papers as dealing with business cycles and economic crises were raised, and it is worthwhile to revisit these now to shed some more light on the potential implications of the empirical results from Sections 3.1 and 3.2. This is important because empirically identifying actual associations between economic and bibliometric variables in line with PPT requires two things: first, that the hypothesized relations actually exist in the data; and secondly, that appropriate proxies to measure these are used. The rather weak support for PPT which much of the empirical findings indicate could then just be a consequence of bad proxy variables, e.g. wrong identifications of the relevant set of economics literature on business cycles and economic crises. The following paragraphs therefore take a closer look at this aspect of our operationalization and its implications.

Owing to the short time period for which JEL codes or other kinds of key terms to classify papers are available (mostly not dating back further than the

1990s), we identify the literature of interest – that part of economics and neighbouring disciplines which deals with business cycles and economic crises – by the terms that appear in an article. Specifically, for example, if a paper from the *AER* uses the term "business cycle", it becomes part of BCTC_dE, etc. In doing so, we do not account for how often the term in question appears within the same paper, and especially not for the way that notion is used or qualitatively discussed. This is particularly problematic in the case of various terms which refer to similar concepts, such as 'recession' and 'depression', and all the more so if – as the historical time series indicate – there are shifts in which of these terms is the most prevalent over time. We did combine 'depression' and 'recession' with 'crisis' for the DOWNSWING index, but this is not enough to account for potential changes in the use of the notions. For example, if 'depression' was replaced by 'recession' as the preferred term for the same thing (such as a downswing), then during that transition episode, the relevant variable of interest to capture discussions of business cycles or crises would be the frequency of either term, whereas those of only one single term might not be associated with economic series individually. Furthermore, as it turned out, the DOWNSWING index was fractionally co-integrated with and statistically caused by an economic variable only once, namely with SPC in sBE.

Therefore, the items counted and relative frequencies derived thereof include cases of papers which dealt with different topics, but happened to use a similar terminology, as well as those which do not really contain a substantial discussion of business cycles and economic crises, but merely refer to related events in passing, e.g. to motivate the research (what we here refer to as "lip service" to business cycles and economic crises). As an illustration, consider the first introductory paragraph of Chapter 1: it contains several of the terms which are central to our analysis (see Subsection 2.4.2.1), without providing any BCCT arguments or the like. In fact, more generally, it might even be argued that the present book, strictly speaking, is not a kind of text the PPT hypothesis would predict to sprout during contractions, but it would nonetheless be counted as such by our methodology due to the terms it employs.

Arguably, these problems could be avoided – or at least, their relevance could be reduced – if relevant papers were classified by JEL codes (or similar metadata). An author is probably less likely to label their paper as discussing business cycles with a JEL code if a recent contraction merely serves as the motivation in the beginning, than they are to touch upon related vocabulary in passing. Similarly, a semantic analysis that accounts for word co-occurrences could avoid related problems. As argued at several points in Sections 2.3 and 2.4, both were not feasible for our approach here. What, then, can be said about these issues of semantics and the possible biases in attributing and counting items within the framework of the present analysis?

At the very least, there are two general points which can be made. The first is that, compared with an analysis that classifies papers by JEL codes or similar metadata, we would expect a larger fraction of papers that do not belong to our, so to speak, "ideal" sample. Secondly, the numbers and relative frequencies we observe are probably an upper bound to the frequencies of actual discussions of business cycles and economic crises, especially when the indexes are concerned. Owing to the various different terms we can consider, we are likely to capture a large majority of all papers that substantially deal with business cycles and economic crises in some way or another, and additionally, due to the inaccuracies in the method, we are also likely to include many papers in which the reference to business cycles and economic crises is mere "lip service". For example, even if there was increased activity in BCCT in response to the Great Depression, it is quite likely that the large increase in the frequency of 'depression' in the 1930s includes cursory remarks to the severe contraction. A similar argument might be brought forward to explain why the 'recession' series mostly displayed larger relative fluctuations than their BCTC counterparts in the same category (especially see Figure 3.3 on page 67). When a contraction does occur, "lip service" is more likely to be made by mentioning the 'recession', not the business cycle as a whole.[6]

On the other hand, occurrences of the terms in a paper's title are less likely to be "lip service" and more likely to actually reflect a research interest concerning business cycles and economic crises. This probably holds although, even in the absence of "lip service", false attributions are still possible, especially for terms that are used in other contexts as well, such as 'crisis' or 'depression'. For example, as already pointed out in the respective paragraphs in Subsection 3.1.3, not all of the most cited papers in the tBCTC_WoS, tDOWNSWING_WoS and tOVERALL_WoS sets are concerned with business cycles in a narrow sense; but at least they are concerned with economic crises in some way or another. In total we conjecture that the risk of falsely attributing a paper to a category (such as discussions of business cycles and economic crises) is much lower for occurrences in titles than for words featured anywhere in the documents. On the other hand, however, clearly far from all contributions on business cycles and economic crises will use a term from our list in their title. As illustrative examples, consider Schumpeter's (1935) summary of his approach to business cycle theory ("The Analysis of Economic Change"). Similarly, Frisch's (1936) "On the Notion of Equilibrium and Disequilibrium", a discussion of basic aspects concerning the method of business cycle analysis, is not included in any of the bibliometric series based on titles here. And the seminal contribution of Kydland and Prescott (1982) to Real Business Cycle theory, "Time to Build and Aggregate Fluctuations", would only be included because it contains "fluctuations" in the title, but does not feature among the sets focused upon in the present analysis (BCTC, 'crisis', 'depression', 'recession'). Therefore, identifying the relevant items by term occurrences in titles is likely to result in a smaller set (at least as far as true positives are concerned) than the ideal sample.

Already in the introduction, it was argued that the economics literature on business cycles and economic crises, and BCCT in particular, need not necessarily react to economic fluctuations. Instead, economists might be expected to discuss these relevant matters independent of contemporary context. However, an increase in "lip service" – similar to reports on the events in newspapers – seems to be a somewhat plausible reaction of the literature. Changes in the bibliometric series associated with economic data could to a large part reflect such "lip service" then. Therefore, the methods we used to identify the relevant sets of papers would be expected to be more likely to generate associations in line with PPT, because they capture both "lip service" and changes in the frequency of substantial contributions on business cycles and economic crises. It is thus even more noteworthy that not many positive relations were found in Section 3.2. Assuming that it is mostly "lip service" which reacts to economic fluctuations, and given the differences between the series for frequencies anywhere and only in titles of documents, a testable hypothesis emerges. Observations in line with PPT should be less frequent in the title series (which should contain a lower fraction of "lip service" items) than in the other series. Interestingly, however, this could not be concluded from the econometric results either.

3.3.2 Generality of different findings

In Section 3.1, time series for various bibliometric data were compared across different categories, and their potential associations with economic data were assessed in the econometric analysis of Section 3.2. There were various positive results, but, overall, it was quite clear that the specific results frequently differ between one and another category. For example, INCPC was statistically affecting Recession_sE, an observation in line with PPT, but was not associated in the same way with any of the other 'recession' series. In general, there was much more positive evidence in favour of PPT in the subject categories than there was in the discipline categories. Therefore, it is worth discussing the results' generality – or lack thereof – and how these findings can be interpreted in light of the PPT hypothesis.

3.3.2.1 Term frequencies inside and outside of contraction years

One surprising finding at the beginning of the descriptive overview in Subsection 3.1.2 had been that aggregate term frequency statistics implied a rejection of PPT, because relative frequencies of most of the terms associated with BCCT are lower during contraction years than outside of them. On average, the frequency of major terms such as BCTC and 'crisis' has been higher outside of contraction years than in the years of and immediately following a contraction over the 1855–2012 period. Even more surprising, the frequency of 'prosperity' – a notion clearly referring to the upswing – has been considerably higher during and throughout the years immediately following a contraction than it has been outside of contractions. However, a closer inspection shows that the results cannot be interpreted so easily. Once the nature of the data is taken into account, it becomes clear that there is a potential for a major bias. Indeed, combining Table 2.2 on page 22 and Table 3.3 on page 62 with Figure 3.1 on page 57 shows that, on the one hand, contraction years are much more frequent before than after World War II (of the 64 contraction years in 1855–2012, 49 are in 1855–1945). On the other hand, the total number of papers is much higher in more recent years than it was a century ago. Therefore, forming aggregates across all years from both earlier and later in the observation period heavily skews the results, with contraction years being more seldom after World War II, but potentially still having a larger weight due to the greater number of items.

What is more, aggregates are further skewed by the prevalence of trends in the time series of relative term frequencies, as was evident from Figure 3.3 on page 67. Quite clearly, the time series for BCTC and 'crisis' in particular are characterized by distinct upward trends. Relative frequencies are thus much higher during the decades after World War II which have been characterized by less frequent and shorter recessions. Therefore, the descriptive results based on averages are biased towards indicating a negative relation between contraction years and term frequencies. Since average frequencies were higher in the second half of the observation period, but those years also coincided with less contractions, the average annual frequencies in non-contraction years relative to contraction years over the whole 1855–2012 period are quite likely overestimated by simply taking a number out of Tables 3.2 and 3.3. While it primarily affects the annual average, such a trend also skews the total weighted average, especially if the distribution of the different types of years (contraction or non-contraction) is uneven in different periods of time (e.g. before or after World War II): in that case, many contraction years with relatively low (absolute) numbers (from before World War II) enter the total weighted average for contraction years, whereas the average for non-contraction years is to a larger extent affected by a big number of non-contraction years from the post-war years. A similar logic may be employed to partly explain why some terms, especially 'distress', 'embarrassment' and 'glut', did display a frequencies pattern in line with what PPT implies: for those three, relative frequencies were generally higher before than after World War II, i.e. they were higher when contraction years were more frequent. This contributes to the large differences between non-contraction and contraction years that are observed for these terms' annual averages in sE in particular (e.g. see Figure 3.2 on page 65).

It deserves to be noted that these observations (term frequencies being higher, on average, outside of than during contractions for most terms) are not a peculiar result of the contraction year specification from Subsection 2.2.8, namely defining contraction years as those where at least four consecutive months were part of a downswing. To test the robustness of the findings, we also calculated the same averages for all 15 terms in sE and dE based on contraction year definitions where either three or six consecutive downswing months were required.[7] Based on four months, there were 64 (49 for 1855–1945, 15 for 1946–2012) contraction and 94 (42/52) non-contraction years. With three months as the criterion, this changes to 72 (55/17) contraction and 86 (36/50) non-contraction years; and there are 55 (43/12) contraction and 103 (48/55) non-contraction years if the definition is based on six months. In general, the resulting average frequencies only change remarkably little, and this also applies to their relative sizes between non-contraction and contraction years. In the three-months sample, both averages are higher outside of than during contraction years in most cases, with the notable exceptions being 'depression' (but not its annual average in dE), OVERALL_sE, 'distress', 'panic' and 'prosperity'. When defining contractions based on a six-month downswing period, the general results are virtually identical. Therefore, the weak affirmative evidence concerning PPT which these overall numbers provide can hardly be explained as a byproduct of the definition of contraction years alone – if anything, the other points elaborated on above need to be taken into consideration as well.

A similar descriptive overview as for term frequencies during and outside of contractions was provided for citation frequencies with Figure 3.12 on page 82 in Subsection 3.1.3. Since this covers only the second half of the JSTOR sample, the large disparity in contraction frequencies does not apply here. However, the CCDFs did not provide strong evidence in favour of PPT either, even after publication lags are considered. In sum, therefore, while the aggregate descriptive statistics both for term frequencies as well as for citation counts did not necessarily imply a rejection of PPT when considering the qualifications pointed out in this subsection, they certainly do not constitute very affirmative evidence either.

A more general and more precise measure of the relations between economic and bibliometric variables over the course of business cycles therefore was the aim of the more sophisticated econometric analysis. However, the results of the FCVAR analysis in Subsection 3.2.1 did not provide very strong support in favour of PPT either. In particular, only a relatively small number of pairs implied causality running from economic to bibliometric variables, especially in the dE and dBE categories (see the next Subsection 3.3.2.2 for a more detailed discussion of this point). What is more, most cases of an association in line with PPT were not robust across the different categories, i.e. many fractionally co-integrated pairs with causality running from economic to bibliometric variables were specific to one of the categories of interest and even displayed contradictory results in other categories: for example, INCPC was found to cause Recession_sE, but in turn was found to be caused by Recession_dBE. Furthermore, no individual bibliometric variable proved to be one which was particularly frequently and systematically caused by economic variables, and, on the other hand, no economic variable systematically caused a large number of bibliometric variables across all four categories (especially see Subsection 3.2.1.3). For example, accounting for WN, there were seven fractionally co-integrated pairs for CPI in sE, and five such pairs in dBE. Four of those in sE displayed causality in the expected direction, but none of those in dBE did. In general, assuming validity of PPT, one might have expected a higher degree of clustering.

A closer look at repeated findings across different categories further highlights the limited support even these results provide for a comprehensive theoretical interpretation of PPT. The most robust positive finding in line with PPT was in cell E11 of Tables 3.5–3.8, i.e. changes in the frequency of bankruptcies were found to statistically cause changes in the relative frequency of papers containing the term 'glut'. Not only is this the only cell in the BANKR column with relevant findings, it is also an association which, arguably, would not be the first that one names when predicting which pair of economic and bibliometric variables would display a strong association in line with PPT. A similar argument may be brought forward to evaluate the frequency of bibliometric variables caused by the CPI: more (respectively almost as many when accounting for WN) than for three major real economic variables with prominent appearances in many business cycle theories – UNEMP, INDP and INV – taken together. What is more, with one exception (namely Recession_sBE), the latter three were associated with other bibliometric variables than CPI was. Interestingly, Recession_dE and UNEMP were neither causally associated nor fractionally co-integrated in the first place – despite the close fit observed in the descriptive assessment of Figure 3.10 on page 78. Among the repeated positive findings, the most interesting ones from a theoretical perspective which considers the terms' respective prominence are probably in cells D1, F2 and F4. Cell D1, for example, indicates that, in both sE and sBE, BCTC was statistically caused by investment activity – which seems intuitively appealing, given the prominent role of investment in much of BCCT. However, it is questionable whether such individual findings constitute compelling evidence in favour of PPT when many of the other pairs are not even fractionally co-integrated or indicate quite contrasting findings (e.g. that Depression_dE and Crisis_dBE were found to cause INV). Therefore, the FCVAR analysis of frequencies anywhere in documents, taken as a whole, does not provide very strong evidence in favour of PPT either. The following subsections will further highlight specific issues of this general point by discussing differences between the various categories and their implications.

Concerning the FCVAR analysis of frequencies in titles, Table 3.9 on page 91 exemplarily showed results for the sBE category. Here, the number of fractionally co-integrated cases, and especially of pairs in accordance with PPT, was considerably higher (about twice that documented in Table 3.6 for bibliometric series of frequencies anywhere in documents). However, other problems need to be considered, which go back to the uneven distribution of contraction years and items in the frequency series over time once again. There is a notable difference between the four series in the top half of the table, and the three in the lower half. For the INCPC, UNEMP, INDP and INV series which have only been available since 1929, 1948, 1919 and 1929, respectively, there are only six (four when accounting for the WN results) positive findings, whereas the other 19 (respectively 18 when accounting for WN) are found in the bottom half for the series which go back to 1900 (BANKR), 1855 (CPI) and 1871 (SPC). Considering the low absolute frequencies of matching items in the earlier parts of the respective title series, even in the largest category sBE, it is quite surprising to find so many results for the longer series, whereas the shorter ones, despite their generally high relative coverage (see Table 3.4) returned fewer fractionally co-integrated cases. This especially holds for INDP, which contains a full decade before the Great Depression, but returned no positive finding in line with PPT. On the other hand, Figures 3.4–3.7 have documented just how volatile the title series were – even after using five-year moving averages – until the early 20th century. At the same time, as documented in Table 2.2 on page 22, contractions (and consequently contraction years) were much more frequent during this period. Indeed, of the 75 years between 1855 and 1929, 43 (i.e. considerably more than half) are contraction years. This means that, for the analysis of frequencies in titles, highly volatile bibliometric series – in part due to the generally low coverage and the nature of term frequencies in titles – are combined with economic data that are subject to more frequent fluctuations. On the other hand, the economic series which are available only for a shorter time period cover years with less frequent contractions, and are combined with less volatile bibliometric series (i.e. where fluctuations due to the coverage are less likely). Therefore, it can be argued that, despite the more comprehensive coverage, the results for BANKR, CPI and SPC in Table 3.9 are more likely to be error-prone than the others, i.e. less reliable. Taken together, then, the overall evidence concerning the validity of PPT based on the FCVAR analysis remains inconclusive.

3.3.2.2 Economics articles and economics journals

Whereas the overall results across all variables and categories thus provide little support for PPT, the analysis and discussion so far has also identified some systematic differences which warrant a closer inspection, for they might reflect theoretically plausible underlying mechanisms. This specifically holds for differences between the bibliometric categories, which is why the following paragraphs discuss the divergent findings found for subject and discipline categories, respectively. To interpret these results, it is important to reiterate the difference between the JSTOR categories (see Subsection 2.3.2): subjects are identified for each paper individually based on the words it uses, whereas disciplines are attributed to a paper based on the journal. Therefore, sE contains all papers, regardless of where they are published, which feature economics terminology ("economics papers"), whereas dE contains all papers that were published in an economics journal, regardless of their actual content.

In the descriptive overview of Section 3.1, where term frequencies in subject categories were plotted next to those in the corresponding discipline categories, the series had appeared to display fairly similar general trends and major points of fluctuations. However, one of the clearest results from the econometric analysis was the much smaller number of findings in accordance with PPT in the discipline categories dE and dBE than there were for sE and sBE. This warrants a closer look at the similarities – or differences – between the respective categories. Figures 3.15 and 3.16 therefore show the same time series of frequencies anywhere in documents from Figures 3.3, 3.6 and 3.7, but arranged differently, so that each panel contains a term's frequencies in either sE or sBE, and, correspondingly, dE or dBE. Each of the two tables contains six panels, for BCTC, 'crisis', 'depression', 'recession', DOWNSWING and OVERALL. Figure 3.15 compares sE with dE, and Figure 3.16 does the same for sBE and dBE.

At first glance, the figures seem to reaffirm the original impression of a close fit in both general trends and fluctuations from the descriptive overview. However, a closer look reveals notable differences: in Figure 3.15, the black lines corresponding to sE are almost consistently above the grey lines representing dE. This is especially pronounced for BCTC after 1970, 'depression' from 1920 to 1940 and since about 1970, and 'recession' since the mid-1970s. Together with their higher levels, the sE series also display larger absolute changes than the dE series. Considering how the categories are defined, the latter observation – greater absolute changes in sE as compared with dE – may be seen as an indication that some of the increased writing activity in response to contractions is "lip service". For example, during and following the Great Depression, in the 1930s up to 50% of economics papers featured the word 'depression', whereas only about 35% of papers in economics journals did. However, a paper which briefly references the Great Depression may end up in the sE category, whereas it need not feature in dE. Therefore, sE contains all items from non-economics journals which sprout up following a contraction, but these do not necessarily contain BCCT. Be that as it may, one might expect a reaction of the sE literature to business cycles and economic crises, even if PPT did not strictly apply to the economics literature in a more narrow sense (specifically dE), because changes in the bibliometric data are a compound of "genuine" PPT effects and lip service, and the latter is likely to be more prominent in sE than dE (also see Subsection 3.3.1). This line of reasoning could then reconcile the large difference in positive findings between subject and discipline categories as observed in the econometric analysis.

Quite interestingly, however, the comparison of sBE and dBE in Figure 3.16 provides a rather different picture. Frequencies are fairly similar, but with the notable difference that dBE frequencies are mostly higher than sBE frequencies. The most pronounced differences in levels – while the series still show similar fluctuations – can be found for BCTC, 'depression', DOWNSWING and OVERALL from between the first half of the 1930s to the second half of the 1960s. During this period, a paper in a BE journal (dBE) was more likely to feature one of the respective terms than any paper which was concerned with BE topics (sBE). This is the opposite of what was found for Figure 3.15 and the comparison of sE with dE. However, a few additional points need to be taken into account which could explain at least part of the discrepancy between sE and dE, on the one hand, and sBE and dBE, on the other. A major difference is the relative share of E within BE – over 70% for dE in dBE, and only about 22% of sE in sBE. The large share of dE in dBE and relatively smaller size of sE in sBE can be observed overall, and over time as well, i.e. it is not just a result skewed by more recent years where publication numbers were much higher than a century earlier. This means that the other categories, such as F or

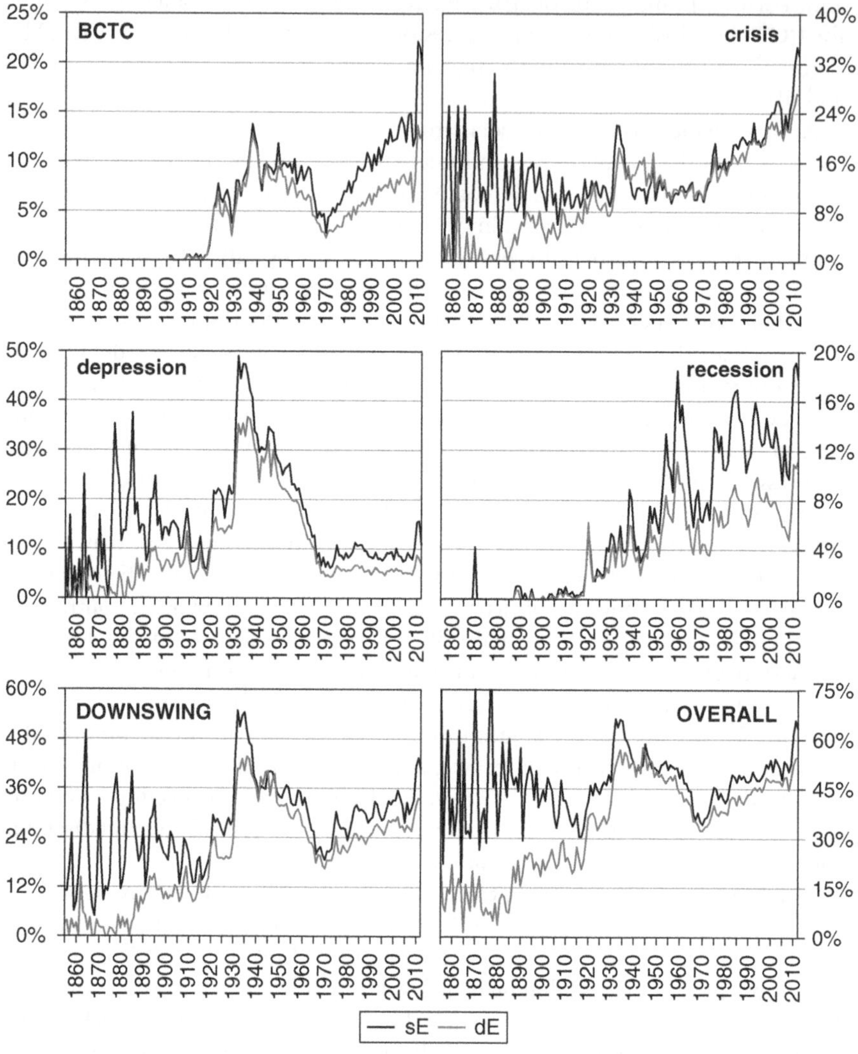

Figure 3.15 Comparison of term frequencies, sE vs. dE, 1855–2012.

Note: Each panel shows time series of the four central terms (BCTC, 'crisis', 'depression', 'recession') and two indexes (DOWNSWING, OVERALL) anywhere in documents in the sE (black) and dE (dark grey) categories.

"business" – especially without intersections with E – make up a much larger share in sBE than they do in dBE. In general, the comparison of Figures 3.15 and 3.16 shows that frequencies in E are higher than in BE, meaning that the other, non-E categories use the respective terms less often. The small share of sE in sBE can therefore explain at least partly why sBE frequencies are below dBE in the aforementioned cases. While sE reacts more strongly than dE, this

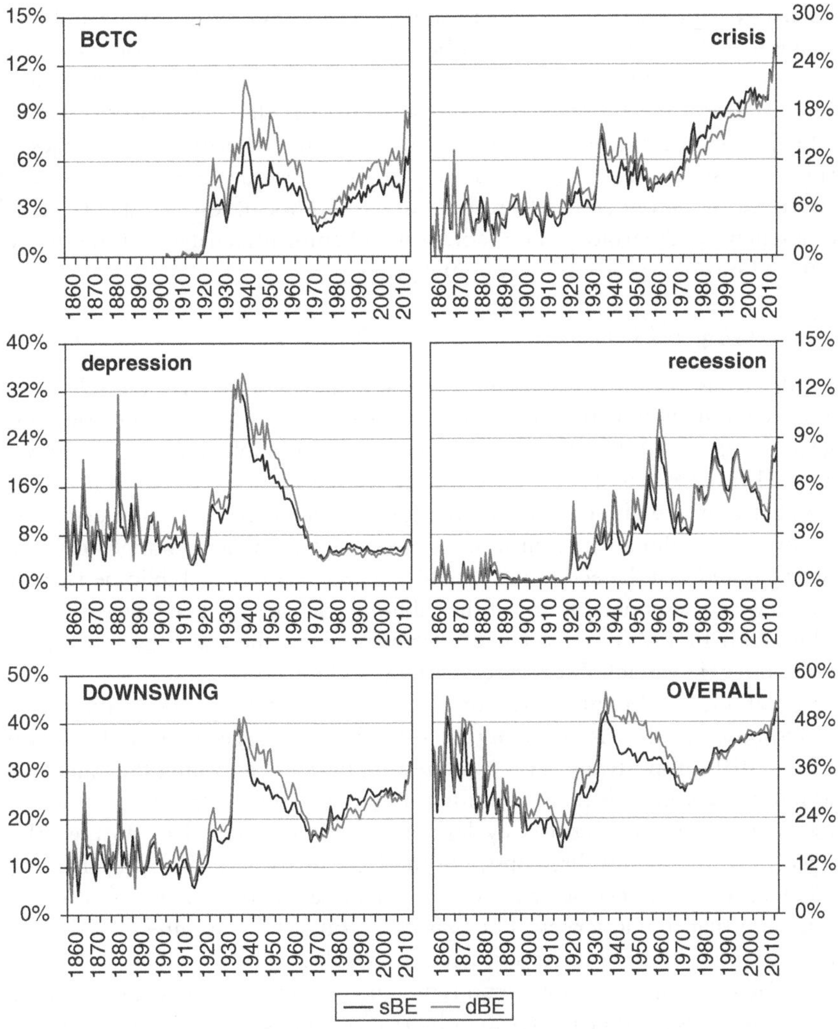

Figure 3.16 Comparison of term frequencies, sBE vs. dBE, 1855–2012.

Note: Each panel shows time series of the four central terms (BCTC, 'crisis', 'depression', 'recession') and two indexes (DOWNSWING, OVERALL) anywhere in documents in the sBE (black) and dBE (dark grey) categories.

might not be enough to overcompensate the lack of or weak reaction in non-E categories, which have a much higher weight in sBE, and therefore contribute to sBE frequencies being lower than dBE, where the change in dE, although smaller than that in sE, has a much larger weight.

Overall, however, it is clear that there are differences between subject and discipline categories, especially between economics articles and economics journals. These cannot be fully and comprehensively explained by the data available for and used in the present study, but it does not seem implausible to assume that the stronger association between economic and bibliometric variables – especially concerning causal relations in line with PPT – in sE relative to dE indicates the prevalence of "lip service", i.e. that a potentially considerable part of the reaction of the academic literature to economic variables, at least where such a reaction is statistically observed, is due to increased usage of specific words and reference to recent events, and not necessarily due to actual comprehensive discussions and theoretical and empirical analyses of the subject matter of business cycles and economic crises.

3.3.2.3 Magnitudes of measured effects

In order to assess not just whether economic and bibliometric variables were associated, but also whether their connection – if any – was in the direction predicted by PPT, and how strong measured effects are, Subsection 3.2.2 showed a few select IRFs based on a VAR model. While there were also some differences between the different IRFs, even for the same combination of economic variables and bibliometric terms, six of the seven pairs where Granger-causality tests suggested that the economic variable Granger-causes the bibliometric variable showed a response pattern of the bibliometric variable that was very much in line with PPT. A more detailed interpretation of the strengths and timings of bibliometric variables' responses warrants a closer look.

First of all, in all plotted cases of Figures 3.13 and 3.14, the coefficients of the responses in the IRFs are about 5–10 times as large in sE and dE as in sBE and dBE, respectively. This is interesting because, assuming the validity of the results, this implies that economics itself reacts much stronger in a way as suggested by PPT to business cycles and economic crises than do the other subjects and disciplines that constitute the BE categories (otherwise, this large difference would not arise, with E being a subset of BE). This, of course, is something that might very well be expected from a PPT argument, and it also fits very well with the previous subsection's results.

The lag of the most notable responses – one period in four cases, two periods in two cases – is another interesting observation. These findings imply that the strongest reaction of discussions of business cycles and economic crises in the economics literature, in response to economic developments such as inflation rates above trend, occurs between one and two years after the change in economic data. In their analysis of publishing delays in different disciplines, Björk and Solomon (2013) find a fairly large publication lag of about 18 months in economics. Now this seems to fit very well with the observed delays in the responses and would thus provide a qualitative backing of the PPT argument: a contraction sets in, and 18 months later the work dealing with that contraction is published. However, it should be noted that these 18 months do not contain the full process which would be part of the PPT logic. Overall, an author's reaction to a contraction presupposes that the contraction set in, that the relevant data and records are published so the scholar becomes aware of the contraction, and that they decide to write a paper and then submit it to the journal – and, from that point on, the average delay is still 18 months. Therefore, it seems plausible to assume that, for papers which are actually conceptualized and written in response to a crisis or contraction, a larger delay of maybe up to three years would be reasonable. On the other hand, it is possible for "lip service" to the recent events to enter papers which are already in the peer-review process, if an author decides, in preparing the final manuscript, to add additional motivation by reference to recent events. Therefore, one would expect the "lip service" component of PPT to have a shorter delay than the effect on actual analyses of business cycles and economic crises. The observed delays of one or two years thus lend themselves to the interpretation that the "lip service" component is the bigger part of the reaction of the economics literature to business cycles and economic crises. A comprehensive analysis of this issue requires a proper semantic analysis, which the data used in this book unfortunately could not provide.

It is also worthwhile to embed these findings in the broader context of the FCVAR analysis (see Subsection 3.2.1). Neither CPI and BCTC nor UNEMP and 'recession' are fractionally co-integrated in any of the JSTOR categories. SPC and 'crisis' are fractionally co-integrated in three categories (sE, dE, dBE), but in none of these cases do the long-run exogeneity tests suggest causality running from the economic to the bibliometric variable. INV and Depression_dE are fractionally co-integrated, but the long-run exogeneity tests suggest causality running in the opposite direction to what PPT implies. While the VAR analysis and the IRFs, when considered in isolation, therefore provide some compelling evidence in favour of PPT, the FCVAR results once more point to the general observation of a lack of conclusive and systematic evidence. Since FCVAR is arguably the better specification to tackle our research question (see Subsection 2.4.4), the VAR findings need to be interpreted with caution.

3.3.3 Comparison with findings from earlier research

3.3.3.1 Kufenko and Geiger (2016)

The results documented in Tables 3.5 and 3.6 of Subsection 3.2.1.1 can be directly compared to those reported by Kufenko and Geiger (2016: 64–66). Kufenko and Geiger (2016) worked with basically the same economic and bibliometric data. Except for systematic differences as in the 'crisis' series (where the plural "crises" is also considered in the records for this book), the bibliometric variables, although independently constructed from scratch for the present analysis, are mostly identical with those from Kufenko and Geiger (2016). There are more differences in economic data. For example, the industrial production series uses a different base year (2012 instead of 2007), and relative changes are also different in detail. In the income per capita series, there are very small differences of much less than 0.1% in 2010, 2011 and 2012. However, they are still basically the same series from the same data source. To analyse the data, Kufenko and Geiger (2016) worked with an earlier version of the FCVAR package, but employed the same method. Also, the FCVAR analysis uses logarithmic transformations of all economic series except for the unemployment rate in both studies. The comparison of results therefore serves as a kind of robustness check to test the reliability of the findings and whether considerable differences can ensue from small changes in the underlying data and econometric tools.

For the seven economic and 15 bibliometric variables employed here, Kufenko and Geiger (2016: tables 12 and 13) find 23 fractionally co-integrated pairs in the sE category. Among these, the long-run exogeneity test suggests causality in line with PPT in nine cases, the reverse direction in seven cases, and both ways three times. Four fractionally co-integrated pairs do not display any significant results in the long-run exogeneity test. Eight of the fractionally co-integrated pairs identified by Kufenko and Geiger (2016: tables 12 and 13) can be found in Table 3.5 with the same suggested order of causality (C9, E11, F2, F4, F11, F13, F14, G7). Another six fractionally co-integrated pairs feature in both studies, but with different results in the long-run exogeneity test (A7, C7, C13, F9, G2, G8). Therefore, eight (respectively 14) out of 23 pairs identified by Kufenko and Geiger (2016: tables 12 and 13) were replicated here – which means that 15 of those reported in Table 3.5 had not been identified in the highly similar study before. This sheds serious doubt on the reliability and therefore the general applicability of the findings – the previous ones as well as the new results from Subsection 3.2.1.1.

The comparison of sBE findings from Table 3.6 with those by Kufenko and Geiger (2016) leads to a similar interpretation. Kufenko and Geiger (2016: tables 10 and 11) had identified 29 fractionally co-integrated pairs, where the long-run exogeneity test suggested causality in line with PPT 11 times, the opposite way seven times, both ways eight times, and with no significant results in three cases. Here, only two of the 18 fractionally co-integrated cases from Table 3.6 were not already reported – and for 12 cases, the same kind of causality was found as well (B2, B6, C6, D1, D8, F2, F4, F8, F9, F11, F14, G5). Consequently, four fractionally co-integrated pairs identified in both studies returned different results in the long-run exogeneity tests (A4, B15, C4, C13). Whereas many of the findings from Table 3.6 therefore constitute a replication of the earlier results by Kufenko and Geiger (2016: tables 10 and 11), this argument does not hold the other way around. Concerning sBE, only 16 out of 29 co-integrated pairs documented by Kufenko and Geiger (2016: tables 10 and 11) were identified again in Table 3.6, i.e. just over half of the earlier results were replicated (and less than half when the order of causality is considered).

For one economic variable, this comparison highlights a very robust result: in both sE and sBE, long-run exogeneity tests reported in Kufenko and Geiger (2016: tables 10 and 13) had documented causality running from consumer prices to 'crisis', 'recession', 'glut' and 'stagnation'. All of these were confirmed in Tables 3.5 and 3.6 (F2, F4, F11, F14). Overall, however, comparing the findings of Subsection 3.2.1.1 with those of Kufenko and Geiger (2016: 64–66) implies low reliability. Furthermore, this is also true when comparing the few select pairs from the VAR analysis in Table 3.12 on page 101 with the corresponding results in Kufenko and Geiger (2016: 59–61). The data sources are the same in both analyses, and especially the bibliometric series are mostly identical. If the causality suggested by PPT was indeed a very general phenomenon, and if the method employed in both studies was an appropriate tool to capture this effect, small differences in the underlying data should not affect the results of the statistical analysis much. As already indicated, the tools here differ slightly from Kufenko and Geiger (2016) due to the newer version of the FCVAR package that was employed. Since positive results in line with PPT amount to only around 10% of the total number of pairs that were compared in sE and sBE, and these are generally uniform neither across different categories, nor between Kufenko and Geiger (2016) and the present book (i.e. specific economic–bibliometric pairs mostly did not show uniform result patterns in the FCVAR and long-run exogeneity tests), this raises the serious question of whether some of the results might just be statistical artefacts. It is worthwhile, then, to discuss the research strategy more generally with a focus on the issue of potential false positives. Subsection 3.3.4 elaborates on this point in detail.

3.3.3.2 Besomi (2011)

While the analysis in the present book greatly extends the empirical effort of Besomi (2011), it was very much inspired by that earlier work (especially see Subsection 2.4.2.1), which was the first notable attempt to quantitatively assess PPT. Therefore, it is interesting to compare the methods that were used and the respective results. Besomi (2011: 113ff.) tracks and graphically displays, for the period 1815–2009, absolute frequencies of various terms connected to BCCT in the titles of a large set of documents. (Since we follow Besomi in this respect, the terms are mostly identical with the ones we used; but see Besomi (2011: 57ff.) for the detailed documentation.) The items that Besomi (2011) screens for his analysis are books, pamphlets and articles. Articles from periodicals are mostly available (and therefore included in the database) from the end of the 19th century onwards, and Besomi (2011: 55) uses JSTOR and EconLit records from the 1930s onwards. For the earlier years, Besomi (2011: 55) has compiled a database of not only various books, treatises and pamphlets, but also journal articles and other items, on crises and cycles, which contains about 2700 items in the 19th century, and about another 3000 for the first four decades of the 20th century. These records include items in French, German and Italian, and word occurrences of the corresponding non-English terms of these are also included in tracking the absolute frequencies. Besomi (2011: 56) interprets the resulting figures to confirm PPT by noting that "[t]he number of writings on crises and cycles clearly peaks immediately after the outbreak of each crisis" and by linking many individual episodes to peaks in his frequency data. For example, Besomi (2011: 56) notes the very high frequencies during the Great Depression, and the decreasing frequencies of all terms during the 1960s and 1970s. Especially throughout the 19th century, the many individual episodes of economic turmoil that Besomi (2011: 56f.) points out can be traced in Besomi's (2011: 113f.) figures quite well indeed.

Besomi's method differs from ours in various respects. First of all, Besomi (2011) provides absolute frequency counts, whereas our analysis uses relative measures. Besomi's sample is also more diverse, and dates back further in history, whereas our sample of the journal literature from JSTOR is more comprehensive overall, and consistent in the sense that we include only research articles. The most apparent difference, however, is in the different methods employed, especially for how the bibliometric series are compared with the economic data, respectively, in Besomi's work, the timings of particular economic crises and downturns. Whereas Besomi refers to historical episodes to date contractions in his figures, we use econometric tools to find them in the changes in the data. Besomi (2011: 118, fn. 4) is, of course, aware of the superficial nature of his approach, and points out that his figures "are not meant to substitute for serious statistical analysis". Be that as it may, the statistical analysis presented here provides quite different findings, and we therefore also favour another interpretation regarding PPT.

Despite similarities, even our descriptive results from Section 3.1 already show notable differences to Besomi (2011). For example, during and after the Great Depression, Besomi (2011: 115) finds a higher frequency of "panic" than of "depression" in most years in the 1930s, and "crisis" also appears more frequently in many of these years (even though "depression" also reaches unprecedented levels). Concerning our records, Figure 3.4 on page 68 has shown that, in journals on JSTOR, 'depression' did indeed peak in the 1930s, but at much higher levels than 'crisis' in almost every year across all categories. The numbers for 'panic' (not in Figure 3.4) did not even show extraordinarily high frequencies in any of the JSTOR categories. More generally, however, the econometric analysis in Section 3.2 has produced little comprehensive support for PPT, and even the more conclusive findings for title frequencies have to be interpreted with care (see Subsection 3.3.2.1). Therefore, based on our systematic assessment, we cannot argue as strongly in favour of PPT as was done in that earlier work.

Potentially, much of the difference between our findings and interpretation and those of Besomi (2011) can be traced to the different samples. Already, in the introductory remarks of Chapter 1, it has been pointed out that PPT might not necessarily be the most plausible hypothesis for the economics literature, because a topic as central as business cycles and economic crises should be worthy of academic discussions independently of current events. Until the first four decades of the 20th century, however, Besomi's sample includes much literature like pamphlets and similar texts. Arguably, these can be expected to be more prone to a PPT effect. Both results taken together can then be interpreted to support PPT in the non-academic literature, while constituting a lack of evidence for PPT in scientific writings, at least as far as substantial work on business cycles and economic crises is concerned.

3.3.4 Test power, false positive rates and implications

The generally low robustness of the results for associations between economic and bibliometric variables calls for a discussion of a more fundamental issue, namely the question of whether or not, and to what extent, it is possible that the findings reported in Section 3.2 are merely false positives. Even though this is without doubt an important issue, it is rarely considered in empirical research across all kinds of scientific disciplines.[8] We wish to address it here, for a very simple example already illustrates the problem's relevance. Given the significance benchmark we used in our analysis (the 95% level, i.e. an α of 5%), even if there were no underlying relations at all (i.e. even if no bibliometric variable was fractionally co-integrated with an economic variable) we would expect significant results in 5% of all the relations we investigate, i.e. in 5.25 of the 105 pairs of each category – and all of these would be false positives. The method employed in Section 3.2 is more complicated, of course. In particular, positive findings in line with PPT are the result of a two-stage process, in which a pair of one economic and one bibliometric variable needs to be fractionally co-integrated, and also display the right pattern in the long-run exogeneity test. Nonetheless, a closer inspection of the results seems warranted, since the absolute numbers of both fractionally co-integrated cases, and causalities in line with PPT, are not very high either way.

Very generally, the probability of reporting false positives depends on three components: the significance level used as a benchmark, α; the statistical power $1-\beta$ of the test employed to identify the relation (where β is the probability of a type II error, i.e. false negative), i.e. the probability of correctly identifying a positive association present in the data; and the *a priori* probability π of a positive relation actually existing in the plane of all possible relations of interest. For any specific relation, e.g. between two variables, the probability of correctly identifying a positive association (i.e. a true positive) is then given as $\pi(1-\beta)$; whereas the probability of a false positive is $\alpha(1-\pi)$. The false positive report probability (FPRP) is the relative frequency of false positives among all positives, i.e. $\alpha(1-\pi)/[\alpha(1-\pi)+\pi(1-\beta)]$.

Given the familiar standard level of $\alpha = 0.05$ which is employed in all of the various tests conducted in Section 3.2, it is possible to illustrate the FPRP for any combination of test power and π. Figure 3.17 does just that, with FPRPs shaded in a β–π diagram (the resolution is 250 × 250). Darker areas correspond to higher FPRPs, with black areas representing FPRPs between just over 90% and 100%, whereas white areas represent FPRPs of 0% (only given for $\pi = 1$), and the lightest grey corresponds to FPRPs just above 0% and at most 10%. The shading highlights the rather obvious and intuitively clear insight that the frequency of false positives among all positive findings decreases with both test power and π. To apply this observation to discussions of the results from the previous section, it is feasible to superimpose lines representing the total number of positive findings (as per the results presented in Section 3.2, where, for each JSTOR category, 105 pairs of economic and bibliometric variables were tested). Doing this not just for the number of fractionally co-integrated cases, but for the results in line with PPT, presupposes, of course, a major simplification of the econometric method and the assumption that positive findings in the long-run exogeneity test are the result of one test on the whole sample (whereas, in fact, they are the result of a second test on an already preselected subsample). The probability of a long-run exogeneity test result in line with PPT, however, is zero for pairs which are not fractionally co-integrated (because, then, the test cannot be applied). More generally, the probability of a significant result in the long-run exogeneity test is not independent of that of a significant result in the FCVAR test. Therefore, this simplification is helpful to illustrate the general issue of false positives.

Overall, we sketched six lines which delineate three bands in Figure 3.17. The solid lines indicate combinations of test power and π for which the expected number of positive results $\alpha(1-\pi)+\pi(1-\beta)$ with $\alpha=0.05$ in 105 tests is between 18 and 29. This corresponds to the number of fractionally co-integrated cases found in sBE and sE. The 20, respectively 21, pairs from dBE and dE could be represented as similar lines inside that band. For illustrative purposes, the dotted lines similarly correspond to the 11 (as in sBE), respectively 12 (sE), pairs in line with PPT, under the simplifying assumption that they were identified from a one-stage statistical test. Likewise, the dashed lines correspond to two (dE), respectively three (dBE), positive findings.[9]

Considering the band delineated by the solid lines, i.e. those corresponding to the number of positives in the FCVAR tests, Figure 3.17 shows that the FPRP is likely below 20%, so we expect the large majority of fractionally co-integrated pairs to be fractionally co-integrated indeed. Assuming validity of the simplification mentioned above, Figure 3.17 further lends itself to the interpretation that the results observed for sE and sBE in Section 3.2 are unlikely to come about from a combination of $\pi=0.9$ and $1-\beta=0.5$. On the other hand, they could result from very high π combined with a rather low test power of between 0.1 and 0.2; for $0.2\leq\pi\leq0.3$ and $0.25\leq1-\beta\leq0.35$ (in which case FPRPs would be rather high, likely somewhere between 20% and 40%); or from very high test power combined with very low π (in which case there would also be a similarly high FPRP).

As a further analysis of the results shows, long-run exogeneity test power for the large majority of fractionally co-integrated cases from Section 3.2 was larger than 0.9, and most of these, especially those where the long-run exogeneity test suggested causality according to PPT, even turned out to have a test power of 1. A test power of 1 means that, if a positive association exists in the data, e.g. between an economic and a bibliometric variable, it will be identified. These are rather clear and maybe surprisingly strong results, but they cannot be directly connected to the previous argument. First of all, these and the illustration of Figure 3.17 assumed an implicit average test power over

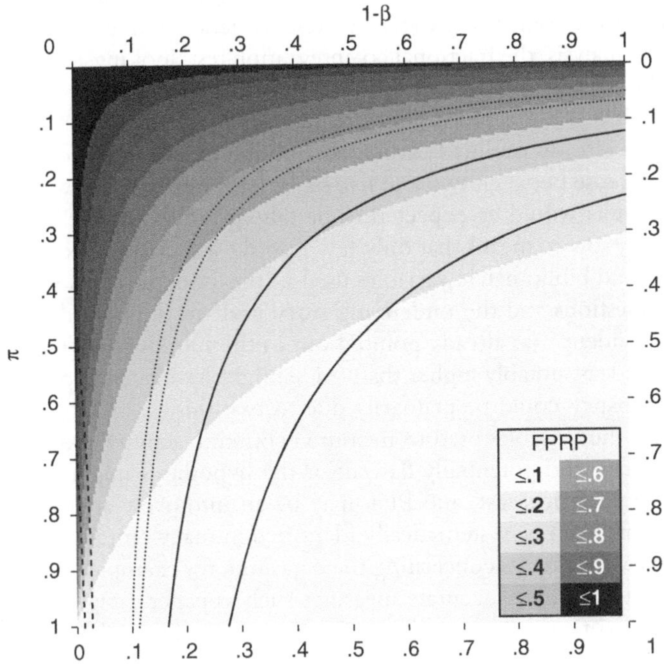

Figure 3.17 Hypothetical and estimated FPRPs.

Note: Shaded areas indicate FPRPs resulting from combinations of test power and π for $\alpha = 0.05$. The two solid lines delineate the band into which all results from Subsection 3.2.1.1 fall. Broken lines correspond to the bands obtained if findings in line with PPT could be directly related to all (i.e. not just the fractionally co-integrated) pairs, specifically for sE and sBE (dotted) and dE and dBE (dashed).

all tested relations of a category, and no such value can be readily calculated here. Secondly, estimated test powers are those from just a small subset of each category, namely those cases (between 18 and 29 of the 105) which were fractionally co-integrated (otherwise no long-run exogeneity test would be conducted). This means that the test power results are those for a sample which, by its pre-selection, is more likely to generate positive findings, respectively within which it is exceedingly likely that, if a positive association exists, it will be identified.

Especially when implications concerning the validity of PPT are to be drawn, π is the crucial variable: it represents the *a priori* probability that an economic and a bibliometric variable are associated. The size of π quite generally depends on two factors: first, the level of confidence in the theoretical argument that such an association between the variables exists; and secondly, the quality and appropriateness of the empirical measures for the theoretical constructs they operationalize (economic activity and the spread of discussions of business cycles and economic crises). Making the simplifying assumption that the high test power from the long-run exogeneity tests is generalizable to include the first step of the analysis, the fractional co-integration test, looking at Figure 3.17 shows that the actually observed number of positives is likely to result from comparatively low *a priori* probabilities of potentially less than 10%, coupled with FPRPs, as already outlined earlier, that might well be between 20% and 40% – in which case between two and five of 12 (sE), respectively two and four of 11 (sBE), results would be expected to be false positives. At the same time, the implied very low π means that only few positive associations exist between the economic and bibliometric variables used in this book to assess PPT. Since the research questions and the underlying story itself are supported by plausible anecdotal evidence (as already pointed out in the introductory Chapter 1), a high π – or at least notably higher than 0.1 – might have been expected. The resulting discrepancy could be primarily due to two things, or a combination of them: either the variables used to measure economic activity and the literature are inaccurate and potentially flawed; or the hypothesis might simply not hold up to the empirical test, and PPT may be an intuitively appealing story, but not one which can be systematically identified in many empirical relations.

Given the various caveats concerning the data, and, for example, the regret of not being able to use more accurate measures such as paper categories defined by JEL codes, it is of course very well possible that the quality of the data and the inaccurate measure of BCCT and related discussions they represent correspond to a lower π than might be expected from an ideal construct. Nonetheless, it is probably too much to conclude that this is the only explanation for the implied low π. This point is strengthened when widening the scope a bit and taking the validation results from the previous subsections into account. There, it was shown that, when comparing categories, and despite a few notable exceptions, it is often different pairs of economic and bibliometric variables that display a positive association. This can be read as an indication of false positives, because there may not be consistent underlying relations which return reproducible results – and instead, given the large number of pairs, the tests find a random few false positive results every time.

Overall, therefore, the analysis of test power, false positives and what may be, as it were, derived retrospectively about the "expected" *a priori* probability of PPT further adds to the observation that, based on the data and results from Section 3.2, one can hardly argue for a strong association between business cycles and economic crises and their discussions in the literature as measured in the present analysis. Across the different JSTOR categories, no more than between two and 12 associations in line with PPT were identified among 105 associations, at a FPRP of potentially between 20% and 40%. Under simplifying assumptions, given the high estimates for test power, the results, if not solely attributed to problems with the data, then imply a rather low probability of the original PPT hypothesis being an accurate description of the association between economic data and the economics literature.

3.3.5 Assessing the effect of changes in underlying citation data

The descriptive results presented for the citation data in Subsection 3.3.5 were, at best, tentative. Indeed, the trends in Figure 3.11 on page 80 could reflect shifting patterns of interest in the literature on business cycles and economic crises – or be statistical artefacts resulting from changes in the metadata. For example, if the average number of WoS-indexed references per paper increases every year – which, as our data show, is indeed the case – then, even if cited items were randomly drawn, one would expect more and more items to cite at least one other paper from a given set. Secondly, the said given sets (tBCTC_WoS, tDOWNSWING_WoS, tOVERALL_WoS) were very small near the beginning of the observation period (indeed, starting at two, 14 and 28 items in 1956), and continuously grew larger throughout. Furthermore, the fraction of all BCTC, DOWNSWING and OVERALL papers published between 1956 and a given year relative to all WoS economics papers until that year was generally increasing until 2015, too. This holds even if WoS papers before 1956 are considered (which, indirectly, is the case through documented citations), for there are no BCTC, DOWNSWING and OVERALL papers (and their fraction among all economics papers is thus 0%) before 1956. Therefore, even if the absolute number of references in the economics literature published every year had remained unchanged, one would expect an increase in the fraction of papers citing at least one from a particular underlying set, even if references were drawn at random, as long as that underlying set's fraction of the total literature is continuously increasing (which, on average, is the case).

Given the data used here, a quantitative assessment of the potential chance effect is possible. The average number of references in economics papers indexed on the WoS has increased from about 4.6 in 1956 to just over 40 in 2015, and has steadily increased at a fairly constant growth rate since the second half of the 1960s in particular. Furthermore, again comparing 1956 and 2015, the cumulated relative frequency of BCTC papers increased from under 0.1% to over 0.3%, from about 0.5% to over 1.2% for DOWNSWING, and from over 1% to over 2.5% for OVERALL. Therefore, over the observation period, the average number of references has increased to more than eight times its original level, and the relative frequency of relevant citable papers in the overall body of citable economics literature has increased to about two to three times the original level. If references were drawn completely at random, their selection can be approximately described by a binomial distribution $B(k \mid p, n)$, with the fraction of papers containing BCTC, DOWNSWING or OVERALL as the success probability p, the average number of total references as the number of draws n, and the number of relevant references (i.e. references to the BCTC, DOWNSWING or OVERALL sets) as the number of successful draws k. The probability of any paper containing at least one reference to the relevant citable set is then given as the complementary probability to that of zero relevant references, i.e. $1 - B(0 \mid p, n) = 1 - (1 - p)^n$. Neglecting economics papers listed on the WoS, but published before 1956, these simple calculations imply that, given the observable changes in the underlying coefficients, the relative frequency of tBCTC_cit would be about 31 times, and those of tDOWNSWING_cit and tOVERALL_cit about 15 and 13 times their 1956 levels in 2015. Furthermore, a simulation over the whole observation period, based on each year's average citation counts and cumulated relative frequencies, can also replicate the remarkable trend increase in the DOWNSWING and OVERALL series in the mid-2000s. This alone may not fully explain the trend in panel (e) of Figure 3.11, but it does go a considerable way towards doing so. Therefore, the method and data presented in Subsection 3.1.3 cannot reliably distinguish between plausible alternative hypotheses for explaining the rising trend (at least pre-2000s) in relative citation frequencies to all three series, and indeed it seems likely that changing patterns in the metadata have a major effect.

The series depicted in the bottom right panel (f) of Figure 3.11 can be analysed in a similar fashion. Indeed, if the average number of references per document increases, one would also expect an increase in the average absolute number of references to a given set such as tBCTC_WoS. Both the analytical and numerical solutions are more complicated here for two reasons. From a binomial distribution, the expected number of relevant references per citing item if references were randomly drawn would be given as np, i.e. the average number of total references per item times the fraction of citable papers. However, this includes papers with zero relevant references, which were not featured in panel (f) of Figure 3.11. The expected number of references per paper with at least one reference is therefore given by normalizing to the fraction of those papers among all papers, i.e. dividing by the complementary probability of having zero relevant references, which results in $np/[1-(1-p)^n]$. However, the second problem remains: the binomial distribution implies an urn model in which items are returned after drawing. Citations, however, correspond to an urn model where items (i.e. references) are not returned once they were drawn (i.e. cited), for a paper can only feature in another's bibliography once (this is also why the calculations above are an approximation). Therefore, the following estimate of average citation frequencies at best approximates an upper bound to that measure.

The data already used in the previous calculation imply 1.001 BCTC references per citing item with at least one relevant reference in 1956, 1.06 in 2015, and 1.03 in 2000 near where the trends in panel (f) of Figure 3.11 became flatter and values were already close to (in the case of BCTC even higher than) those of 2015. Given the larger set of citable papers, numbers for DOWNSWING and OVERALL are naturally higher, but still considerably lower (especially considering that these are upper bounds for the expected numbers) than those in panel (f) of Figure 3.11, particularly in 2000, where DOWNSWING is at 1.09 and OVERALL at 1.26. It is also worth pointing out that these values are considerably lower than those estimated for the end of the observation period (1.26 and 1.62, respectively). Especially the peak and subsequent decline in the BCTC series around 2000 cannot be found in the simulated time series, which in light of increasing average numbers of references per item and the increasing fraction of relevant citable items among all items instead follows a fairly steady upward trend. Therefore, this historical development and the particular trend cannot be explained as readily as a potential random byproduct of changes in the underlying factors as the trends in frequencies of citing papers. While actual levels for the latter are overpredicted by the simulation, the general development is replicated fairly well. On the other hand, however, the simulation results based on the assumption of a random drawing of references underpredict the clustering of citations to papers from the same underlying set – which, of course, would be expected given that references are indeed usually not drawn at random, but depend on a specific research topic. However, it should be noted that these observations provide no evidence of cyclical citation behaviour (e.g. as could be expected from PPT, higher citation frequencies in contraction periods).

Notes

1 Concerning the rightmost parts in all three panels, one more note on the 2012 cut-off date for this analysis is in order. The declines in all time series in the top two panels near the end of the depicted period are not due to some sudden change in publication habits, loads of journals disappearing or similar issues, but mainly and primarily due to JSTOR's "rolling wall" (see Subsection 2.3.2) of journal issues only becoming available several years after publication. The years after 2012 indeed document even lower absolute numbers in the associated records. Among the top journals, all but the *JEL* (only until 2011) are covered until 2012 (see Table 2.3 on page 38). However, due to the *JEL*'s low number of research articles, this does not visibly affect the series in 2012.

2 Owing to the remarkably clear-cut results, the detailed tables do not contain much information, which is why they are left out here to save on space.

3 In general, some caveats need to be taken into account when interpreting the smoothed data. First of all, the smoothing increases the probability of detecting cycles, since what might otherwise be considered as shocks is cumulated (for example, see Kufenko 2016). However, in the analysis here, the smoothing is used purely for illustrative purposes, and the econometric analysis in Section 3.2 starts with the original data. Owing to the larger sample size, the WoS series in Figure 3.9 were not smoothed.

4 Spearman's rank correlation coefficients of papers' citation frequencies for a pair of years of one and another between C and the following three years are all greater than 0.9 and always greatest between C and C+1 (0.974 for BCTC; 0.986 for DOWNSWING; 0.981 for OVERALL).

5 The simultaneous effect may be a result of hidden mixed-frequency processes (literature or economic variables interacting at frequencies higher than the annual ones).

6 While their short available time frame prevented us from presenting data on keywords in our empirical analysis, one related result is of interest here. In keywords of WoS economics papers (see Subsection 2.3.3), BCTC was – until 2008 in author-provided, and until 2013 in automatically generated, keywords – more frequent than 'crisis'. Since these keywords are arguably a better proxy of a paper's actual topics than the mere occurrence of a term, this observation might serve as a hint that mentions of 'crisis' anywhere in an article's text are more often "lip service" (see Section 2.4) than those of BCTC.

7 The corresponding average frequencies are not reported in the form of tables or figures here due to their general similarity to the original four-months definition. However, they are available from the authors upon request.

8 See, for example, Wacholder et al. (2004) and Ioannidis (2005). Further, see the more recent discussion on the "replication crisis" and publication bias (e.g. Open Science Collaboration 2015; Camerer et al. 2016; Christensen and Miguel 2016; Clemens 2017) as well as several contributions in the May 2017 *AER* issue (e.g. Berry et al. 2017; Duvendack et al. 2017; Hamermesh 2017; Höffler 2017; also note Hamermesh 2007). Andrews and Kasy (2017) provide parametric estimates of the conditional publication probability based on a study's empirical results and show, for example, that results significant at the 5% level are 10–50 times more likely to be published than insignificant results.

9 It should be noted that, in addition to the simplification of neglecting the two-stage process of the econometric methods, the bands thus delineated are of course not a perfect measure of the range of positives covered by the results from Section 3.2, because these are specific test outcomes which are superimposed onto expected values (such as the FPRPs) in Figure 3.17. Nonetheless, relating the specific results with the expected values seems to be a decent approximation to provide at least some kind of benchmark to assess and discuss the results.

4 Conclusion

This book was dedicated to analysing the empirical association between business cycles and economic crises, on the one hand, and the economics literature on the other. Specifically, its research question built on the "panics produce texts" (PPT) hypothesis, i.e. the suggestion that economic crises and subsequent downswings induce increased writing on those events (such as theoretical and empirical work on business cycles and economic crises), whereas prosperous economic times have the opposite effect. Both aspects of interest – economic fluctuations and developments in the economics literature – were operationalized by referencing several relevant data sources. Business cycles in historical economic development were identified in various time series for economic variables such as income per capita, investment activity and consumer prices in the United States. The economics literature on business cycles and economic crises was identified via proxy: first and foremost, sets of papers featuring relevant terms (such as "business cycle") were selected, and their frequency counted, from the journal literature archived on JSTOR. Secondly, citation records for papers concerned with business cycles and economic crises were built from Web of Science (WoS) data. These economic and bibliometric data were arranged and compared with each other in both a descriptive and an econometric analysis which used vector autoregression (VAR) and fractionally co-integrated vector autoregression (FCVAR) in order to find out whether any associations between the series in line with PPT could be identified.

Overall, our empirical analysis primarily covered the years 1855–2012. Over that period, more than 630 000 journal articles on business and economics and almost 280 000 articles from economics journals were indexed on JSTOR. Terms such as "business cycle" or "trade cycle" (BCTC), 'crisis', 'depression' and 'recession', which were selected as the most relevant ones for our analysis, appeared in thousands of these items, and in many hundreds of their titles. Since the distribution of journal articles over time is very uneven, with more recent years archiving more journals, issues and items, the analysis primarily worked with relative frequencies (i.e. occurrences relative to all items in the comparison category).

The main methods to test the association between economic and bibliometric variables in the descriptive analysis were to compare these relative frequencies inside and outside of contraction years, and to search for notable fluctuations in the historical time series. Quite surprisingly, average frequencies of many terms (including BCTC, 'crisis' and 'recession') were actually considerably higher outside of than during contraction years, i.e. a result opposite to what PPT suggests. On the other hand, the expected pattern was shown by frequencies of 'depression' – and, somewhat unexpected, because it implies a correlation of contractions and increased talk of the upswing component of business cycles, 'prosperity'. The data further showed that one year after a contraction, most average term frequencies were higher than during contractions, but this trend did not generally persist into the second and third year after a contraction. Similar results were found for citation data, where normalized citation counts (i.e. averages per year) of papers related to discussions of business cycles and economic crises were not systematically higher in contraction years than outside of contractions. A closer inspection showed, however, that for the large majority of papers in the citable set, citation counts do at least increase in the first year after a contraction. Nonetheless, this was not enough to establish a uniform pattern of contractions being correlated with higher citation counts.

However, the discussion on these average numbers also pointed out that they have to be interpreted with care due to the uneven distribution of both items and contraction years (independently of how exactly they were defined) over time. Contraction years were much more frequent in the first half of the observation period, especially before World War II, when the annual number of journal articles was much lower than during the 2000s especially. This argument can also partly explain why some terms do display a frequency pattern in line with PPT. Notions such as 'distress' were much more common before than after World War II, i.e. when contraction years made up about 50% of all years (as opposed to the only 20% after World War II). Nonetheless, considering these factors cannot fully solve the somewhat paradoxical nature of the observation that, for many terms, average frequencies are higher outside of than during contraction years. Another aspect which might matter in this context is publication lag. Taken alone, however, this did not seem to offer a comprehensive explanation to the observation either.

In the other part of the descriptive content analysis, the very high frequencies of 'depression' in the 1930s constituted the first notable pattern in the time series. During the Great Depression, almost half of all economics articles and well over 30% of articles in economics journals featured 'depression'. The frequency of 'depression' subsequently decreased, and, in more recent decades, 'crisis' has become the most frequent term. The frequencies of BCTC and 'recession' were generally lower and quite close to one another throughout. During the 1960s and 1970s, the relative frequencies of BCTC were at historically low levels, which coincides with Bronfenbrenner's (1969) volume and the question of whether or not the business cycle may be obsolete. The data suggest that, around this time, discussions of business cycles indeed seemed to be fairly uncommon.

At some points, the descriptive analysis therefore already provided a few impressions of how economic developments and bibliometric variables might be related. Even though results from overall frequency records seemed to contradict PPT, observations such as the high frequencies of 'depression' in the 1930s, and clearly identifiable and recurring peaks and troughs in series such as 'recession', which also showed a very similar pattern over time to the unemployment rate, indicated that there might indeed be relevant associations to be found between the variables – or that, at any rate, a more systematic econometric analysis was necessary in order to gauge whether those highlighted patterns were just exceptions.

Overall, the econometric analysis provided very diverse findings, but a lack of systematic and comprehensive support for PPT, especially when taking various caveats into account. Concerning term frequencies anywhere in documents, 420 potential associations between economic and bibliometric variables were analysed across four JSTOR categories. Of these pairs, 88 were fractionally co-integrated, and 28 of these suggested causality in line with PPT, i.e. that the economic variable statistically causes the bibliometric variable, while the bibliometric variable does not statistically cause the economic variable. However, in 24 cases, the opposite order of causality – from bibliometric to economic variables – was suggested; and for 27 pairs, the test results indicated that bibliometric and economic variables simultaneously caused each other. What is more, despite major overlaps between the different JSTOR categories, there was not much clustering of positive results, i.e. many findings in line with PPT could only be identified in one category, so that most results were not robust across different categories. Additionally, the comparison of the results with earlier research which used virtually the same data and econometric methods added further qualifications to the reliability of what little positive findings there were. Comparing the present study with that of Kufenko and Geiger (2016) showed that the intersection of pairs which displayed the same order of causality in both analyses was only about half of the overall findings, and indeed there are also various cases where pairs were fractionally co-integrated in one analysis, but not in the other. The only economic variable for which consistently many associations with bibliometric variables were identified was consumer prices, especially its association with 'crisis', 'recession', 'glut' and 'stagnation', which was found in both sE and sBE, and in both Kufenko and Geiger (2016) as well as the present study.

The other two categories, namely economics, and business and economics journals (dE and dBE), had not been included in previous research. There were only very few results in line with PPT (five out of 210 pairs), and more instances of other orders of causality. Overall, therefore, no individual bibliometric variable turned out to be one which was particularly often associated with economic variables; and, on the other hand, no economic variable (with the possible exception of consumer prices) systematically caused a large number of bibliometric variables across all four categories. If anything, the total evidence in favour of PPT thus seems to be not very strong. It is rather weak for the subject categories; and for discipline categories, there is even more evidence of an effect in the opposite direction, i.e. bibliometric affecting economic variables.

This finding of differences between subject and discipline categories, on the other hand, proved to be very robust across various comparisons. In the discussion, it was therefore argued that the fact that more bibliometric variables in subject categories – e.g. economics papers – are associated with economic variables than in discipline categories – e.g. papers from economics journals – can be read to imply that those associations between economic and bibliometric variables which are identified often constitute "lip service". In general, our operationalization of PPT which built on the occurrence of central notions in papers captures two potential reactions: changes in genuine discussions of analyses of business cycles and economic crises; and references to recent events, e.g. to motivate a paper (i.e. what we call "lip service" to business cycle and economic crises theory, etc.). Now, if a contraction causes authors of articles in non-economics journals to refer to recent events, this constitutes a reaction of the sE or sBE literature, without necessarily showing the same effect in dE or dBE. The observed differences between subject and discipline categories could therefore result from such behaviour.

While the FCVAR analysis provides a measure of association and of the order of statistical causality between two variables, it does not quantify the strength and direction of the effects where a causal relation is identified. To this end, four combinations of economic and bibliometric variables were exemplarily examined across the same four JSTOR categories in a VAR framework with impulse response functions (IRFs). While the VAR results on Granger-causality among variable pairs were often far from identical to the FCVAR results, which shed further doubt on whether the data provide proper support for PPT, they were at least generally in line with PPT when considered on their own. Among the seven IRFs of pairs where the bibliometric variable was Granger-caused by the economic variable, but did not Granger-cause the economic variable in turn, six impulses to the economic variable were followed by clear responses from the bibliometric variable in the direction suggested by PPT. For example, a 1% change in consumer prices above trend was followed by a 0.05 percentage points increase in the frequency of articles in economics journals that contain BCTC one year later. Similarly, if the S&P stock market index decreases by 1% below trend, the IRF simulation suggests that the frequency of business and economics papers which contain 'crisis' increases by 0.023 percentage points in the next year. And an increase of the unemployment rate by 1 percentage point above its trend is followed by a 0.6 percentage points higher frequency of economics papers featuring 'recession' one year later. In general, economics categories showed much stronger responses of the bibliometric variables than the overarching business and economics categories. What is more, the observed delays of one or sometimes two years between the original impulse and the strongest response seemed to provide further evidence of "lip service". Considering the relatively high average lag between the submission of a paper and its publication in an economics journal, an author who writes on business cycles and economic crises in response to such events would be expected to need more time than one or two years to publish the paper in a journal. On the other hand, it does not seem far-fetched to assume that the authors of papers already in the review process might want to add references to recent events (i.e. "lip service") in the introductions to provide further motivations of their work.

Both the original research interest as well as part of our empirical research strategy were inspired by Besomi (2011). Summarizing his own descriptive empirical work which had used a different sample, (Besomi 2011: 56) had argued in favour of PPT. Likewise, this is also how (Kufenko and Geiger 2016: 57f.) had tentatively summarized the results from their econometric analysis, which was very similar to that in the present book. Some of the findings in this book point in the same direction, for example when considering that the Great Depression was closely associated with large increases in the relative frequencies of terms relevant to the analysis of business cycles and economic crises. However, taken as a whole, the more comprehensive analysis conducted here suggests a different interpretation of the statistical association between economic and bibliometric variables over the course of business cycles and economic crises. Indeed, it is hard to argue convincingly that both the descriptive, and in particular the econometric, results of Chapter 3 provide strong and comprehensive support of the PPT hypothesis at the core of our research question on the association between economic fluctuations and the economics literature. What is more, it was also argued that much of the support in favour of PPT that was found can be read to imply that the reaction of the economics literature to business cycles and economic crises happens to a large part in the form of "lip service", and not so much by increased activity in substantial works on business cycles and economic crises. At the very least, there are two ways to rationalize this finding. First, the operationalization could be flawed, meaning that the variables we used as proxies for economic activity and the economics literature might be inaccurate and not properly represent what we do want to measure. Secondly, despite its intuitive appeal, PPT might indeed be a hypothesis that does not hold up to the empirical test. While the first argument seems very plausible, especially in light of the various issues concerning semantics which were raised several times throughout the book, the second possibility cannot be ruled out either, as was, for example, suggested in the discussion on false positives.

Bearing the various caveats in mind, we would therefore argue conclusively that, despite the scope of the analysis in this book, there is still much more to be learned from further research on the nexus between business cycles, economic crises and their discussion in the economics literature. For example, it was pointed out already in the introduction that the economics literature on business cycles and economic crises need not necessarily react to economic fluctuations in the way suggested by PPT, because such a central and important topic should be expected to attract attention by researchers independently of the specific contemporary context. In this light, the lack of support in favour of

PPT, and the finding that many of the associations that were identified might be attributed to "lip service", is actually not that surprising and does not necessarily require further explanation. Nonetheless, it may be worthwhile to dig deeper here, and especially extend the part of the analysis which deals with issues of semantics. Indeed, this highlights an issue which was already pointed out in the presentation of our methods, namely that research on the history of economic thought can benefit greatly from a combination of an empirical analysis using bibliometric data with a well-founded, qualitative reading of the relevant literature. Applied to the research question at hand, a promising next step could be to devise a better method of reliably identifying economics papers as belonging to a category of interest, such as the analysis of business cycles and economic crises, and generate new bibliometric time series based on this method. These new series can then be compared with economic data by the methods we used here, which would allow for a better impression of the literature's reaction as far as substantial works on business cycles and economic crises are concerned, and thereby also provide a better estimate of the degree of "lip service" that can be found. Such a method of classifying papers would also allow for a closer look at differences between various categories, both within the academic literature as well as from other sources, such as newspapers. In general, therefore, further research should aim not just at answering the question of whether or not "panics produce texts", but also more closely look at what kind of texts panics supposedly produce.

References

Abderrezak, A. (1998). Long Memory in Cyclical Fluctuations. *Nonlinear Dynamics, Psychology, and Life Sciences 2* (3), 243–251.

Aftalion, A. (1913). *Les Crises Périodiques de Surproduction.* Paris: Rivière.

Aimar, T., F. Bismans, and C. Diebolt (2010). Le Cycle Économique: Une Synthése. *Revue Française d'Économie 24* (4), 3–65.

Akaike, H. (1974). A New Look at the Statistical Model Identification. *IEEE Transactions on Automatic Control 19* (6), 716–723.

Alberts, B. (2013). Impact Factor Distortions. *Science 340* (6134), 787.

Allsopp, C. J. (1971). Review: Is the Business Cycle Obsolete? *Economic Journal, 81* (324), 951–953.

Andrews, I. and M. Kasy (2017). Identification of and Correction for Publication Bias. *NBER Working Paper 23298.*

Backhouse, R. E. (1998). The Transformation of U.S. Economics, 1920–1960, Viewed Through a Survey of Journal Articles. *History of Political Economy 30* (Supplement), 85–107.

Baillie, R. T. (1996). Long Memory Processes and Fractional Integration in Econometrics. *Journal of Econometrics 73* (1), 5–59.

Baumol, W. J. (1967). Macroeconomics of Unbalanced Growth: The Anatomy of Urban Crisis. *American Economic Review 57* (3), 415–426.

Becker, M. and T. Knudsen (2004). The Role of Entrepreneurship in Economic and Technological Development: The Contribution of Schumpeter to Understanding Entrepreneurship. *Centre for Research on Entrepreneurship and Entrepreneurs Working Paper Series.*

Beckmann, M. and O. Persson (1998). The Thirteen Most Cited Journals in Economics. *Scientometrics 42* (2), 267–271.

Beran, J., Y. Feng, and S. Ghosh (2013). *Long-Memory Processes.* Berlin, Heidelberg: Springer.

Berry, J., L. C. Coffman, D. Hanley, R. Gihleb, and A. J. Wilson (2017). Assessing the Rate of Replication in Economics. *American Economic Review 107* (5), 27–31.

Besomi, D. (2011). Naming Crises: A Note on Semantics and Chronology. In D. Besomi (Ed.), *Crises and Cycles in Economic Dictionaries and Encyclopaedias*, 54–132. London: Routledge.

Biddle, J. E. (1996). A Citation Analysis of the Sources and Extant of Wesley Mitchell's Reputation. *History of Political Economy 28* (2), 137–169.

Biddle, J. E. and D. S. Hamermesh (2016). Theory and Measurement: Emergence, Consolidation and Erosion of a Consensus. *NBER Working Paper 22253.*

Björk, B.-C. and D. Solomon (2013). The Publishing Delay in Scholarly Peer-Reviewed Journals. *Journal of Informetrics* 7 (4), 914–923.

Blaug, M. (1986). *Great Economists Before Keynes: An Introduction to the Lives & Works of One Hundred Great Economists of the Past.* Brighton: Wheatsheaf.

Board of Governors of the Federal Reserve System (2017). Industrial Production Index [INDPRO]. Retrieved from FRED, Federal Reserve Bank of St. Louis. March 4th, 2017.

Böhm-Bawerk, E. (1898). Rezension: Eugen von Bergmann, Die Wirtschaftskrisen. Geschichte der Nationalökonomischen Krisentheorieen. *Zeitschrift für Volkswirtschaft, Sozialpolitik und Verwaltung* 7, 132–133.

Bordo, M. D. and D. Landau (1979). The Pattern of Citations in Economic Theory 1945–68: An Exploration Towards a Quantitative History of Thought. *History of Political Economy 11* (2), 240–253.

Borokhovich, K. A., R. J. Bricker, K. R. Brunarski, and B. J. Simkins (1995). Finance Research Productivity and Influence. *Journal of Finance 50* (5), 1691 1717.

Borokhovich, K. A., A. A. Lee, and B. J. Simkins (2015). From Psychology, Law, Accounting and Economics: Measuring the Influence of Finance Journals in the Social Sciences. *Journal of Financial Education 41* (3), 1–25.

Box, G. E. P. and D. A. Pierce (1970). Distribution of Residual Autocorrelations in Autoregressive-Integrated Moving Average Time Series Models. *Journal of the American Statistical Association 65* (332), 1509–1526.

Brogaard, J., J. Engelberg, and E. Van Wesep (2018). Do Economists Swing for the Fences After Tenure? *Journal of Economic Perspectives 32* (1), 179–194.

Bronfenbrenner, M. (1966). Trends, Cycles, and Fads in Economic Writing. *American Economic Review 56* (1/2), 538–552.

Bronfenbrenner, M. (Ed.) (1969). *Is the Business Cycle Obsolete?* New York: Wiley.

Burton, M. P. and E. Phimister (1995). Core Journals: A Reappraisal of the Diamond List. *Economic Journal 105* (429), 361–373.

Cahlik, T. (2000). Search for Fundamental Articles in Economics. *Scientometrics 49* (3), 389–402.

Camerer, C. F., A. Dreber, E. Forsell, T.-H. Ho, J. Huber, M. Johannesson, M. Kirchler, J. Almenberg, A. Altmejd, T. Chan, E. Heikensten, F. Holzmeister, T. Imai, S. Isaksson, G. Nave, T. Pfeiffer, M. Razen, and H. Wu (2016). Evaluating Replicability of Laboratory Experiments in Economics. *Science 351* (6280), 1433–1436.

Cardoso, A. R., P. Guimarães, and K. F. Zimmermann (2010). Trends in Economic Research: An International Perspective. *Kyklos 63* (4), 479–494.

Caspari, V. (2008). John Maynard Keynes. In H. D. Kurz (Ed.), *Von Vilfredo Pareto bis Amartya Sen*, vol. 2 of *Klassiker des Ökonomischen Denkens*, 161–186. Munich: C. H. Beck.

Cherrier, B. (2017). Classifying Economics: A History of the JEL Codes. *Journal of Economic Literature 55* (2), 545–579.

Christensen, G. S. and E. Miguel (2016). Transparency, Reproducibility, and the Credibility of Economics Research. *NBER Working Paper 22989.*

Claveau, F. and Y. Gingras (2016). Macrodynamics of Economics: A Bibliometric History. *History of Political Economy 48* (4), 551–592.

Clemens, M. A. (2017). The Meaning of Failed Replications: A Review and Proposal. *Journal of Economic Surveys 31* (1), 326–342.

Colander, D. (2004). The Strange Persistence of the IS-LM Model. *History of Political Economy 36* (Supplement), 305–322.

Costas, R., T. N. van Leeuwen, and A. F. J. van Raan (2010). Is Scientific Literature Subject to a "Sell-By-Date"? A General Methodology to Analyze the "Durability" of Scientific Documents. *Journal of the American Society for Information Science and Technology 61* (2), 329–339.

Cronin, B. and H. B. Atkins (Eds.) (2000). *The Web of Knowledge: A Festschrift in Honor of Eugene Garfield*. Medford: Information Today.

Diamond, A. M. (1986). What Is a Citation Worth? *Journal of Human Resources 21* (2), 200–215.

Diamond, A. M. (2000). The Complementarity of Scientometrics and Economics. In B. Cronin and H. B. Atkins (Eds.), *The Web of Knowledge: A Festschrift in Honor of Eugene Garfield*, 321–336. Medford: Information Today.

Diamond, A. M. (2009). Schumpeter vs. Keynes: "In the Long Run, Not All of Us Are Dead". *Journal of the History of Economic Thought 31* (4), 531–541.

Diamond, A. M. and D. R. Haurin (1995). Changing Patterns of Subfield Specialization Among Cohorts of Economists from 1927–1988. *Research in the History of Economic Thought and Methodology 13*, 103–123.

Diamond, A. M. and R. J. Toth (2007). The Determinants of Election to the Presidency of the American Economic Association: Evidence from a Cohort of Distinguished 1950's Economists. *Scientometrics 73* (2), 131–137.

Dimand, R. W. (1994). Irving Fisher's Debt-Deflation Theory of Great Depressions. *Review of Social Economy 52* (1), 92–107.

Duarte, P. G. and Y. Giraud (2016). The Place of the History of Economic Thought in Mainstream Economics, 1991–2011, Viewed Through a Bibliographic Survey. *Journal of the History of Economic Thought 38* (4), 431–462.

Durbin, E. F. M. (1933). *Purchasing Power and Trade Depression. A Critique of Underconsumption Theories*. London: Jonathan Cape.

Duvendack, M., R. Palmer-Jones, and W. R. Reed (2017). What Is Meant by "Replication" and Why Does It Encounter Resistance in Economics? *American Economic Review 107* (5), 46–51.

Egghe, L. (2006). Theory and Practise of the *g*-Index. *Scientometrics 69* (1), 131–152.

Elsevier (Ed.) (2016). *Scopus Content Coverage Guide*. Amsterdam: Elsevier.

Engle, R. F. and C. W. J. Granger (1987). Co-integration and Error Correction: Representation, Estimation, and Testing. *Econometrica 55* (2), 251–276.

Fabian, A. (1989). Speculation on Distress: The Popular Discourse of the Panics of 1837 and 1857. *Yale Journal of Criticism 3* (1), 127–142.

Fisher, I. (1932). *Booms and Depressions: Some First Principles*. New York: Adelphi.

Franceschini, F., D. Maisano, and L. Mastrogiacomo (2016). Empirical Analysis and Classification of Database Errors in Scopus and Web of Science. *Journal of Informetrics 10* (4), 933–953.

Frisch, R. (1936). On the Notion of Equilibrium and Disequilibrium. *Review of Economic Studies 3* (2), 100–105.

Gagolewski, M. (2013). Scientific Impact Assessment Cannot Be Fair. *Journal of Informetrics 7* (4), 792–802.

Garfield, E. (1955). Citation Indexes for Science: A New Dimension in Documentation Through Association of Ideas. *Science 122* (3159), 108–111.

Garfield, E. (1972). Citation Analysis as a Tool in Journal Evaluation. *Science 178* (4060), 471–479.

Garfield, E. (1979). *Citation Indexing – Its Theory and Application in Science, Technology, and Humanities*. New York: Wiley.

Garfield, E. (2007). The Evolution of the Science Citation Index. *International Microbiology 10*, 65–69.

Garrett, T. A. (2007). The Rise in Personal Bankruptcies: The Eighth Federal Reserve District and Beyond. *Federal Reserve Bank of St. Louis Review 89* (1), 15–37.

Geiger, N. (2014). Cycles "Versus" Growth in Schumpeter – A Graphical Interpretation of Some Core Theoretical Remarks. *Cahiers d'Economie Politique/Papers in Political Economy 67*, 35–54.

Geiger, N. (2017). The Rise of Behavioral Economics: A Quantitative Assessment. *Social Science History 41* (3), 555–583.

Gerrity, D. M. and R. B. McKenzie (1978). The Ranking of Southern Economics Departments: New Criterion and Further Evidence. *Southern Economic Journal 45* (2), 608–614.

Gläser, J., W. Glänzel, and A. Scharnhorst (2017). Same Data – Different Results? Towards a Comparative Approach to the Identification of Thematic Structures in Science. *Scientometrics 111* (2), 981–998.

Gnewuch, M. and K. Wohlrabe (2017). Title Characteristics and Citations in Economics. *Scientometrics 110* (3), 1573–1578.

Guerrero-Bote, V. P. and F. Moya-Anegón (2012). A Further Step Forward in Measuring Journals' Scientific Prestige: The SJR2 Indicator. *Journal of Informetrics 6* (4), 674–688.

Hamermesh, D. S. (2007). Viewpoint: Replication in Economics. *Canadian Journal of Economics/Revue Canadienne d'Économique 40* (3), 715–733.

Hamermesh, D. S. (2013). Six Decades of Top Economics Publishing: Who and How? *Journal of Economic Literature 51* (1), 162–172.

Hamermesh, D. S. (2015). Citations in Economics: Measurement, Uses and Impacts. *NBER Working Paper 21754*.

Hamermesh, D. S. (2017). Replication in Labor Economics: Evidence from Data, and What It Suggests. *American Economic Review 107* (5), 37–40.

Hamermesh, D. S., G. E. Johnson, and B. A. Weisbrod (1982). Scholarship, Citations and Salaries: Economic Rewards in Economics. *Southern Economic Journal 49* (2), 472–481.

Hamilton, J. D. (1989). A New Approach to the Economic Analysis of Nonstationary Time Series and the Business Cycle. *Econometrica 57* (2), 357–384.

Hannan, E. J. and B. G. Quinn (1979). The Determination of the Order of an Autoregression. *Journal of the Royal Statistical Society 41* (Series B), 190–195.

Hansen, G. D. (1985). Indivisible Labor and the Business Cycle. *Journal of Monetary Economics 16* (3), 309–327.

Harzing, A.-W. (2007). Publish or Perish. Software available from http://www.harzing.com/pop.htm.

Harzing, A.-W. and S. Alakangas (2016). Google Scholar, Scopus and the Web of Science: A Longitudinal and Cross-Disciplinary Comparison. *Scientometrics 106* (2), 787–804.

Hicks, J. R. (1950). *A Contribution to the Theory of the Trade Cycle*. Oxford: Clarendon Press.

Hirsch, J. E. (2005). An Index to Quantify an Individual's Scientific Research Output. *Proceedings of the National Academy of Sciences 102* (46), 16569–16572.

Ho, M. H.-C., J. S. Liu, and K. C.-T. Chang (2017). To Include or Not: The Role of Review Papers in Citation-Based Analysis. *Scientometrics 110* (1), 65–76.

Höffler, J. H. (2017). Replication and Economics Journal Policies. *American Economic Review 107* (5), 52–55.

Hoover, K. D. (2004). Lost Causes. *Journal of the History of Economic Thought 26* (2), 149–164.

Hoover, K. D. (2014). On the Reception of Haavelmo's Econometric Thought. *Journal of the History of Economic Thought 36* (1), 45–65.

Hurst, H. E. (1951). Long-Term Storage Capacity of Reservoirs. *Transactions of the American Society of Civil Engineers 116*, 770–808.

Hurst, H. E. (1957). A Suggested Statistical Model of Some Time Series That Occur in Nature. *Nature 180*, 494.

Ioannidis, J. P. A. (2005). Why Most Published Research Findings Are False. *PLOS Med 2* (8), 696–701.

Jacsó, P. (2010). Metadata Mega Mess in Google Scholar. *Online Information Review 34* (1), 175–191.

Johansen, S. (1991). Estimation and Hypothesis Testing of Cointegration Vectors in Gaussian Vector Autoregressive Models. *Econometrica 59* (6), 1551–1580.

Johansen, S. and M. Ø. Nielsen (2012). Likelihood Inference for a Fractionally Cointegrated Vector Autoregressive Model. *Econometrica 80* (6), 2667–2732.

Johnson, H. G. (1971). The Keynesian Revolution and the Monetarist Counter-Revolution. *American Economic Review 61* (2), 1–14.

Jovanovic, F. (2012). Bachelier: Not the Forgotten Forerunner He Has Been Depicted As: An Analysis of the Dissemination of Louis Bachelier's Work in Economics. *European Journal of the History of Economic Thought 19* (3), 431–451.

Kalman, R. E. (1960). A New Approach to Linear Filtering and Prediction Problems. *Transactions of the ASME – Journal of Basic Engineering 82* (Series D), 35–45.

Kaminsky, G. L. and C. M. Reinhart (1999). The Twin Crises: The Causes of Banking and Balance-of-Payments Problems. *American Economic Review 89* (3), 473–500.

Kaur, J., F. Radicchi, and F. Menczer (2013). Universality of Scholarly Impact Metrics. *Journal of Informetrics* 7 (4), 924–932.

Keynes, J. M. (1936). *The General Theory of Employment, Interest, and Money*, vol. VII of *The Collected Writings of John Maynard Keynes* (1973). London: Macmillan.

Kim, E. H., A. Morse, and L. Zingales (2006). What Has Mattered to Economics Since 1970. *Journal of Economic Perspectives 20* (4), 189–202.

King, A., B. Simboli, and K. Rom (2012). JSTOR's "Data for Research": A Bibliometric Analysis of Mathematics in Economics. *Issues in Science and Technology Librarianship 71*, fall.

Krugman, P. (1979). A Model of Balance-of-Payments Crises. *Journal of Money, Credit and Banking 11* (3), 311–325.

Kufenko, V. (2016). Spurious Periodicities in Cliometric Series: Simultaneous Testing. *Violette Reihe Arbeitspapiere 48/2016.*

Kufenko, V. and N. Geiger (2016). Business Cycles in the Economy and in Economics: An Econometric Analysis. *Scientometrics 107* (1), 43–69.

Kufenko, V. and N. Geiger (2017). Stylized Facts of the Business Cycle: Universal Phenomenon, or Institutionally Determined? *Journal of Business Cycle Research 13* (2), 165–187.

Kurz, H. D. (2006). Whither the History of Economic Thought? Going Nowhere Rather Slowly? *European Journal of the History of Economic Thought 13* (4), 463–488.

Kydland, F. E. and E. C. Prescott (1982). Time to Build and Aggregate Fluctuations. *Econometrica 50* (6), 1345–1370.

Laband, D. N. and M. J. Piette (1994). The Relative Impacts of Economics Journals: 1970–1990. *Journal of Economic Literature 32* (2), 640–666.

Laibson, D. and R. Zeckhauser (1998). Amos Tversky and the Ascent of Behavioral Economics. *Journal of Risk and Uncertainty 16* (1), 7–47.

Levine-Clark, M. and E. L. Gil (2009). A Comparative Citation Analysis of Web of Science, Scopus, and Google Scholar. *Journal of Business & Finance Librarianship 14* (1), 32–46.

Leydesdorff, L. and S. Milojević (2015). Scientometrics. In J. D. Wright (Ed.), *International Encyclopedia of Social and Behavioral Sciences* (2nd edn.), vol. 21, 322–327. Oxford: Elsevier. arXiv: 1208.4566.

Ljung, G. M. and G. E. P. Box (1978). On a Measure of Lack of Fit in Time Series Models. *Biometrika 65* (2), 297–303.

Lotka, A. J. (1926). The Frequency Distribution of Scientific Productivity. *Journal of the Washington Academy of Sciences 16* (12), 317–323.

Lucas, R. E. (2003). Macroeconomic Priorities. *American Economic Review 93* (1), 1–14.

Mandelbrot, B. (1972). Statistical Methodology for Nonperiodic Cycles: From the Covariance to R/S Analysis. In S. V. Berg (Ed.), *Annals of Economic and Social Measurement*, vol. 1 (3), 259–290. New York: National Bureau of Economic Research.

Mandelbrot, B. and J. W. Van Ness (1968). Fractional Brownian Motions, Fractional Noises and Applications. *SIAM Review 10* (4), 422–437.

Mandelbrot, B. and J. R. Wallis (1968). Noah, Joseph, and Operational Hydrology. *Water Resources Research 4* (5), 909–918.

Marcuzzo, M. C. (2008). Is History of Economic Thought a "Serious" Subject? *Erasmus Journal for Philosophy and Economics 1* (1), 107–123.

Merton, R. K. (1968). The Matthew Effect in Science. *Science 159* (3810), 56–63.

Merton, R. K. (1979). Foreword. In E. Garfield, *Citation Indexing – Its Theory and Application in Science, Technology, and Humanities*, v–ix. New York: Wiley.

Merton, R. K. (1988). The Matthew Effect in Science, II: Cumulative Advantage and the Symbolism of Intellectual Property. *Isis 79* (4), 606–623.

Michel, J.-B., Y. K. Shen, A. P. Aiden, A. Veres, M. K. Gray, J. P. Pickett, D. Hoiberg, D. Clancy, P. Norvig, J. Orwant, S. Pinker, M. A. Nowak, and E. L. Aiden (2011). Quantitative Analysis of Culture Using Millions of Digitized Books. *Science 331* (6014), 176–182.

Mills, J. (1868). On Credit Cycles and the Origin of Commercial Panics. In *Transactions of the Manchester Statistical Society*, 11–40. Manchester: J. Roberts.

Mitchell, W. C. (1951). *What Happens During Business Cycles: A Progress Report*. NBER Book Series Studies in Business Cycles. New York: National Bureau of Economic Research.

Neumark, F. (1975). Zyklen in der Geschichte ökonomischer Ideen. *Kyklos 28* (2), 257–285.

Nordhaus, W. D. (1975). The Political Business Cycle. *Review of Economic Studies 42* (2), 169–190.

Oehler, K. (1990). Speaking Axiomatically: Citation Patterns to Early Articles in General Equilibrium Theory. *History of Political Economy 22* (1), 101–112.

Officer, L. H. and S. H. Williamson (2017). The Annual Consumer Price Index for the United States, 1774–2015. Accessed on March 4th, 2017.

Open Science Collaboration (2015). Estimating the Reproducibility of Psychological Science. *Science 349* (6251), 943.

Oswald, A. J. (2009). A Suggested Method for the Measurement of World-Leading Research (Illustrated with Data on Economics). *Scientometrics 84* (1), 99–113.

Palacios-Huerta, I. and O. Volij (2004). The Measurement of Intellectual Influence. *Econometrica 72* (3), 963–977.

Peritz, B. C. (1990). The Citation Impact of Funded and Unfunded Research in Economics. *Scientometrics 19* (3–4), 199–206.

Perry, M. and P. J. Reny (2016). How to Count Citations If You Must. *American Economic Review 106* (9), 2722–2741.

Petris, G. (2010). An R Package for Dynamic Linear Models. *Journal of Statistical Software 36* (12), 1–16.

Phillips, P. C. (2007). Unit Root Log Periodogram Regression. *Journal of Econometrics 138* (1), 104–124.

Pieters, R. and H. Baumgartner (2002). Who Talks to Whom? Intra- and Interdisciplinary Communication of Economics Journals. *Journal of Economic Literature 40* (2), 483–509.

Pitt, C., C. Goodman, and K. Hanson (2016). Economic Evaluation in Global Perspective: A Bibliometric Analysis of the Recent Literature. *Health Economics 25*, 9–28.

Price, D. J. D. S. (1963). *Little Science, Big Science*. New York, London: Columbia University Press.

Price, D. J. D. S. (1978). Editorial Statements. *Scientometrics 1* (1), 3–8.

Qin, D. (2011). The Phillips Curve from the Perspective of the History of Econometrics. *History of Political Economy 43* (Supplement), 283–308.

Quandt, R. E. (1976). Some Quantitative Aspects of the Economics Journal Literature. *Journal of Political Economy 84* (4), 741–755.

Radicchi, F., S. Fortunato, and C. Castellano (2008). Universality of Citation Distributions: Toward an Objective Measure of Scientific Impact. *Proceedings of the National Academy of Sciences 105* (45), 17268–17272.

Richter, F. E. (1923). Recent Books on Business Cycles. *Quarterly Journal of Economics 38* (1), 153–168.

Romer, C. D. (1999). Changes in Business Cycles: Evidence and Explanations. *Journal of Economic Perspectives 13* (2), 23–44.

Sandelin, B. (2001). The De-Germanization of Swedish Economics. *History of Political Economy 33* (3), 517–539.

Sandelin, B. and S. Ranki (1997). Internationalization or Americanization of Swedish Economics? *European Journal of the History of Economic Thought 4* (2), 284–298.

Sandelin, B. and A. Veiderpass (1996). The Dissolution of the Swedish Tradition. *History of Political Economy 28* (Supplement), 142–164.

Schumpeter, J. A. (1935). The Analysis of Economic Change. *Review of Economics and Statistics 17* (4), 2–10.

Schumpeter, J. A. (1939). *Business Cycles. A Theoretical, Historical and Statistical Analysis of the Capitalist Process*. New York, Toronto, London: McGraw-Hill.

Schumpeter, J. A. (1954). *History of Economic Analysis*. New York: Oxford University Press.

Schwarz, G. E. (1978). Estimating the Dimension of a Model. *Annals of Statistics 6* (2), 461–464.

Shiller, R. J. (2015). *Irrational Exuberance* (3rd edn.). Princeton: Princeton University Press.

Silva, E. G. and A. A. Teixeira (2008). Surveying Structural Change: Seminal Contributions and a Bibliometric Account. *Structural Change and Economic Dynamics 19* (4), 273–300.

Skidelsky, R. (2009). *Keynes: The Return of the Master*. London: Allen Lane.

Stigler, G. J. (1965a). *Essays in the History of Economics*. Chicago: University of Chicago Press.

Stigler, G. J. (1965b). Statistical Studies in the History of Economic Thought. In *Essays in the History of Economics*, 31–50. Chicago: University of Chicago Press.

Stigler, G. J. and C. Freidland (1975). The Citation Practices of Doctorates in Economics. *Journal of Political Economy 83* (3), 477–507.

Stigler, G. J. and C. Freidland (1979). The Pattern of Citation Practices in Economics. *History of Political Economy 11* (1), 1–20.

Stigler, G. J., S. M. Stigler, and C. Freidland (1995). The Journals of Economics. *Journal of Political Economy 103* (2), 331–359.

Sun, Y. and B. S. Xia (2016). The Scholarly Communication of Economic Knowledge: A Citation Analysis of Google Scholar. *Scientometrics 109* (3), 1965–1978.

Sutter, M. and M. G. Kochner (2001). Power Laws of Research Output. Evidence for Journals of Economics. *Scientometrics 51* (2), 405–414.

US Bureau of Economic Analysis (2017a). Real Disposable Personal Income: Per Capita [A229RX0A048NBEA]. Retrieved from FRED, Federal Reserve Bank of St. Louis. Accessed on March 4th, 2017.

US Bureau of Economic Analysis (2017b). Real Gross Private Domestic Investment (Chain-Type Quantity Index) [A006RA3A086NBEA]. Retrieved from FRED, Federal Reserve Bank of St. Louis. Accessed on March 4th, 2017.

US Bureau of Labor Statistics (2017). Civilian Unemployment Rate [UNRATE]. Retrieved from FRED, Federal Reserve Bank of St. Louis. Accessed on March 4th, 2017.

US Bureau of the Census (1975). *Historical Statistics of the United States: Colonial Times to 1970, Bicentennial Edition*. Washington, DC: US Government Printing Office.

Vernon, R. (1966). International Investment and International Trade in the Product Cycle. *International Executive 8* (4), 16–16.

Wacholder, S., S. Chanock, M. Garcia-Closas, L. El Ghormli, and N. Rothman (2004). Assessing the Probability That a Positive Report is False: An Approach for Molecular Epidemiology Studies. *Journal of the National Cancer Institute 96* (6), 434–442.

Walsh, C. E. (1999). Changes in the Business Cycle. *FRBSF Economic Letter 1999-16*.

Wang, J., R. Veugelers, and P. Stephan (2016). Bias Against Novelty in Science: A Cautionary Tale for Users of Bibliometric Indicators. *NBER Working Paper 22180*.

Wight, J. B. (2002). The Rise of Adam Smith: Articles and Citations, 1970–1997. *History of Political Economy 34* (1), 55–82.

Zipf, G. K. (1935). *The Psycho-Biology of Language*. Boston: Houghton-Mifflin.

Zipf, G. K. (1949). *Human Behaviour and the Principle of Least Effort: An Introduction to Human Ecology*. Cambridge, MA: Addison-Wesley.

Zuckerman, H. (1987). Citation Analysis and the Complex Problem of Intellectual Influence. *Scientometrics 12* (5–6), 329–338.

Index

Page references followed by (t) denote tables and (f) denote figures

For Product Safety Concerns and Information please contact our
EU representative GPSR@taylorandfrancis.com Taylor & Francis
Verlag GmbH, Kaufingerstraße 24, 80331 München, Germany